Outdoor Life

DEER HUNTER'S YEARBOOK 1987

Outdoor Life Books, New York

Stackpole Books, Harrisburg, Pennsylvania

Cover photo: Leonard Lee Rue III

Copyright © 1986 by Times Mirror Magazines, Inc.

Published by

Outdoor Life Books
Times Mirror Magazines, Inc.
380 Madison Avenue
New York, NY 10017

Distributed to the trade by

Stackpole Books
Cameron and Kelker Streets
P.O. Box 1831
Harrisburg, PA 17105

ISSN 0734-2918

ISBN 0-943822-77-7

Second Printing, 1987

Manufactured in the United States of America

Contents

Preface

As a veteran senior editor of *Outdoor Life,* I'm often asked why the magazine publishes so many deer-hunting articles. My answer is very simple: "In most of the United States, deer hunting is a very new sport and hunters want to learn as much as they can about it."

But everyone knows that the original settlers living largely on game, as well as the pioneers on the great trek westward, fed their families almost exclusively on venison of one kind or another. This was subsistence hunting, not sport. Settlers and pioneers killed so efficiently that deer were virtually wiped out east of the Mississippi River. Henry David Thoreau, the philosopher, was astounded when he saw a whitetail deer in Massachusetts. The animals were thought to be extinct.

The 1890s and the early 1900s were the low point for America's deer. For instance, as late as 1923, the total deer population of New York State was estimated to be about 30,000. Today, the New York herd totals about 600,000. The same dark time came to most American states, and though the mule deer was not slaughtered to the same horrible extent as the whitetail, the Western animals were eliminated from large portions of their range by the same combination of subsistence hunting and market hunting.

Deer were restored in America mostly because of pressure on legislators brought to bear by sport hunters. Through hunting-license fees, voluntary levies on sporting arms and ammunition, and voluntary contributions, American hunters also provided almost all the money that was used to restore deer through stocking and habitat improvement. Today, there are probably more deer in what became the United States than there were when the first Europeans arrived. One state after another has rebuilt its herd, declared open seasons, and set limits. Many men who had never seen deer as boys now hunt them every year.

Because deer hunting is a growing sport and, to many, a new one, new and newly revived hunting techniques are constantly appearing on the scene.

That accounts for why the two largest sections in the *1987 Outdoor Life Deer Hunter's Yearbook* are those on hunting whitetail deer and hunting mule deer. Here, you'll find the latest techniques for hunting the two most widely hunted North American deer.

It also accounts for why this year's Edition begins with a chapter titled "Man: The Ultimate Stalker," and continues with a broad range of hunting methods, from how to fool a deer's sensitive ears to the closely guarded stalking and tracking secrets of the Benoits—perhaps America's most successful (and most envied) hunting family. Some of these techniques are new; others date back to the dawn of time and have been newly rediscovered.

You'll also find the latest information on guns and shooting and bows and bowhunting, along with an entirely new section called Safety And Survival. It gives you tips to help you stay warmer and more comfortable on even the coldest hunting days, as well as a revealing chapter on game thievery with some simple precautions to help you make sure the buck you shoot winds up on *your* table.

Most articles reprinted in this Edition were originally published in *Outdoor Life* magazine. You'll also find articles from *Deer and Big Game* and *Hunting Guns,* two annual publications edited by the magazine staff, and four articles from *Deer & Deer Hunting* magazine. Also included are 20 easily prepared venison recipes excerpted from a book by well-known outdoor writer John Weiss, giving you even more ways to cook your deer than in the last year's Edition.

We think you'll find the chapters in this Edition of the *Deer Hunter's Yearbook* a pleasure to read as well as highly informative. Because deer hunting is now a sport and not just a means of staying alive, the Yearbook includes humor, dramatic narratives, and atmospheric stories in addition to the hard-core how-to chapters you've come to expect in the series. We hope you enjoy it.

George H. Haas
Senior Editor
Outdoor Life Magazine

Man:
The Ultimate Stalker

By Valerius Geist

The human animal is a stalker so capable that it puts other carnivores to shame. Predatory animals need not be as good as us because they do not need to get as close to their prey before killing it—instead rushing to their intended kill with jetlike speed. Our ancestors, before the days of bow and arrow or spears, could not run down prey like wolves. They could, however, stalk unsuspecting animals and kill them with their hands. An art born of necessity is, however, no longer needed in the day of the scoped deer rifle and elevated tree stand. Nowadays, man is, at best, a clumsy woods walker.

Although by and large unused in this day of tree stands, man is still endowed with the physical characteristics needed for stalking game—characteristics that were so vital to the survival of primitive man.

Can you stand on one leg? Have you ever seen a cat do that? How about a deer? Funny isn't it! What do you think being able to stand on one leg is good for? If you ever want to get within shooting distance of a game animal, you will discover the advantages of standing on one leg. When stalking a feeding deer, for example, you will have to freeze instantly in whatever position you happen to be in when that deer glares in your direction. If you tip, the jig is up. So, man has a superb sense of balance, which is one reason we can, with a touch of training, walk on tightropes.

One scientist recently concluded that human feet, more specifically the pads, are endowed with thousands of nerve endings that are largely unnecessary. Some statement. Had he cause to stalk game as if his life depended on it—like primitive man—he would have known better than to write such rubbish. Our feet are so sensitive precisely because life itself once depended on such sensitivity to get close enough to game to kill and eat it. One tiny stick breaking, one dry leaf crackling, one wobbly pebble gone unexplored by sensitive toes and pads, and man went hungry. So, combine this superb sensitivity of our feet with our capability of balancing, our great self-discipline, our excellent eyesight, and our ability to learn and you have an animal that can sneak like, well, like a human.

As an animal behaviorist, I have had the opportunity to virtually perfect my stalking tactics. I have stalked so close to a blacktail deer that I was tempted to grab its tail. On another occasion, with a low winter sun at my back, I shot a whitetail buck at 20 paces as it rose from its bed in dense aspens. With the bright sun pouring into the thicket, I could see nicely, but that buck was forced to look directly into the sunlight and could not spot my slow approach.

In all the stalks on game I have made, self-discipline has been an overriding factor in my success. When stalking a deer or elk, for example, you may experience a horsefly about to make a meal of you. Swatting it may alleviate the problem but, to take game, you will just have to grin and bear it and get on with the stalk as if nothing in the world could distract you. And nothing in the world must.

Most hunters must learn that one cannot always stalk. In dry leaves, stalking is almost impossible. The best conditions are soft, moist ground.

The art of walking up big game may have taken a back seat to tree stands and scoped rifles, but the physical capabilities used so efficiently by primitive man are still there. All we have to do is use them.

For example, take the bull moose I observed one July. He was a big fellow with a left front leg limp and scraggly antlers. I saw him now and again and quickly discovered that he was easily spooked. He looked as if he had once been shot at and was not fond of it. I found him one forenoon, feeding in a clear-cut. As I slinked along, I suddenly saw his back a couple of hundred yards below, sticking out over some windfalls. He was busy feeding, paying little attention to all that was about him. I could hear him feed as the flowering plants came apart under the pull of his long, black nose. I could not see on what species of plant he fed and wanted to know.

Off went my boots, my creaky packboard, my notes, and all else that could clatter, scrape, creak, or scratch. Since nobody was there to watch, off went my pants as well—worn as they were and fairly soft, they still were far too noisy for an approach on any game, let alone an experienced old bull.

I had to sneak up on the moose through some 200 yards of deadfalls, broken branches, fireweed, willowbrushes, and open rocky patches, thick with pebbles that were poised to click and clack. Let one stone clack or one branch snap and that big bull would vanish.

My route to the bull might sound a bit discouraging, if not impossible. But don't believe it. It was made for stalking. I could see every branch and avoid each pebble. The ground was a blanket of finely rotted wood—soft and pliable. The greenery was moist and wouldn't snap, crackle or pop. All that was required was to watch the quarry, keep some obstruction between it and me, and let the toes and foot pads find the right places to step.

Eyes on the quarry, toes exploring, fingers picking up and holding aside stalks and branches, and ready to freeze in an instant, I began the stalk. Almost instantly, the bull reared up, his nose testing the wind. Nothing detected, his head dropped, but then came up again. Did he hear me? I stood poorly balanced, then spotted a flash—a female mule deer. The bull must have also identified it. He dropped his head, stepped forward, and continued feeding, unconcerned about the deer.

Then came 20 yards of very careful stalking. Only a glance now and again while my exploring feet did the rest. With my hands, I swam through the fireweed, holding stalks still the moment I noticed or anticipated that the bull would raise his head. Never once did I lose sight of him. In a fairly short time, I reached some logs about 15 feet from the animal. He was eating *Senicios* and *Valerina*, selecting the flowering parts from the plants. Initial stalk completed, I had an even more difficult task: Get back without disturbing the animal. After all, I did not want him to leave. I needed him as a study animal. Spooking clients is no way to run a business. So I sneaked back, slower than on the approach.

To become an accomplished stalker, it is vital to practice during the off-season, as I did with the bull moose. All the reading about stalking will do little good if you are unable to put what you have learned into practice. Spend time in the woods and try to walk silently into the thickest places possible. This will help you learn about animal behavior and, above all else, will allow you to study the terrain. In this way, you can better understand the best and the worst stalking conditions.

I was able to sneak up on and back from the bull because the terrain was suitable. In hard snow, frost, and dry leaves, stalking is largely ineffective. The problem is that even when stalking conditions are great, like in a warm drizzle, we often fail to appreciate it as such and cover ourselves with rubber and rubbish in order to stay dry. You might just as well put a flashing police light on your head and siren in your rucksack.

Modern outdoor clothing that is manufactured to keep you dry is usually a miserable encumbrance to the stalker. If the weather is warm and the vegetation is pliable, do as the ancients did; wear as little as possible. Walking silently is far easier with a minimum of clothes and equipment. In cold weather, I dress totally in wool, from pants to a wool hat. Keep in mind, too, that during the rain is one of the best times to be out in the woods. If you can get into some good old-fashioned wool and don't mind a good soaking, go with it and hunt in the rain. Wool

will keep you warm and allow you to stalk quietly. I never wear camouflage clothing. Most camo is made of denim or canvas material and is very loud in the woods.

A fresh blanket of snow also provides good stalking conditions. If the snow is still falling, so much the better. All the tracks you will see will be fresh, and four or five inches of the white stuff should muffle any missteps you make. Game is also easier to see under these conditions. However, once the snow has had a chance to melt and refreeze, stalking is nearly impossible. Crunchy snow is worse than dry leaves.

Stalkers should also pay special attention to hunting boots. Just take a look at the soles of most hunting boots—one cleat beside the other, with huge corrugation for extra traction. They may be fine for hiking or climbing but not for stalking game.

Such soles maximize the amount of dead surface area attached to your feet, that is, surface area that has little or no sensitivity and catches on twigs, crunchy leaves, and other noisy wood litter. For stalking, you need soles that allow the foot to feel the ground beneath it. I prefer leather/rubber pac boots with as little corrugation on the thin leather soles as possible. They are the next best thing to moccasins, which are excellent for stalking but wear out too quickly. Autumn in Canada is cold, and I have found that pac boots provide adequate warmth and dryness.

Most hunters are poor stalkers because they move through the woods too quickly. I've come up with a tactic that has allowed me to sneak up on game consistently.

Most of my kills are made under 20 paces. To do this, I get into the thickest stuff possible by using a zigzag and curving route. The key is to walk slowly. I take three carefully measured steps and then pause for approximately seven seconds while peering into the thickets with my binocular. Before moving again, I slip the binocular into my shirt to keep it from scraping against any noisemakers, such as the buttons on my coat. If I make any accidental noise, I'll freeze in my tracks for five or six minutes before resuming the stalk. Before moving again, I will pick the path very carefully in order to avoid blowdowns, noisy brush, and so on. By zigzagging and taking carefully measured pauses, I can confound deer. I have used this tactic even under crusty snow conditions, but obviously it works best when the woods are quiet.

I don't use scents. I simply can't be bothered with them. If I wear the quietest clothes I can find, I'll get a deer, eventually.

Stalking. If I were advising someone on how to be consistently successful on big game, I wouldn't recommend it. But, for the hunter who wants the ultimate challenge, it is the only way to go. Mankind comes from a long line of stalkers. Whenever I go hunting, I learn more about myself. Each time out teaches me something new about wildlife.

I Go Deerstalking. . . "Just Because"

By Tony Orman

I go deerstalking because I like to. I love the usually beautiful mountains and bush where deer are found. In comparison, the weekday surroundings of the working world are monotonous and ugly.

I go deerstalking sometimes just to escape the urban world and its crowds of people; to escape the artificial world of television and social life; to escape the things most of us tolerate but don't love.

Getting out in the hills is a way of returning to reality where things are logical, fresh, pure, and clean; where there are no interruptions from telephones, television, or other trivialities.

I go deerstalking because it exercises my patience, relaxes my mind, and sheds my daily cares and worries. There is a special quietness and humility among good sportsmen in the hills. I go because I can find sweet solitude yet never be lonely; because a stew in camp always tastes better than one back home; because a cup of tea or coffee becomes the nectar of the gods after a hard slog with a pack; because one day I may find a big, big buck and will decide whether to kill or to show mercy. Going deerstalking is so important. Like all good outdoor sports, once you get out there, the worries and cares of the city are somehow put into perspective and seem less important.

I go deerstalking just to enjoy myself, perhaps for a morning, an evening, a weekend, or occasionally longer. I am a "very average hunter," but like so many who go deerstalking, I go "just because."

*Reflections of a Deerstalker, 1979

How To Read A Big Buck's Mind

By John O. Cartier

The two-track road to my place winds through a quarter mile of mixed hardwoods, birch, and hemlock. Whitetails use my 40 acres of northern-Michigan woods mostly as a bedding area, so I'm likely to see anywhere from one to ten or even more deer whenever I drive up or down my road at dawn or dusk. When there is snow on the ground, they are very easy to spot and I expect to see them.

One early-January morning several years ago, I saw 12 whitetails react to my presence in ways that amazed me.

When I drove toward the house just after daylight one morning, I noticed four whitetails standing near a clump of hemlock about 80 yards from my house. The animals were a striking sight against two inches of snow cover, and they didn't twitch a muscle as I drove by within easy stone-throwing range. Because they would be visible from the picture window in my office, I decided to rush inside the house, grab my binocular, and get a close-up look at those deer.

My parking spot was within view of the animals, and I wondered if they would bolt when they saw me jumping from my vehicle and running into the building. I figured that that was exactly what had happened because I couldn't see the deer through my optics. Then I realized that they might still be in the same spot but hidden from my new vantage point by the clump of hemlocks. The only way to find out was to get back into my vehicle and drive back along the road.

The whitetails were still standing like statues, pre-

A buck pawing in the leaves with head low isn't likely to run, so there's no rush about shooting him.

cisely where they had been before. So they hadn't moved, even though they had watched a nearby human drive back and forth and run 20 yards in two directions. Because I was worked up by the sight of those deer, I carefully looked for more as I slowly drove farther along the road. I spotted two more on a ridge 60 yards away just before I reached the place where my road joins the county road. There I turned around and drove back. Just before I got near the original four deer, I noticed an enormous whitetail on the slope just above them. I wondered how I could have missed seeing that deer earlier. It occurred to me that I should be able to easily see that animal through another window in my house.

I parked, ran back indoors, grabbed the binocular, and zeroed for a close-up look at that big deer. I expected to see antlers but found myself looking at one of the biggest does I've ever seen. I watched that deer for a while to see how long she would stand still before moving.

She didn't move a hair for ten minutes and 13 seconds by my watch. Then she cocked her ears forward and turned her head for a straight-on look at my house. During the next several moments, the doe moved only her head while looking toward all points

of the compass. After that, she did something that I had never seen before.

Deer often wag their tails, of course, but this one raised her tail to a horizontal position and then stiffly wagged it from side to side several times. Within seconds, I began seeing more deer.

Obviously, the wagging stiff tail was an all-clear signal. That's important. Suppose you're on stand and spot a deer that acts as though it's suspicious about possible danger. If the deer stays still for several moments, and then makes that stiff-tail wag, you can be sure of two things: Your deer is signaling other deer in the immediate area, and the deer that you're watching is no longer alarmed.

I've told many deer-hunting friends about all this and one of them used the information last fall to kill a fine six-pointer.

"I was watching this doe," he told me. "She stopped moving and, when she began moving again, she gave that odd tail wag. I remembered what you had said and immediately started looking carefully for other deer. Behind her and to the left, I spotted the legs of another whitetail below the branches of several small cedars. That deer just stood there while I looked through my binoculars. I finally made out the antlers and dropped the buck in his tracks. I never would have seen him if I hadn't remembered what you said."

On the day when I first noticed the doe's tail-wag signal, I had spotted only seven deer, even though I had driven up and down my road three times. After she signaled and began browsing, however, I spotted five more deer within minutes. In my deer hunting articles, I have often said that most hunters probably fail to see at least 80 percent of the whitetails that are within relatively clear view. I'll never know how I could have missed seeing those extra five animals against that new snow background in bare woods. No matter how experienced you are at deer hunting, you're still going to miss seeing a lot of deer. We all do it and we always will, but you can spot more of them if you know how.

Three of those extra five deer were between me and the four that I had originally seen. They weren't more than 30 yards away from the place where I had parked my vehicle. They had watched me run into my house, back out, and run back in again. Why didn't they panic and bolt when they saw a human so close? Any deer watching a stillhunter becomes alerted long before the human gets as close as I did, and most of them bolt at more than twice that distance. My friends and I put on a lot of drives in my woods. I don't even see most of the deer that I jump when I'm a driver, and the others usually show no more than a white flag flashing in the distance. Why did those three whitetails choose not to bolt?

Most likely, it was because they sensed that I was totally unaware of their presence and therefore was unlikely to harm them. Whitetails pay little heed to human beings if there is no threat. A farmer in his yard or on his tractor hardly rates a second glance by deer. But if that same farmer is in deer woods in the fall, he is suspect.

There are statistics that show deer are well aware of whether or not they're being hunted. One research project conducted over a period of several years in Wisconsin showed that, for every 100 whitetails seen by unarmed human beings in deer habitat, bowhunters saw 83 and firearms hunters saw only 41.5. Further, firearms hunters saw only 1.94 bucks per 100 hours of hunting, while bowhunters saw 5.45, and unarmed persons saw 7.28, on the average.

One of my most knowledgeable deer-hunting friends has a blind in an abandoned orchard. For several evenings just before deer season, he sat in his blind and saw an average of 18 deer per evening. On the first day of the gun season, he saw 17, of which one was a buck that he couldn't get a shot at. The next day, he saw four and, during the next two days, he didn't see any.

He didn't use the blind again until the December muzzleloader season was coming to an end. By the end of this season, the regular gun hunters have long since left the woods, and the deer have again resumed normal behavior patterns. On the last day of that special December season, my buddy spotted 23 whitetails.

All of this shows that deer are masters of the disappearing act when they don't want to be seen. This is why preseason scouting is so important. Any area where there are lots of deer before the hunting season opens normally harbors lots of deer during hunting seasons. The average hunter just doesn't see

them because the animals fade away into dense cover and dark shadows. Many studies involving radio-collared deer have proved that whitetails never flee long distances when hunting pressure becomes heavy. They simply use the terrain and the vegetation to conceal themselves. Suppose, for instance, that a stranger hunted for several days during the middle of firearms deer season from my friend's blind. Very possibly, he might not see a single deer and could easily conclude that there weren't any in the area. The smart hunter scouts until he finds a place with a relatively high deer population. Then he sticks with it and hunts it hard, and he employs hunting methods that give him the best opportunities to see deer in that situation.

An unseen hunter has the best odds, of course, and to remain unseen almost always involves taking a stand. It has been said many times that you can increase your view tenfold if you can gain five feet of height. This is why tree stands are so effective. A hunter on a ground stand or blind can't see as well, but he'll see far more deer than any hunter who is moving. The odds are stacked heavily against the stillhunter.

The moving hunter also makes sounds, some of which deer ignore and some of which put them into instant flight. They have an uncanny way of knowing which sounds mean danger. The snapping of a twig or dead branch almost always puts a whitetail into instant flight. The reason is that all deer predators, including man, weigh enough to snap a fairly thick twig by stepping on it.

Deer almost never show fear of noises made by automobiles, trucks, farm machinery, or other me-chanical equipment. They don't even pay much attention to distant gunshots. A gunsmith friend of mine fires hundreds of shots near one end of a 40-acre field. Many times, he has seen deer entering the field and beginning to feed while he was firing big-bore rifles. And deer pay almost no attention to lumbermen cutting trees with chain saws. I've often thought that a hunter with a running chain saw might actually be able to walk within easy shooting range of deer.

All of this is meant to point out that deer do not react like human beings. Their thinking differs from ours. Let's go back to the three deer that I watched through my office window. Although only a little more than ten minutes had passed after I parked my vehicle and went into my house, the deer had already forgotten about me as a possible source of danger.

Even though I was less than 30 yards away and I had been in plain view, the deer simply ignored the fact that I had to be nearby. They couldn't see, hear, or smell me, so they forgot me. Within moments after the big doe waved the all-clear signal, all of those whitetails were completely relaxed. And that situation enabled me to observe some of their other common reactions.

I've often felt that deer don't always travel upwind so that they can scent danger ahead. Of the 12 deer that I was watching, only two finally left the area by slowly walking directly into the west wind. Five left in a southeasterly direction; two went northwest; and others headed straight south. I believe that deer travel in the direction they want to go at any given time, without reference to the wind. I have observed this many times while watching deer from stands. This tells me that I should expect to see deer coming into view from just about any direction, except directly downwind, as long as my stand is surrounded by typical whitetail habitat. The stand hunter who expects to see deer only on or near runways, near scrapes, or near escape routes is going to miss seeing a lot of deer.

Many studies of radio-collared whitetails show that most of the deer lived out their lives within 1½ square miles of where they were born, and that they were very reluctant to enter strange territory. This means that any deer must react quickly to the availability of various foods in its limited area. The average mature whitetail requires about 15 pounds of forage to fill its paunch, and the animal may eat that much twice every day. Two of the most favored whitetail foods in my area are corn and apples. The very best place to hunt is near an unharvested cornfield, but that information doesn't help you if corn isn't grown where you hunt. It's up to you to find out about the most favored deer foods in your part of the country and then to scout the places where those foods are most abundant.

There are two other things that you should keep in mind about deer foods. Deer in farm country face a dramatic change in diet as soon as all the crops are harvested. Then they have to switch to natural foods.

The deer shown in the photo at far left has stopped feeding and is raising his head. If his tail twitches suddenly, he will almost certainly run. Meanwhile, buck in facing photo has tail high and rump hairs flared to signal other deer of danger. If he runs, he will probably hold his tail low.

Even in nonagricultural areas, there can be a big difference between the foods the deer are eating when you're scouting before open season and what they eat later when you're hunting. In addition, bountiful natural foods that existed last fall may be in very short supply this year. In my area, for instance, there was an excellent crop of acorns one year ago but very little the next. I hunted a lot of oak ridges when acorns were abundant, but I knew that this would be a waste of time when acorns were scarce.

Once you know how deer react to the food supply, you have a key to success. You have to know where the preferred deer foods will be in your hunting area when you'll be hunting it. The smart hunter selects stand sites accordingly.

Many hunters will never take a trophy buck because they underestimate how craftily big bucks react to gun pressure.

If a buck survives his first hunting season, he is well aware of what's happening a year later. If you want a trophy rack, you should realize that your quarry becomes totally concerned with survival. Staying alive is his number one objective at all times, and that's why older deer are adept at remaining unseen when firearms begin roaring in the fall. Once you respect that ability, you can really appreciate what it takes to become a really good deer hunter.

Whitetails react quickly to the fact that there are always some places that the average hunter seldom bothers with. One prime example is a rock area along a fence row in an otherwise open field. Even though that small path may be as little as the floor of your bathroom, there may be a depresion and some high weeds and grass in it. It could hide a big buck, but not one deer hunter in 50 would bother to check it out. Tiny islands of thick cover, no bigger than a small house, are good bets, too. If the cover is so small that you can't imagine a buck hiding in it, it is often a good bet.

Deer learn that humans seldom bother them in certain spots, and they always react to that knowledge by hiding in those places. Farmland whitetails don't avoid an area just because buildings are nearby. Many a big buck is alive today because he learned to bed in weeds behind a barn. The deer sense that hunters seldom hunt close to buildings.

Near where I live, there is a large state park. Most of the park is open to firearms deer hunting, but there is a buffer area near the campgrounds and buildings where no firearms are allowed for obvious reasons. During most of the year, there are very few whitetails in that safety zone but, after the first day of gun season, that area is full of deer. I often wonder why most hunters are aware that wild geese quickly learn refuge boundaries but don't appreciate that deer react the same way. Deer know enough to go where they're not hunted.

I've harped enough on how difficult it can be to see deer, but once you do spot one, it's extremely helpful to know what the animal is likely to do next. A whitetail's intentions are often revealed by body language. Knowing these reactions can make you a more successful hunter. Earlier, I described the stiff tail wag used by a big doe to make an all-clear signal. A somewhat similar swishing of the tail indicates relaxation, but the tail is not stiff nor is it held in a horizontal position. If you see a deer swishing its tail that way, you're looking at a deer that is not alert for potential danger. Further, deer that are routinely browsing, scratching themsleves, and interacting with herd members are not alert.

A deer that stands stiffly erect with its head high and its ears cupped is very concerned about immediate danger. The animal may bound away immediately but, the longer it stands still, the more likely it is to relax. All deer have short attention spans. They react quickly to what may be dangerous, but they soon calm down if no problems develop. Hunters often feel that they should take a quick and perhaps poorly aimed shot at a buck as soon as they spot him standing in an alert position. You'll often get a far better shot if you wait for him to resume his unalarmed routine. If you spot a relaxed tail wag, a relaxing of the deer's cupped ears, or the erect head being lowered, your buck will soon return to his normal routine.

If, on the other hand, the first thing that you see is the all-too-familiar fully raised white tail flashing through the cover, you can be sure that the deer is running for its life. Many studies have shown that does are far more likely to show the white flag than bucks. Bucks tend to flee danger holding their heads and tails low. If you jump several deer and one is running with its tail down, you're probably looking at a buck. If you have tracking in mind, that's the deer to go after.

A whitetail that stamps or paws the ground with one of its front feet is signaling other nearby deer that potential danger is at hand, and it is trying to make that danger show itself. The deer has not yet identified you as a human predator. If you can continue to remain unidentified, the animal may revert to normal routine. If you move or in some other way reveal your presence, the deer will bolt.

A feeding deer almost always twitches its tail before raising its head to look around for danger. That's something to keep in mind if you're stalking a buck in relatively open country. Freeze as soon as you see the twitch.

A deer's tail can tell you many other things, too. Unalarmed deer normally carry their tails low, but they usually raise them with the first sign of trouble. A deer that greatly suspects danger will often raise its tail high and flare the white hairs. In most situations, a deer with erect tail hairs is split seconds away from bolting. If panic takes over, the animal will also flare its white rump hairs. This is signal enough to shoot, especially if the deer also lays back its ears. A flared tail and laid-back ears are sure signs of immediate flight. Shoot!

For your copy of John O. Cartier's latest book, *How To Get Your Deer: A Practical Guide For The Dedicated Hunter,* please send $24.95 plus $2.64 for delivery and handling to Outdoor Life Books, Dept. DHY7, Box 2018, Latham, NY 12111.

Megabucks

By Kathy Etling

The big whitetail buck was tired. The rut was nearly over and his energy was spent. Every year it took more to maintain his dominance and breed the does. And this year a hunter was hot on his trail. The man was using every trick in the book to reduce the buck to a year's supply of venison and a trophy of heroic proportions for his family-room wall.

The buck knew about hunters. He'd been shot at earlier in his life, before he'd grown such spectacular antlers. Always he had come away from these encounters a little wiser and a whole lot warier. But this hunter was different.

The first hint of the man's presence in the buck's woods came when the leaves began to change from green to gold. The deer couldn't know that his tremendous rub trees had attracted the man's attention, or that late one evening, the hunter had watched as the huge buck stepped cautiously from cover. But from that moment on, the buck knew what it meant to be hunted.

Everything a whitetail buck requires was to be found within the deer's 200-acre home range: does, food, water, and cover. A small but growing deer population ensured that the buck did not have far to travel during the breeding season.

The buck usually moved at night. During the day, he bedded down in dense thickets. And always, before making any move, he used his incredible nose.

The days were very short now. Gun season had come and gone, and the buck sensed that it was only a matter of days before he'd be safe for another year. The hunter had switched to a bow, but the big deer knew he couldn't drop his guard, even for an instant. Even now the hunter searched the buck's range for the fat, round tracks.

A breeze carried the hunter's scent to the buck's nose. Within thick briers, the buck lay still, neck stretched out flat along the ground. His antlers were motionless in the fading light, when the whisper of the hunter's feet on fallen leaves reached his ears. The hunter stopped to look and listen, less than ten feet away from the whitetail's head. Heart pounding dully, the buck waited for darkness, when the hunter would leave.

Finally, the hunter sighed and trudged slowly away. The buck waited several minutes and then moved out of the thicket. He went deep into the woods to another part of his range.

Storm clouds gathered, and the buck felt a vague discomfort in his chest while he walked, but he only moved faster, trying to find a place to rest without the hunter dogging his tracks.

Large raindrops pelted the thick gray coat. Soon a downpour drenched the ground, erasing all signs. The buck shivered, but kept plodding along until he reached a bluff, screened by a dense curtain of mountain laurel. Stepping behind the undergrowth, the buck wearily shook the water from his shoulders. He was so tired. Now he would rest. He sank to his knees and closed his eyes.

The buck died that night in his sleep. The hunter was baffled. He looked high and low, but the buck had seemingly vanished. All the next year, he searched, but found nothing, not even a fat, rounded track. The hunter was bitterly disappointed. Never before had he seen a rack to compare with that buck's. He guessed it would score at least 220 Boone and Crockett points, a new world record typical.

The rack? It was gone by the next hunting season, chewed by rodents. There was nothing left; nothing to indicate that one of the largest bucks ever had passed this way. A trophy was lost forever.

Incredible? It's not. This drama is taken from real

life. Consider the No. 1 nontypical whitetail, a monster buck that broke a record that had stood for 90 years, and did so by 47⅞ points. Like the deer in my story, the great buck died of natural causes during the hunting season in St. Louis County, Missouri. The difference between the two is that the Missouri buck was found, and reigns as the current world record.

Superbucks are freaks. They become superbucks through a series of lucky breaks, but there are lots of them out there right now. In the past, the lack of solid information on giant whitetail bucks has contributed to the aura of mystery, the trace of the supernatural that enhances any superbuck tale.

The real-life story of the monster Missouri buck will never be known, but may have paralleled my fictional buck's life and death. Several points made in my dramatization have been substantiated by deer researchers who specialize in big bucks. Learning why a deer develops into a superbuck, and what makes him tick once he does, may help you locate, and eventually take, a trophy whitetail.

Of the top 50 places in the Boone and Crockett typical category, 34 are occupied by bucks that were taken during the 1960s and 1970s. Sixty-eight percent of all large typical whitetails were, in fact, killed fairly recently.

The story is the same in the nontypical category: 33 of the bucks that qualified for the top 50 spots were taken in the 1960s and 1970s. And many heads that qualify haven't made it into print yet. Still others haven't even been scored, because many people are unaware of the competition or don't care to enter it. There's always a catch-up period, and it's a sure bet that several more heads from the '70s and '80s will qualify for the top 50 in both categories. Big bucks aren't a thing of the past. They're out there now for those hunters willing to get out and hunt them.

There's superbuck potential in every state, but big-buck experts agree that there are certain areas in each, where no amount of management will ever produce a superbuck. Dr. James C. Kroll, of Stephen F. Austin University in Nacogdoches, Texas, told me, "If you've got a place where the soil's poor, the nutrition needed for good antler growth is not available. Two areas that immediately come to mind are the extreme southeast portion of Georgia and the panhandle of Florida. A buck from either place is lucky to develop forked antlers. The superbuck hunter should take a good look at the soils in his state. He can call the local SCS (Soil Conservation Service) agent, who can help him with the various soil profiles. What he should be looking for is fertile soil that has enough calcium and phosphates for good antler growth. A good place to start is any area that's produced good bucks in the past."

Sixteen to 17 percent of a deer's diet should be high-protein foods, especially during the antler growing months of late spring and early summer. Excellent sources of protein, at this time, are agricultural products. Soybeans, with nearly 40 percent available protein, and alfalfa are two crops that fit the bill nicely. Milo and clover are also good.

Naturally occurring high-protein browse includes honeysuckle, greenbrier, and blackberry, in the south, and pokeweed, jewel weed, aster rosettes, lespedeza, and wild lettuce, in more northerly ranges. Asters are the small sunflower-type blossoms seen in fallow fields during early summer. Scouting trips, at the height of the growing season, can determine whether or not high protein browse is available in a potential hunting area.

Good nutrition is the first requirement for fantastic antlers. Age and genetics are the other two. Surprisingly, the last five Boone and Crockett bucks Dr. Kroll has examined were only 3½ to 4½ years old. This is a bit lower than some earlier studies suggested for optimum antler growth attainment. These bucks might have sported even better antlers later in life, but at 3½ to 4½, their headgear was good enough to make the book. Still, to reach that age in some areas is almost impossible for the average whitetail buck.

To find a buck in this age bracket, look for an area that isn't heavily hunted. The areas that sustain the most pressure are usually the areas with the most deer. Concentrate on an area with a new, or building, population of whitetails. Locate an almost inaccessible area. In such places, the hunter has the best chance of taking a superbuck.

Another good place to check out is an area that looks like it *should* support deer, but where there is no hunting pressure. Dr. Harry Jacobson, a big-buck researcher at Mississippi State, knows of several tremendous bucks, taken recently, that he jokingly refers to as "fence-row deer," "backyard deer," or "city-limits deer." The hunters who shot these animals suspected the big bucks were to found where no one else expected them to be, and hunted accordingly.

Dr. Jacobson told me, "Anyone who is serious about bagging a good buck must remember that whitetails are very adaptable, and a superbuck is the most adaptable whitetail of all."

Genetics are least important. Both Dr. Kroll and Dr. Jacobson emphasized that the overwhelming majority of bucks, given a proper diet and the opportunity to live longer than 18 months, will eventually develop excellent antlers. They call this allowing the buck to develop to his "full genetic potential." The potential exists in most bucks; it's programmed in their chromosomes.

Jacobson and Kroll also feel that does have been protected, on some ranges, to the point of negative impact. Up to 90 percent of 18-month bucks may be shot in a given area every year. That leaves very few to grow to superbuck age. The protected does expand to fill the available range, and the population gets severely out of balance. Too many deer compete for too little food, with the result that there's not enough nutrition to go around. Stunted bodies and antlers are the end products. Shooting does, to swing the pendulum back the other way, often works wonders in establishing a quality deer herd. Rather

Many trophy whitetails die of old age. That should be the ultimate clue that most hunters simply don't know how to hunt deer with record-book racks.

than a big, unbalanced population resulting, more superbucks would develop.

It takes a series of lucky breaks for a deer to become a superbuck, and he learns from every one of them. Since a ''bucks only'' mentality endures in many areas, the bucks are shot at when they first develop antlers. Even a spike, most often the young of the preceding year, is fair game in many states, and many hunters believe that all spikes are genetically inferior.

In no time, a buck, any buck, has made the connection between human scent and whizzing projectiles. After one or two near misses, the deer becomes cautious. He becomes warier and warier and soon limits his movements to avoid hunters. He becomes increasingly nocturnal, since there's little chance of running into a human in the woods at night. But both researchers also believe that many big bucks feel safe moving around during the *middle* of the day.

"Deer are usually shot at early and late in the day," Dr. Kroll says, "and they adjust their activity to avoid hunters. That means that many darn good bucks move around in the middle of the day. A hunter who stays put *all* day long increases his chances of scoring on a superbuck. A hunter's chances for a big buck are best on opening day, and dwindle as the season wears on. Big bucks are extremely elusive. Even when they're not being hunted, they spend most of their time laying low. When a buck does decide to move, he knows where he's going and how he's going to get there. There's very little random travel involved in a big buck's lifestyle. It's like a zone defense in football when hunters enter the picture. A smart old buck can adjust his activity to completely avoid the hunters."

Dr. Jacobson added, "I think a superbuck is probably more sedentary than the average deer, and is therefore more likely to survive. The less a big buck moves, the less likely he'll be seen. But a lot of this superbuck mystique is created by the hunters themselves. You hear how smart, how elusive these critters are, and how ol' So and So shot at a giant buck the other day and the buck just took off and never stopped. First of all, very few hunters won't get flustered when shooting at a big whitetail, so there are bound to be many stories about the trophy buck that got away. No mystery there. Second, because of a big buck's size, his sheer strength is amazing. When you shoot a yearling, he may run 100 yards before dropping. When you shoot a superbuck, an animal conditioned to survive, you're shooting at a superior specimen. He's likely to react very differently when shot. He may hide right away, or he may run a heck of a lot farther than you'd ever figure he could. He might even run uphill—he just might have the strength—and if a buck does that, some hunters won't bother to check, because they can't believe they hit the deer. This is how a lot of giant bucks get away and how the mystique develops. Those bucks may die out there and never be found. Always be sure you follow up any shot at a superbuck. He may be lying dead just over the next ridge."

When a whitetail population is out of balance, scrapes don't always mean what they should. In fact, scrapes sometimes aren't even made by a dominant buck. Dr. Jacobson has witnessed this with some of

his study deer.

"I don't put as much faith in scrapes as some other biologists do. I've got one dominant buck that's never made a scrape in his life. Other bucks in the same area scrape, but not the dominant one, I put my faith in scent glands and rubs. Rubs are signposts that have been liberally doused with forehead gland scent. They serve as visual and olfactory warnings. Tree branches that bucks have chewed on and rubbed are also good. I've seen does stand up on their hind legs so they could lick the branches where the bucks have rubbed. If I found a bunch of big rubs, I'd hunt right there."

The top Missouri nontypical buck was found dead, not shot, as was another of the top five Boone and Crockett nontypicals. In addition, still another big nontypical recently came to light, and it was also found dead. No autopsy was done on any of these deer. How many superbucks die of natural causes and are never found?

Dr. Kroll and Dr. Jacobson think there are quite a few. "Once the bucks establish dominance during the summer, they have to stay on top. Dominance isn't decided in the fall, with head butting and fighting. It's decided earlier, while the antlers are still in velvet. Two bucks stand up on their hind legs and flail away at each other with their forefeet. This is how the pecking order is determined. The top male, or alpha buck, must maintain that dominance or lose his position.

"A dominant buck has a rough go of it. He's so busy asserting his dominance that he'll run himself into the ground. During the rut, he expends more calories and uses up fat reserves by breeding and running off other bucks. They don't feed enough to build up new reserves. When winter arrives, they're at low ebb and survival becomes harder. And when a dominant buck shows any sign of weakness the subordinate bucks jump all over him. They jump him, push him around, and even gore him if they can. They gang up on him and do anything to edge him out of his dominant position. The cause of the buck loss that results from this kind of activity is called 'post-rut mortality,' and is probably the reason why so many superdeer just seem to disappear."

A superbuck's magnificence lies in the eyes of his beholder. Any buck large enough to qualify for Boone and Crockett, with 170 typical points, is unquestionably a real trophy. But there are many beautiful bucks, with fine antlers, that will never qualify for Boone and Crockett. This doesn't diminish their value in the least. Any whitetail that sports a rack in excess of 130 Boone and Crockett points is a buck to be proud of. My husband, Bob, killed a buck that scored 133, a far cry from the minimum Boone and Crockett score, but everyone's impressed when they see the rack.

Superbucks *are* alive and well and just about everywhere. Hunters who long to match wits with one stand a good chance of doing so. A superbuck can be *yours!*

Mystery Of The Muley/Whitetail

By Jeff Murray

Ordinarily, I try not to get too fired up over stories about mystical bucks with massive racks and cagey personalities. I don't need any more adrenaline pumping through my veins than I've already got. Mention the words *big buck*, in-season or out, and I become an instant Walter Mitty, fantasizing about my next conquest. It's an uncontrollable Pavlovian response, pure and simple.

So when Leo Faber gave a crew of Minnesota whitetail hunters—some on their first Western hunt—the grand tour of his sprawling 7,000-acre Montana ranch, I tried to temper my ever-so-vivid imagination as he spun yarn after yarn about the big deer taken over the years by family and friends on his land.

"Looky here," he'd say as he pointed a finger at a procession of 17 mule deer, mostly does and fawns, heading down an aspen-choked draw. "For every ten muleys you see, there's probably a whitetail to match down in that coulee. They love those bottom-lands, you know."

Indeed, the ranch was ideal deer habitat for both muleys and whitetails. And it was postcard pretty. Pine-studded slopes of the Bear Paw Mountain Range gradually melted into rolling foothills and open grazing fields. Ribbons of brushy creek beds laced the perimeter of almost every hill.

Frequently, Faber would slam on the brakes of his Chevy pickup and show us exactly where a heavy-racked buck had rubbed shoulders with a 150-grain bullet, and lost. Some were muleys; some were

With antlers like a whitetail, except for the forked tips, this Montana buck also sported muley-type ears and tail.

whitetails. But one—the one that ended up on his wall—was something else.

Back at the house, I gawked at the "whitetail" mount that was the No. 3 Boone and Crockett in Montana for a spell. It was intriguing, to say the least. The tines weren't forked like a mule deer's—except for the tips of the main beams—but the snout sure looked like a mule deer's.

"You should have seen the tail," Faber said. "It was a flag like a whitetail's, only about half as long as you'd expect, with the coloration of a mule deer.

"When I first spotted him, he was with 20 or 30 muleys on the edge of a field, and I didn't think that he was a crossbreed until I talked with a biologist long after the buck had been field-dressed."

Now, it was a considerable adjustment for an Easterner to make, hunting mule deer in high altitudes in fairly open country, but throw in this stuff about half-and-half deer and I just knew that something weird was going to happen on this trip. And sure enough, it did—to me.

The story continues with me forgetting about this nonsense of half-breeds and concentrating on how to get within range of a good mule deer buck. After three days of sneaking around (and scaring away) herds of baldheaded animals, I finally located a decent rack. Actually, there were four of them together, but I didn't know that until it was too late.

After tracing the muley's route for the better part of a morning, always one hill behind, my big chance to score came when I spotted the buck moseying over the crest of the next ridge. I ran for it. Gasping for air, I crawled up the hilltop and quickly glassed the other side. Egads, there were three of them and all were fine bucks! With the composure of a veteran outfitter, I calmly picked out the widest rack and lowered for the shoulder area. That's when the fourth animal appeared. It was at least as big as the

one that I had in my crosshairs, but its rack was definitely unbroken, just like those on all the whitetails that I'd hunted back in the Midwest. What was this buck doing, running with muleys up on a ridge where whitetails didn't belong? It so riled me that I didn't come close to squeezing the trigger; my only reward was a fleeting glimpse of a stubby flag wagging over the horizon with three other respectable but retreating bucks.

It all happened so fast that I talked myself out of what I thought I had seen within the hour. For two years, it was just a mirage to me, until I talked to Leo Faber again over the telephone. We talked about past hunts and big bucks and plans for next year's hunt . . . and his hybrid mount. He had me convinced that my mirage was a real live mule deer/whitetail hybrid.

"Talk to Al Rosgaard, the state's biologist up in Havre," he said. "He's seen a lot more crossbreeds than I have."

Sure enough, I called Rosgaard and he backed up Leo's testimony to the letter. Rosgaard said that he had seen more hybrids south of the Big Timber Mountains along the Boulder River than up in the Bear Paws. At least to this professional, the phenomenon was a fact of life, not someone's fancy.

"Wherever the two habitats overlap," Rosgaard explained, "you'll have a good chance of sighting these hybrids."

In Montana, that means river bottoms in mountainous areas, according to Rosgaard, but the eastern half of the state could also provide opportunities as the ever-adaptable whitetail extends its range westward from the Dakotas.

The Montana experience is far from an isolated one. Kansas officials have also documented the occurrence of hybrids. Terry Funk, a biologist at the Hays regional office, told me that a unique method

HYBRID HABITAT

Crosshatched area on map is where muley/whitetail hybrids have been documented. As whitetail range expands, incidences of crossbreeding are likely to increase. Hybrids have also been spotted in Washington.

Illustration by Tom Moore

Anywhere muley and whitetail habitats overlap, hybrids will probably exist. Here a whitetail and muley spar.

had been developed by Kansas Fish and Game personnel to accurately determine both the age and the species of a particular deer.

"The technique is virtually foolproof for animals up to 3½ years old," he said. "A mule deer's front incisors are shaped like a light bulb, while a whitetail's look like a human's."

In recent years, Kansas biologists have been experiencing a few surprises when they get feedback from hunters who send their deer's incisors in for study. According to Funk, a good number of teeth samples haven't jibed with what the hunter said his buck looked like. Of course, the fault doesn't lie with fish and game officials, but with the fact that the specimens analyzed were hybrids that shared characteristics of both species.

Prior to the "tooth period," Kansas employed check stations similar to those found in other states. Bill Peabody, a Ducks Unlimited regional director, had worked as a biologist for the state for a dozen years as well as participating in the state's checking operations.

"We always suspected that hybridization would occur," Peabody told me. "Wherever the two species came in close contact with one another, especially in our transition zone around Hays, there would be reports of obvious hybrid specimens that didn't fit either category."

The Kansas story is a relatively recent one. Peabody grew up on a farm in southeastern Kansas. When he got out of the service in 1965, he rarely saw a whitetail. Today, whitetails outnumber mule deer

by a ratio of 4 to 1, with the state's overall herd hovering around 100,000 animals and still expanding. Again, the ever-adaptable whitetail had pushed its way into the farm country and western plains of mule deer territory.

Other states, such as Nebraska, Wyoming, South Dakota, and Washington, have recorded sightings of "mule-tail" hybrids. But, to date, no blood tests involving chromosome/DNA analysis have been conducted. Perhaps the most comprehensive, detailed study comparing several hybrids was done on Alberta deer by William D. Wishart, who is the head of wildlife research for the province's fish and wildlife division in Edmonton. Muscle tissue from two hybrids that Wishart examined personally were analyzed by electrophoresis, and it was found that they each had two albumen bands—one characteristic of mule deer and one characteristic of whitetails.

What exactly does a hybrid look like? According to Wishart's findings, it can look mostly like a whitetail, or it can look mostly like a mule deer, or it can be an "intermediate" and share equally the characteristics of both species. One uniform characteristic observed in all hybrids, though, was the appearance of the tail—larger than a muley's, smaller than a whitetail's, with a brown-merging-to-black outer body and a white underbelly.

Overall body musculature appears to be a blend of both species, in most instances. Weight and coloration fall in the intermediate category, although some very large hybrids have been sighted. This, however, may be due to the simple fact that the

"You should have seen the tail," Faber said. "It was a flag like a whitetail's, only about half as long as you'd expect, with the coloration of a mule deer."

larger animals of a given area will always attract the most attention.

Hunters rely mainly on antler configuration and body traits to distinguish the two species. That's why hybrids will mess you up every time. One such buck from British Columbia that was cited by Wishart in his study was reported to have troken tines, while the Alberta bucks were mainly unbroken. Ear length and the rump patch are also dead giveaways for muleys. Most crossbreeds documented, however, sported in-between ear lengths and had inconspicuous or nonexistent rump patches.

Trained biologists usually fare no better. The color of the metatarsal tuft, for instance, is a constant white for whitetails and always brown on mule deer. Hybrids are most often white; one particular animal was brown and white. As mentioned earlier, teeth samples can't be relied upon, nor can the preorbital gland; a blend of characteristics from both species is usually the result.

An interesting footnote to the Alberta study is the fact that all the hybrids were found to associate with mule deer and not whitetails. According to Wishart, the probability of mule deer does mating with whitetail bucks is more likely because muley does are far less elusive than whitetail does when approached by a rutting buck.

No doubt, physical attributes of these hybrids are

fascinating. Leo Faber's trophy and the one that I saw in the wild were handsome, worthy specimens. But what engrosses me most about them is how these animals are apt to act.

For starters, we know that they travel in bunches. So instead of dealing with one pair of eyes and ears, you've probably got 20 or 30 to contend with; alert one and you'll scatter the herd. And if they end up with the muley's eyesight and hearing, it won't be easy to get within range. Shots in excess of 200 yards can be counted on.

If the hybrids continue to traffic predominantly with mule deer, or if they colonize in muley country, you can expect to be in for one of the most grueling hunts of your life. To boot, they migrate more than a circus, and pinning down their location isn't likely to be a weekend affair.

But the scary thing about these deer is how their nature could complement these attributes and habits. Injecting a little whitetail nerve, smarts, and unpredictability could give them a few addded stunts that muleys don't usually pull—like crawling on their bellies, or sitting tight until just the right moment, or hiding out in cover barely thick enough to conceal a garter snake, or circling on a backtrack . . . the list is almost endless!

Again, only time will tell exactly what kind of quarry these hybrids will be, but already reports are circulating about a super race of almost unhuntable trophy bucks in certain counties across the United States and Canada. One recent story that I heard while attending a Deer Classic get-together centered around the antics of a particular buck that, by its description, had to be a crossbreed. The hunter, who had bagged both Pope and Young and Boone and Crockett bucks, told of how he had never had so many close chances on a buck without scoring; each ended with yet another twist and a daring last-minute escape.

"I'd never seen anything like it," he said. "It was almost as if he was toying with me. If it hadn't been for his massive rack, I would have given up . . . but a 190- to 200-point rack isn't easy to find or forget."

To be sure, there were other stories of strange-looking whitetails at the Classic, and I'm sure that we are just beginning to scratch the surface.

Practical problems are sure to arise with increasing frequency when hybrids are matched with game laws and the record book. Which tag do you put it under? Which species in the book? Should we consider a separate listing?

"Whenever an identification problem arises," Boone and Crockett's Executive Director Hal Nesbitt explained, "standard procedure is to use the higher scoring category for minimum requirements. So you're looking at 195 points instead of 170, if the species is in doubt. So far, it hasn't been a problem. I've seen very few instances, myself."

Well, that could be changing. If current trends continue to escalate, both state and private game officials are going to have a few things to consider. It's only a matter of time.

Deer's Ears And How To Fool Them

By John Weiss

Not enough press is given to a whitetail's sense of hearing. The popular subjects these days seem to continually focus on either their ability to see or the use of bottled potions to fool their highly refined sense of smell.

Consequently, many hunters assume that if they simply avoid crashing through the woodlands, they'll get their buck. Yet this can be a big mistake because a whitetail's ears are indeed a more formidable defense mechanism than that. A deer's ears can easily cause a hunter's undoing. The key element in using this insight to one's advantage is understanding that there is a tremendous difference between *what a deer is capable of hearing* and *what a deer hears that is likely to warn or frighten it*. It is how the deer interprets what it hears that makes the difference to hunters.

This point was driven home more than 20 years ago when I was an infantryman at Fort Benning, Georgia. Like most military installations, where hunting is restricted or prohibited altogether, the terrain was alive with too many whitetails for the animal's own good. During maneuvers, we'd see them grazing by the dozens like so many beef steers. But what was really significant, to me anyway, was what regularly happened on the artillery range.

I had two MOS designations (MOS being an acronym for Military Occupation Specialty): I was a range-plotter on a mortar crew and a loader on a two-man bazooka team. It was more than just a little awe inspiring to take our turn on the firing line to

Photo by Richard P. Smith

All hunters know how well whitetails can hear, but it's how they enterpret what they hear that spells the difference between hunting success and failure.

This large whitetail is engaging in a three-step hearing process involving recognition, classification, and reponse.

lob rounds downrange, where they absolutely annihilated derelict tanks and armored personnel carriers with outrageous explosive sounds and flames that leapt skyward.

The intriguing thing about all of this was that it was relatively common to see groups of whitetails placidly feeding on distant hillsides, seemingly oblivious to the deafening noises created by our weapons. Occasionally a deer would briefly look up, but then, very shortly and apparently out of boredom, it would return to the more important matter of nibbling on this or that.

Unquestionably, generations of deer living on that particular military base had long since become quite used to all manner of loud explosive sounds and re-

lated fireworks. Because those goings-on never posed any threat to their immediate well-being, they simply paid them little mind.

Scene II: Many years have passed; I've long since been discharged from the U.S. Army, and I'm hosting a party of deer hunters on my farm in southern Ohio. There is one special tree stand where I want my good friend Al Wolter to station himself on opening day, but he is apprehensive about sitting there. On this particular morning the wind is a bit stronger than usual, and the stand's wooden platform is making creaking noises. Understandably, Al is certain that any bucks in the vicinity will avoid the unnatural sound permeating their bailiwick.

At first, I agree that perhaps this morning the

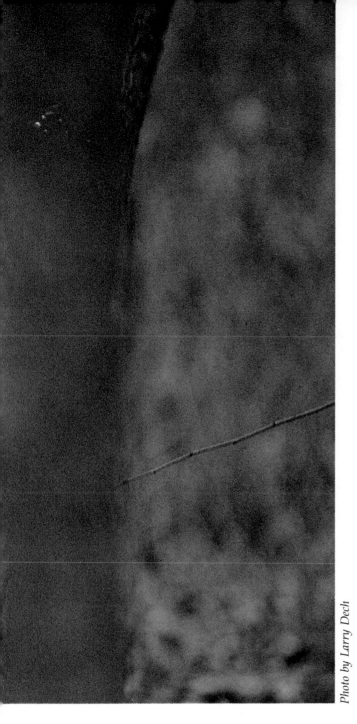

Photo by Larry Dech

Recurring incidents like these hold a wealth of hunting knowledge for those who witness them firsthand and who have the foresight to file that information away in one's memory locker.

But exactly how acute is a whitetail's hearing? Moreover, how does it compare with our own hearing, and, of critical concern, how do deer catalog specific sounds as harmless while others are instantly recognized as potentially threatening?

In his classic book *Deer Of North America,* naturalist Leonard Lee Rue explains that deer are particularly adept at distinguishing high-pitched sounds extending to 30,000 cycles per second. The significance of this readily comes to light when one considers that an average human's hearing limit is a mere 16,000 cycles per second.

Even more noteworthy is the enormous reflective surface of a whitetail's ears—each encompasses approximately 24 square inches and can be instantly swiveled 180 degrees. A human ear, by comparison, encompasses only about 3½ square inches of sound-catching surface and cannot be swiveled. It's no wonder deer are able to so keenly detect even the faintest sounds over surprisingly long distances.

Yet there is much more to understanding a whitetail's sense of hearing than simply respecting its ability to detect sounds. The animals actually engage in a three-step hearing process involving *recognition, classification,* and *response* (and, depending upon the nature of the first two elements, the third item—response—may entail no behavioral reaction whatsoever). Moreover, it's primarily the influence of the so-called Doppler effect that determines the varying distances at which deer are capable of detecting those particular sounds that are most likely to elicit responses from them.

As an analogy, using our own hearing as a base of reference, consider the pitch of a locomotive's whistle as it approaches and then passes you. As the train draws nearer and nearer, the pitch of the whistle deceptively seems to rise. When the locomotive passes, the pitch of the whistle deceptively begins dropping until eventually you cannot hear it at all.

What has really happened—the Doppler effect—is that as the locomotive was approaching, the whistle's sound waves became compressed, causing an increase in the number of cycles per second reaching your ear. This became translated into a higher pitch. After the locomotive passed, the sound waves became spaced wider and wider apart, with fewer and fewer cycles per second reaching your ear; this resulted in a lower pitch. Actually, the pitch of the whistle never changed at all, only your perception of that pitch in accordance with the varying distances at which the sound was heard.

From an anatomical standpoint, whitetails hear in the same manner as humans. But because the neural channels linking their ears to their brain are attuned to much higher-pitched sounds than we are capable of discerning, they tend to overreact to those noises occurring closest to them, which may not necessarily

stand is not a wise choice, but then I have a flashback to my Fort Benning memories.

"Al, I wouldn't worry about the stand making so much noise," I explain. "From the very day I nailed down the first board, that stand has creaked and groaned under the slightest breeze. Multiply that daily occurrence by the ten years the stand has been in existence, and I'm sure the local deer no longer pay any attention to it. That stand has long since become a natural part of the forest's woodwork, so to speak."

Two hours later, Al climbs down from the stand in the old beech, hikes 40 yards, kneels, and with a wide smile on his face attaches his tag to a splendid 11-pointer.

be loud noises but are characterized by higher numbers of cycles per second. This is quite understandable, of course, because the closest of noises are the ones most likely to influence both their immediate safety and the effectiveness with which members of the same species communicate with each other.

Conversely, our own human survival is geared to a much broader world of sensory recognition, and the neural passages connecting our own ears to our brain must consequently be attuned to both close-range and distant sounds.

You may be watching a doe, for example, and notice with surprise that she doesn't react at all to the thud of a distant gunshot, the sound of which immediately draws your notice, and yet she'll instantly turn her head in the direction of her nearby fawn at its faintest mewing for attention. In performing casual experiments, I've also seen a buck reveal no alarm reaction at all to the clearly audible voices of two hunters on a distant ridge yet, at the barely discernible *clink* of my cigarette lighter from ten feet away, almost turn himself inside out trying to leave the area.

Of special curiosity to scientists is trying to understand the function, if any, behind a whitetail's mysterious ability to hear those especially high-pitched sounds that are far beyond the frequencies humans can hear.

We do know, however, that whitetails seldom rely upon any one of their senses exclusive of all others. Any stimuli received by a particular sense generally must receive confirmation from at least one of the other senses before a reaction is forthcoming.

But when it comes to a deer's sense of hearing and the detection of sounds in the absence of confirmation from the other senses, the chink in a whitetails's armor is a very short memory, which scientists say is limited to about three minutes.

This insight is of tremendous value to all hunters who occasionally cough or make some other sound. It is of even greater importance to those hunters who enjoy sneak-hunting, stillhunting, and stalking deer but commonly experience the frustration of not being able to move along as silently as they'd like. Not only are these periodic noises inevitable, but in typical whitetail habitat they constitute only a small percentage of the sounds that bombard deer every minute of every hour of every day.

The critical thing, when you do indeed cough, snap a twig, or crunch upon dry leaves, is to instantly stop and not even blink an eyelid for at least four or five minutes. Then you can begin slowly advancing once again, with the confidence that any deer in the vicinity that heard your initial sound have long since forgotten it and turned their attention to other matters.

One time in South Carolina's Francis Marion National Forest, I had a rare opportunity to witness this firsthand. I was skulking through a lowland swamp when I spotted a buck with a modest six-point rack about 150 yards ahead of me. As I began raising my rifle, my jacket sleeve grated against the rough bark of a cypress branch, and the deer immediately turned and looked squarely in my direction. I almost stopped breathing.

Long minutes later, the deer continued ambling along, browsing on branch tips drooping from willow saplings. I took only one step forward in an attempt to improve my shooting and then silently cursed when my boot made a loud sucking noise as I pulled it out of the swamp muck. Again the deer wheeled around and gave me the once-over, craning his head from one side to the other. Fortunately, the wind was in my favor and surrounding brush adequately broke up my outline. Finally, the deer once again went back to concentrating on the tender willow twigs, and this time I successfully managed to center my crosshairs on his shoulder and drop him.

In going back to their ability to catalog various types of sounds, it's worth repeating that whitetails become intimately familiar with the unique goings-on that characterize their own particular home range. A clear, although admittedly extreme, example of this was evident at Fort Benning. Yet I've observed deer elsewhere and noticed their lack of concern over noises they've become quite accustomed to hearing over long periods of time.

Near where we used to live in southern Florida, armadillos were as thick as flies, and they would root around noisily in dense stands of palmetto with nearby deer almost totally ignoring them. In the brush country of southern Texas, I've often sat in elevated tower blinds and from my vantage point watched javelinas bickering among themselves as they rustled around in thick mesquite. I could see the peccaries but nearby deer couldn't, and yet the deer seemed to register no alarm whatsoever.

Yet one must never lose sight of the fact that whitetails everywhere have nervous, hypertensive personalities that often give rise to behavior mannerisms that are both spontaneous and entirely unpredictable.

One cold dawn while waiting in a tree stand in northern Minnesota, I watched a ruffed grouse drop down from its nighttime roost in a nearby spruce. As it was pecking around on the ground about 25 yards away, a whitetail doe trotted into view. Neither was aware of the other's presence or of mine, but when the deer approached just a bit too closely the grouse whirred from the cover, sending a shower of leaves flying in all directions amid a frenzy of beating wings. The deer fled over the next ridge like she'd just been turpentined. The puzzling thing is that this occurred near the small town of Hinckley, where grouse numbers are exceedingly high, and one would think the local deer would have long since become quite used to the explosive flushing antics of partridge.

Another time, also in Minnesota, a small buck approached my stand, where I'd been amusing myself by watching a chipmunk scurrying around an old log. The deer spotted the movement of the ground squirrel, apparently recognized it as familiar and harmless, and then went back to feeding. For a full five minutes the buck and chipmunk each went about their own business within scant yards of each other. Then suddenly and unexpectedly the chipmunk squeaked, and without even taking a moment to look up the deer was in full flight.

Although I have no evidence to support this, perhaps the chipmunk had become uneasy with my presence and its squeak was some sort of alarm signal the deer recognized. After all, whitetails do have their own ways of communicating danger.

Thus, the smart hunter doesn't concern himself solely with how or what nearby deer may hear but goes to great pains to ensure that he does not spook other creatures as well, which may turn on their own warning sirens.

Yet whitetails also seem to possess an innate curiosity about sounds they've obviously never heard before. One time I was reading a book on small game hunting in which the author recommended loudly kissing the back of your hand to bring shy squirrels out of hiding. On my next bushy-tail outing I tried it, and an eight-point buck sneaked into view, apparently trying to find the source of the sound.

Then there are the sounds that draw no curiosity whatsoever from deer but have the opposite effect of sending them fleeing. The specific nature of the sound doesn't seem nearly as important to whitetails as its cadence. A steady, rhythmic sound, for example, such as a hunter walking along with no occasional pause in his footfalls, is a real spooker, for it serves as advance warning of something sneaking around that's up to no good. In this type of situation the animal needs no additional confirmation from its eyes or nose, for the repeated auditory stimulus has told the brain all it needs to know to make an appropriate response.

This brings us back to once again emphasize the need to move slowly—which all hunters are already aware of—but also to vary the pattern of your footsteps. When a rock inadvertently clinks or dry leaves crunch, come to a halt for that recommended four- to five-minute period described earlier.

Even the times and places where certain sounds occur can have a telling influence on a whitetail's reactions to those sounds.

It stands to reason that a windy or stormy day makes whitetails extremely nervous and jumpy. Not only do the constantly swaying brush, grass, and tree branches make it difficult to classify things that are seen, but the wind also makes identifying intruders by smell equally futile. Add to this the noise of clacking limbs and howling winds, which severely impairs their hearing, and it's no wonder they dive into cover and hide until the weather calms.

For the same reasons, whitetails seldom dawdle around loudly gurgling streams or river courses. They'll come to drink and then leave, or they may cross and continue on their way, but dillydallying increases their vulnerability for the simple reason that the noise of the rushing water competes with a deer's ability to accurately appraise other sounds taking place from time to time.

Yet we have to qualify this, for it is not only the sound of the water itself that is unsettling to deer. Rather, there is an ingrained suspicion of water holes or drinking places along watercourses because these are places where animals customarily preyed upon are most likely to be ambushed.

Without question, there are indeed various areas of the country where timbered river bottoms are like magnets to large numbers of whitetails because of the combination of water, food, and heavy security cover in close proximity to eachother. However, if the water is only serenely gliding along so as not to overly impair a deer's hearing, bucks and does alike may just as well be bedded close to the edge as anywhere else. Yet time and again, from my experience, if the flow of water is loudly bubbling and churning, any deer in the immediate vicinity will predictably locate themselves far back from the actual edge of the water, such as in a hillside thicket or copse of cedars, or perhaps on a terraced bench over the flow. Undoubtedly they choose these spots so they can more easily and effectively distinguish between the sound of the water and other periodic noises that may signal the approach of something that doesn't have their best interests in mind.

Another interesting aside has to do with the way whitetails classify sounds they hear in forest land regions. I find it curious that for years hunters have been scolded as softies for even considering sneaking along on hiker's pathways, fire trails, and old logging roads looking for game. "Be a tough, hardy sportsman and get into the brush!" the critics admonish.

Yet paradoxically, a hunter moving along at a snail's pace on such beaten trails and paths, with long pauses between each forward advance, actually has an excellent chance of getting very close to unsuspecting deer. Staying right on deer trails themselves is even a good bet.

An explanation for this is that such well-established routes generally are tamped down and thereby offer silent footing. But perhaps more importantly, deer themselves use these trails religiously, wending their way along with a minimum of effort and few obstructions to contend with as they travel between feeding, bedding, and drinking locations. Consequently, deer actually come to expect to hear various sounds on such trails, perhaps attributing them to other members of the local deer population as they engage in their own activities. It's the off-trail sounds that strike chords of fear and are most likely to send them hightailing for the next ridge.

With whitetails possessing so many highly refined defense mechanisms, they obviously are never easy quarry under any conditions. But understanding how their sense of hearing works, and how it is continually used in conjunction with their other senses to monitor their surroundings, is sure to help any hunter increase his chances for success.

How Old Is Your Buck?

By Leonard Lee Rue III

Old wives' tales die hard and it is almost impossible to kill some of them off. While there is a great amount of truth in some old beliefs, others are wild misconceptions. When I was a boy, it was common to age deer by the number of points or tines on their antlers. It was believed then, and still is in many areas, that there was a natural progression in the development of the deer's antlers. When a buck was 6 months old, he was a button buck; when he was 18 months old, he had spikes. A buck of 3 years had four points and was known as a Y, a crotch, or a four-point buck. At 4 years of age, a buck was supposed to have six points; at 5 years, he had eight points; at 6 years, ten points, and so on. It is easy to see how this myth got started. It is harder to understand why its fallacy wasn't exposed sooner.

I was raised on a hilltop farm in New Jersey's northwestern Warren County. From time immemorial, farmers checked the teeth of hoofed livestock to determine the age of the animal. It was known that the teeth of browsing and grazing animals were down because of the constant grinding of the vegetation as the animals ate. Aging livestock by looking at the teeth gave rise to that well-known maxim that one should not look a gift horse in the mouth. In other words, you didn't try to age a horse that someone gave you or to take it further, you didn't try to determine its value.

Rural folks knew about tooth wear, but very few of them aged deer that way. It remained for Jack Tanck and C. W. Severinghaus of the New York Conservation Department (now called the Department of Environmental Conservation) to lay the groundwork upon which the system of aging deer by tooth wear was established. This was done in the late 1940s.

When a fawn is born, it has only four teeth. They are in the front of its mouth in the lower jaw and are properly termed incisors. The two center incisors are always larger than the other incisors and are commonly called pincers because they are the main teeth used to clip off the browse that the deer feed upon. Deer, goats, sheep, cattle, and antelope have no front teeth in the upper jaw. Between six and ten days later, four more incisors erupt through the gum line, along with three larger premolar teeth on each side of the mouth at the rear of both the top and bottom jaws. The fawn than has a total of 20 teeth. All of these teeth are deciduous and are often called baby or milk teeth. They are shed and replaced by permanent teeth at a known rate, and knowing this is useful in aging deer.

Most of the hoofed animals have a big gap betwen the incisors in the front of the lower jaw and the rear premolars. This gap is known as the diastema. A fawn has tremendous appeal to humans because it looks cute. This is a human response to the larger-than-normal, slightly bulging skull of most young mammals, including the human baby. The fawn does not look mature until its jawbones have lengthened to accommodate the molar (grinding) teeth in the rear of both jaws. It is only after one year's time that the three molars erupt through the lengthened lower

No, you can't age a buck by counting antler tines. An eight-pointer may only be 1½.

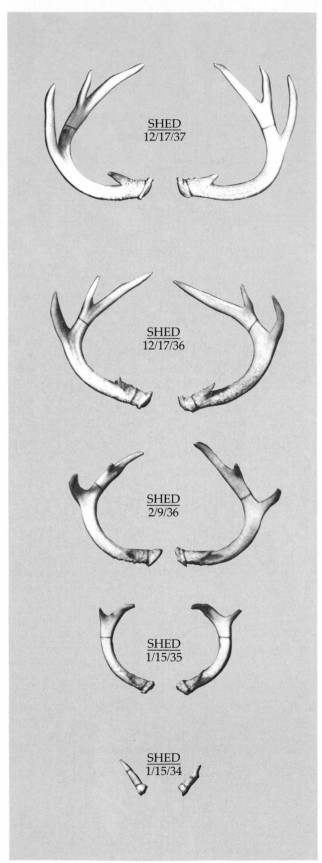

SHED
12/17/37

SHED
12/17/36

SHED
2/9/36

SHED
1/15/35

SHED
1/15/34

Antlers from a tame buck shed in successive winters until age 5½. This has nothing to do with determining age. For instance, if nutrition is good, a 5½-year-old buck may have a 12-point or better trophy rack.

jawbone—three on each side. The first molar erupts at about 6 months of age, the second molar at 9 months of age, and the third rearmost molar is almost completely erupted at 1 year. We are speaking of the lower jaw. There are also six molars in the upper jaw.

With the eruption of the third molars, top and bottom, the deer has a complete set of 32 teeth. The total dentition (both jaws) is described as eight incisors, 12 premolars, and 12 molars. Actually, the two rearmost incisors are more properly known as pseudo-canines. However, these two teeth are identical in size, shape, and function to the incisors.

Occasionally, deer will have two maxillary teeth on each side of the top jaw, toward the front. These are also often classified as canine teeth. These extra teeth are very rare in deer in the North and more common in Southern deer. In New York state, deer having these upper canines make up only .01 percent of the total; in Florida, it is 4.2 percent and, in Texas, it is 17 to 18 percent. These canines are similar to the canine teeth of elk, so avidly sought by some hunters.

Between the fifth and sixth month of age, the center incisors have been pushed out and shed by the emerging permanent incisor teeth. In progession thereafter, working from the inside outward, the other milk incisors are shed and replaced.

Back in the early 1960s, a friend of mine, Bud Disbrow, shot a good-size eight-point buck in Maine. When Bud showed me his buck, I asked him how old it was. His guide had said that it was 6 years old. I said to Bud, "Let's check it out." Using my jaw wrench, I pried the buck's mouth open. Examining the teeth showed that Bud's deer was exactly 17 months of age.

A deer's milk premolars as already mentioned, are also shed and replaced. The third premolar, counting from the front to the rear, has three cusps when it is a milk tooth. A cusp is a point on the chewing surface of a tooth. By the age of 18 months, the premolars are shed and the permanent third premolar has only two cusps. The second and third premolars on Bud's deer had loosened but had not yet fallen out. The permanent two-cusp premolar could be seen pushing the three-cusped milk tooth out. This definitely dated Bud's buck at precisely 17 months.

If you look sideways at the premolars and molars of a deer's jaw, you will notice that each tooth has four slight ridges, with the lowest very near the gum line and each succeeding ridge slightly higher. The first ridge, nearest the gum, is known as the buccal crest; the highest ridge is called the lingual crest. The two ridges in between are the secondary crests. As the teeth wear down with age, you can roughly estimate the deer's age by counting the remaining ridges of the sides of the premolars and molars.

A deer's teeth are covered with enamel, which is very hard. The inner, much darker material is dentine, which is softer. As the teeth wear down and the enamel is worn away, more and more of the darker dentine becomes visible. This is another rough guide to a deer's age. In the photograph that shows the lower jaws of eight deer (page 24), you can see how the teeth gradually wear down and turn darker with age.

To age deer quite accurately from 1½ years of age to 11 years, the amount of remaining teeth showing above the buccal crest is measured with a micrometer. At 1½ years of age, there is about ten millimeters of tooth showing above the gum line. Normal wear accounts for about one millimeter (.039 of an inch) per year. Beyond 11 years, the teeth are usually worn right down to the gum line and can no longer be measured. If you do not have a micrometer, use the accompanying photos to age your deer.

The life span of a whitetail deer is 12 years, so the deer's teeth last as long as it needs them. Because of hunting pressure, however, up to 80 percent of male deer are shot when they are 1½ years old, another ten percent or so at 2½ years, 6 percent at 3½ years, and a percentage point or so per year thereafter. Because a deer does not fully mature until it is 4 years old, most bucks do not have the opportunity to grow old enough and large enough to produce the trophy racks that go in the record books. Of course, very old, declining bucks have smaller and smaller antlers as teeth wear down and their ability to feed themselves diminishes. About one buck in a million makes the book each year.

The aging of deer by tooth wear is the only practical method in the field. It is fairly reliable in most wooded areas but it does not work on coastal plains near the ocean. In such places, sand or grit is often picked up by the wind and deposited on the vegetation. A deer that ingests sand or grit with its food will show excessive wearing of the teeth.

Jack Tanck, whom I greatly admire for his years of field work and observation, clued me in to looking at the secondary ridge below the lingual crest on the first molar. Wear on this tooth is excessive because the deer uses this tooth to cut off the larger twigs it is forced to feed on if browse is scarce. Deer prefer to feed on twigs about the diameter of a wooden match stick. Such twigs are this year's growth and are highly nutritious. They can easily be clipped off by the pincer teeth. During times of starvation, the deer is forced to eat twigs about the diameter of a wooden pencil. This is three- to four-year-old woody growth and contains very little nutrition. The deer ingests a lot of useless lignin cellulose for the small amount of bark covering. These larger twigs cannot be clipped by the pincers and must be chewed off, and the first molar is the tooth called upon to do the job. At 6½ years of age, the secondary ridge on the deer's first molar has been worn off completely. The chances of a hunter or a biologist ever seeing a buck older than 6½ is almost nil.

Although deer have a potential life span of 12 years, most are shot or die long before that age. But there are an increasing number of records of deer that have lived to be more than 20 years old. These are deer that have been raised in captivity and have been fed soft foods, usually in the form of pellets. Wild deer cannot live to such great ages because health deteriorates rapidly once the teeth are worn out. This degeneration usually shows up first in the antlers, which become smaller and smaller once the animal passes it prime at 8 to 9 years. I have seen this happen with both deer and moose.

I have tried, unsuccessfully, to work out an aging system by measuring the base portion of the buck's shed antlers. The convex base of the antler that fitted into the socket on the deer's pedicel is usually oval in shape. Measured across the narrowest diameter, most bucks have a measurement of three-quarters

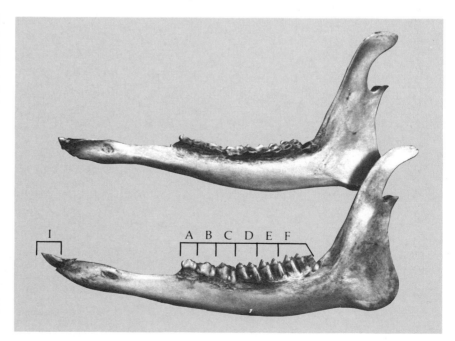

Teeth in an 11½-year-old buck's jaw (top) are so worn down that he could no longer feed efficiently. Natural death was very near. Jaw from 1½-year-old buck (bottom) has teeth almost untouched by wear. Also, the newly erupted third premolar, which comes in last after milk teeth, shows conclusively that the deer was 1½ years old.

A-1st Premolar   D-1st Molar
B-2nd Premolar   E-2nd Molar
C-3rd Premolar   F-3rd Molar
        I-Incisors

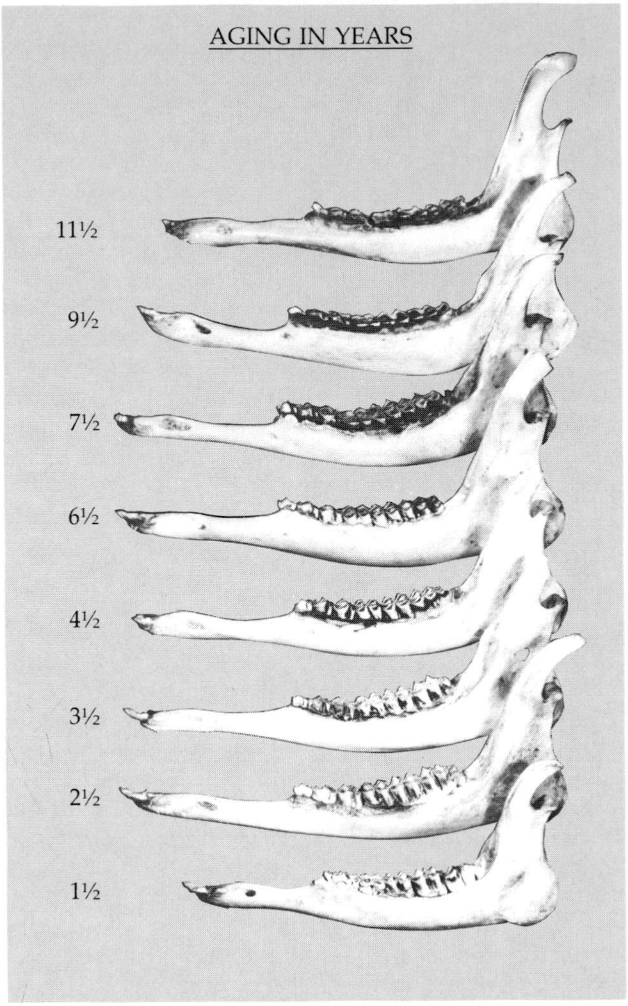

AGING IN YEARS

11½

9½

7½

6½

4½

3½

2½

1½

Aging can accurately be done by noting degree of wear. These jaws are from whitetails ranging from 1½ to 11½ years old. (Some year classes were not available.) Measuring remaining structure above gum line with a micrometer is the way to go, but this photograph can be used to determine approximate age. Guidelines do not hold when grit on food causes abnormal wear.

to seven-eighths of an inch, or 18 to 21 millimeters, at 18 months of age. This discrepancy is what throws the system out of kilter. I could determine no concrete base from which to start my measurements. The discrepancy is caused by three factors: subspeciation, with the antler bases of the larger, Northern deer having a greater diameter than those of deer in the South; the heredity of the deer of any area; and the quality of the food that is available to the individual deer.

One interesting fact that I did discover is that the diameter of that base grows an average of five to six millimeters per year, no matter what the growth of the antler was for that particular year. It is the only segment of the antler to grow larger each year. In a year of good food, the buck will produce good antlers. If a succeeding year produces poor food, the buck's antlers will regress. The base, however, continues to grow larger, regardless. I have a bronze casting of a shed antler owned by Gene Wensel. If that buck had been taken by a hunter during the year that it shed those antlers, it would have become the No. 1 whitetail head. According to my measurements, the buck was 6½ years old when he grew that trophy rack.

Another system for aging deer was tried but discarded, even though it worked. This involved weighing the deer's eye lens. The system was based on studies done by Rexford Lord in conjunction with the aging of cottontail rabbits. The lenses of many eyes, including those of humans, increase in thickness and, therefore, in weight with each additional year. However, using this technique to age deer was abandoned because of the painstaking, time-consuming work that was involved in drying and weighing the lenses.

We are all familiar with the techniques of aging trees by counting their annual rings. We age sheep and goats by counting the dark winter rings in their horns. We age fish by counting the dark winter rings in their scales. I discovered that I could also age fish by the annual growth rings in the flat portions of their vertebrae discs.

In the 1960s, Gilbert and Ransom applied a similar system to deer. It is the most accurate method used in aging most animals, but it can be done only in a laboratory. Winter rings are formed in a deer's teeth because, at that time of the year, the deer is low in blood-serum protein and phosphate, which are needed for tooth formation. A tooth is extracted from the deer's jawbone, usually an incisor. It is taken to a laboratory where it is softened in acid and then sliced into thin layers on a microtome. The slices are then dyed and dried. When checked under a microscope, the bands of lighter-colored cementum stand out in sharp contrast to the dark winter rings.

It is very important to know which tooth has been sliced for the sample being examined. It must be remembered that the premolars are deciduous and show one year less than the deer's actual age. Although the incisors are also shed, they are shed and replaced before the deer's first winter. The molars are not shed, but only the first molar will have all of the winter rings.

Why all this fuss about the accurate age of the deer? It is of vital importance to deer-herd managers because it is the basis for the future hunting seasons. If the majority of the deer are young, this indicates that the population is holding steady or is increasing. When more deer fall into the older categories, it means that the previous winter has been exceptionally hard on deer or that the habitat has deteriorated to the point where the deer herd is about to decline. Knowing the correct age of deer is most important in determining the bag limit and the length of the hunting season.

For your copy of L. L. Rue's *The Deer of North America,* please send $14.95 plus $2.64 for delivery and handling to Outdoor Life Books, Dept. DHY7, Box 2018, Latham, NY 12111.

Amazing Antlers And How They Grow

By Kathy Etling

Antlers and their hidden secrets are being researched like never before and may someday be used to help treat and cure crippling bone diseases.

Primitive people believed that they possessed magical powers. Hunters pursue them relentlessly. Scientists try to discover their secrets. What are they? Antlers!

Antlers are being studied more thoroughly than ever before. Researchers are delving into every detail of antler development. Consequently, more is being learned about antlers all the time.

Researchers have discovered some fascinating facts: They're the fastest form of bone growth known; the blood-rich covering on antlers—called velvet—is the only regenerating skin found among mammals; an antler that is severely injured while growing will heal, although it will be greatly deformed and will "remember" the injury, repeating the deformity every year *for the rest of the buck's life.* An antler is not a horn. A horn is dead and has always been dead. It has no blood supply. Horns grow on both sexes of a species and are made of keratin—a hard protein that also forms the principal matter of fingernails and hair.

Antlers are bone. Male members of the deer families grow them, as do female reindeer and caribou. However, these females shed their antlers two weeks after giving birth. Scientists hypothesize that antlers evolved on these Northern females to help them to protect their calves from wolves in the critical days right after birth.

A buck, however, is programmed to develop antlers before birth. While still in the doe's womb, pedicels—antler growth platforms—start to develop. These pedicels are unique. They're a link between the buck's skull—living tissue—and the antler. Although the antler is living bone for much of the year, it dies once it hardens. The pedicel keeps the dead antler in place on the skull.

Light is the key to antler development, according to Dr. Robert Brown of the Caesar Kleberg Wildlife Research Institute in Kingsville, Texas.

"As days lengthen, the pineal gland—a pea-size gland near the brain's base—receives the message from the eye. Scientists believe that the pineal then releases a hormone—melatonin. When the deer's system contains enough melatonin, the master gland—the pituitary—springs into action. It is speculated that LH [the luteinizing hormone], one of the

Photo courtesy of NORTH AMERICAN WHITETAIL

25

The velvet skin that covers developing antlers is rich with veins and arteries that supply blood to the antlers. As antlers point and harden, the velvet dries and is shed, leaving behind a temporary residue of dried blood. Photos by Dan Brockman

hormones produced by the pituitary, actually triggers the production of testosterone—the male sex hormone—in the testicles. As the testosterone level rises in the buck's blood, the antlers start to grow.''

We know about the pineal gland's contribution because, when it's removed, the buck's antler cycle is thrown out of whack. The buck may then grow antlers during the winter and rub them clean of velvet in the spring.

If the pituitary is removed, the deer won't ever develop antlers—even if artificially injected with testosterone. So far, researchers haven't been able to duplicate the pituitary's function.

One of Dr. Brown's prime objectives was to take samples of growing antler tissue and keep it growing in a test tube, which he has now done. ''By adding or subtracting one hormone at a time, we hope to determine how each affects antler growth,'' he said.

The relationship between light and the antler cycle was discovered by Dr. Dick Goss of Brown University in Providence, Rhode Island. Goss knew that our North American deer had definite antler cycles, but discovered that, at the equator, where day and night are always equal in length, bucks shed their antlers anytime. He found that some even kept their antlers longer than a year. But when relocated in the North, these bucks' antler cycles were identical to those of the native deer.

Dr. Goss even kept laboratory deer indoors to learn about how light governs the antler cycle. If he shortened a year's normal daylight pattern into a six-month period, he found that deer would grow *two* complete sets of antlers per year. Sika bucks can grow up to three sets of antlers per year. But bucks can't grow antlers any faster than three to four months. Once grown, however, the deer immediately rub velvet off the antlers and shed them.

Even at birth, a buck fawn has immature antler bases—the start of pedicels—on his head. Soon, these ''buds'' begin to grow. By autumn, the young buck will have buttons that barely extend above his baby fuzz.

There can be no normal antler cycle without the testes. Aristotle was the first to discover this. If a buck is castrated, many things can happen—depending on the deer's age when castrated. If he's a fawn, he'll never grow antlers. That's because pedicel development is a once-in-a-lifetime event critical to future antler growth.

If an adult buck is castrated, his velvet antlers will continue to grow for the rest of his life. The velvet is never rubbed off, nor are the antlers ever shed—which is why the antlers are so large. In a case such as this, the adrenal gland manufactures just enough testosterone without the testes for antler growth to take place—but not enough for a complete cycle, one that includes shedding of velvet and casting. A deer like this is known as a cactus buck.

If a deer with hard antlers already in place is castrated, he'll lose them within two weeks. He'll grow his cactus set the next spring.

Even does can grow antlers if given shots of testosterone. Recently, a 24-point doe was shot in Kentucky. Biologists discoverd that the doe had undescended testicles in addition to normal female reproductive organs. Such an animal is called a hermaphrodite, meaning that it is of both sexes. The undescended testicles released testosterone and were the reason that the doe sported such flashy headgear.

Dr. Anthony Bubenik of Thornhill, Ontario, has done research in pedicel transplants. If a pedicel is surgically transplanted to another area on the deer's body, a new antler will grow there. Antlers have been successfully grown between deers' eyes, between their ears, and on their foreleg. But an antler grown in this way will never have a brow tine. The transplant procedure destroys the brow tine coding within the deer's nervous system.

Once a fawn grows its first pedicels, the pattern is set for life. A nervous connection has been made between the pedicel and the Antler Growth Center. This center is a site that Dr. Anthony Bubenik's son, Dr. George Bubenik of Guelph University in Ontario, believes exists within the deer's central nervous system, which is composed of both the brain and the spinal cord.

"Once this connection's been made," Dr. George Bubenik explained, "the pedicel itself can be removed or chemically destroyed *and the antler will still grow after healing.* Even if the bone beneath the pedicel is removed, the message to grow an antler will still get through and the buck will grow an antler, although in either case there will be some deformity. New antler growth can only be prevented by destroying such extremely large amounts of tissue that no message is received from the Antler Growth Center."

An antler develops as a lengthening of the skull and it is, in fact, similar to skeletal bone. But growing antlers are cartilage—the pliable substance that you can feel in your nose or your ear.

"The outside of a growing antler is covered with velvet—a skin rich with veins and arteries that supply blood to the antler," according to Dr. Brown. "And the pedicel also acts as a passage that carries blood to the inside of the antler. If you could touch a velvet antler, it would be quite warm because of all this blood. The velvet is also a network of nerves and is very sensitive."

Researchers are trying to unlock the secrets of antler velvet, for they may provide clues to the treatment of burn victims or people afflicted with skin disorders.

As antlers grow, they gradually start to harden. Minerals such as calcium and phosphorus are deposited to form a bony core. Much has been written about adding supplemental minerals to deers' feed to help the animals grow larger antlers.

"A buck can't possibly get all the minerals he needs for the development of his rack from his food," Dr Brown said. "So bucks take minerals from *their own skeletal systems,* especially from the ribs and the sternum, and deposit them in their antlers. The stress to a buck's system is enormous because antlers grow at a tremendous rate.

"When a buck is growing antlers, his ribs become brittle and can break fairly easily," Brown continued. "But wild deer take this in stride—and every year, too. Even if a deer breaks a bone while growing antlers, the break will usually heal smoothly. And when antler growth is complete, the minerals are then restored to the temporarily depleted bones."

This ability to mobilize minerals from one part of the skeleton and deposit them *intact* in another area of the body has scientists excited. Osteoporosis, a disease that depletes minerals in the skeleton, afflicts 25 percent of all Caucasian women over the age of 50. Pelvis, back, and thigh bones become brittle and break easily. Once broken, it's nearly impossible for them to heal.

Osteosarcoma, another bone disease, is a cancer that's difficult to treat and that has a high fatality rate. Massachusetts Senator Edward Kennedy's son lost his leg to this disease several years ago.

The secrets of deer antler growth may help researchers to take a giant step toward understanding and combating these terrible diseases. When a buck depletes his skeletal mineral reserves each spring, he goes through a conditon similar to osteoporosis *every year.* This makes the buck a perfect model to study so that scientists can someday help humans to strengthen diseased bones.

Dr. Brown, along with his associates at the Caesar Kleberg Wildlife Research Institute, is at the forefront of antler growth research. His goal and the goal of other researchers is a major one: to beat both osteoporosis and osteosarcoma by studying antlers.

Research has developed many other interesting observations about deer and their antlers. For example, Dr. Anthony Bubenik writes that every year of a buck's life, the animal will go through three separate stages of sexual development. When a buck casts his antlers, he loses all aggressive tendencies. He becomes timid. It's like a human's infancy. During this time, the pedicels are healing.

As days lengthen, a buck enters the next stage—puberty or adolescence. Buck puberty has two phases: The touch-sensitive phase lasts for about 75 percent of the antler growth period; the second phase, desensitizing, occurs when the antlers point, then harden, and the velvet dies. This stage ends once the velvet is shed. Then the buck enters maturity—the most important part of his yearly cycle. Hardened, polished antlers show that the buck is ready to breed.

During both the infancy and the adolescence stages, the buck doesn't act like a buck at all. His testosterone level is low. Estrogen, the female hormone, is also present in the buck's system and contributes to this odd behavior.

In April a mature whitetail buck shows two nubs where antlers will eventually sprout. By late June, the antlers have already reached partial growth and are covered in velvet.

"During this time, the buck's facial expressions are doelike," according to Dr. Anthony Bubenik. "Males fight like females, standing on hind legs and flailing with forelegs at their opponents' heads. I feel that it's at this time that dominance is decided—not later on when bucks have hardened antlers."

So when deer start the rut, they already know who is head honcho. Perhaps instinctively, they realize that dominance battles with pointed antlers could be dangerous. Because of this, Dr. Anthony Bubenik feels that the battles that do occur when bucks have hardened antlers are more of a ritual than a determination of rank.

However, deer will occasionally use their antlers to fight in deadly earnest. This will occur if a buck wants another buck's doe. This rarely happens in a population where bucks are aware of rank before the rut begins. Sparring may also take place when a buck wanders out of his territory and into the territory of a dominant buck. Fights such as this are short; they end when status is determined.

The last type of fight occurs when a young, inexperiened buck enters a prime male's mating area and challenges him with no regard to threats and warnings. This can be dangerous for the young buck if the prime male is fit. However, after the rut, young bucks can be very aggressive and the dominant buck may be exhausted. The prime male can, in fact, lose and be killed. If the dominant buck is wounded, this makes the younger buck more bloodthirsty. He'll attack relentlessly, often killing the older buck in the process.

Dr. Anthony Bubenik believes that deer spar with each other for one of two reasons: to gain fighting skills for the future, and to determine their antler shape—something that they apparently can't tell until antler growth stabilizes during their prime. This kind of sparring or play-fighting is common among deer that hang out in bachelor bands.

The second kind of sparring, demonstration sparring, lets the bucks test each other's rank, verifying dominance.

Dr. Anthony Bubenik thinks that bucks start soliciting for attention during the rut *while they're still in velvet.*

"They rub the pheromones from the velvet secretion on vegetation throughout their range as a sort of prerut advertising campaign," he explained. "Deer further ensure the connection between their scent and themselves by gently rubbing the velvet over their bodies and scratching it with their hooves. This way, they'll track their pheromones all over the countryside."

Once the velvet is shed, deer lose this means of communication. But Dr. Anthony Bubenik believes that they compensate for this loss by coating their hardened antlers with pheromones from their urine—either deposited directly on the antlers or from treated vegetation.

Bodily injuries also affect antlers. When a buck injures his rear leg while he's in velvet, the antler on the *opposite* side will be stunted. Scientists aren't positive, but some think that they're on the right track with this explanation: A deer hurts his left rear leg. Because deer walk by raising and lowering the opposite front and hind legs simultaneously, the right foreleg and the *injured* left hind leg support the body's weight half of the time. To compensate, the

In September a buck rubs the velvet from his full-grown antlers in readiness for the rut. Shown above are two views of an eight-pointer. The whitetail's antlers are typified by a single main beam on each side with tines growing off each beam.

Illustrations by Doug Allen

Antler Growth Center slows down the right antler's development so that *less* weight is bearing on the affected limb.

If a front leg is injured, the antler on the *same* side will be smaller because the antler on the same side weighs on the injured limb when the animal takes a step.

If the antler itself is injured during growth, it will overdevelop. But the greatest growth doesn't occur the year of the injury. It takes place *the following year.* Again, the antler seems to "remember" the injury from year to year. If the right antler is injured, *only* the right antler will develop excessively. It is known, therefore, that each antler develops independently of the other.

If an antler is injured early in the growing cycle, it will experience the most damage. Such an injury results in the most spectacularly deformed antlers.

Light is apparently the only outside factor affecting the antler cycle. Temperature plays no part at all. And food affects size, but not the cycle itself. However, if a buck has inadequate nutrition, he will shed his antlers early.

Once the buck has hardened antlers, he is ready to fulfill his biological function—fathering the next crop of fawns. The majority of the breeding in a well-balanced population is done by prime males.

Dr. Anthony Bubenik has observed that whitetails, mule deer, and elk use what he calls "deception strategy" at various times.

"In deception strategy," he said, "the antler shape is altered when the buck attacks vegetation with his antlers, then leaves moss, leaves, or grass clinging to them instead of shaking it off. The buck then pa-rades around as if knowing that this will intimidate other bucks by making his antlers appear larger than they really are. Deception strategy is used mainly during long-lasting, evenly matched contests. When a buck practices deception strategy, the other male will give up and retreat. He'll accept the higher rank and be totally fooled by the deception."

Velvet shedding corresponds to the amount of light, so all shedding occurs in a three-week time span. But the antler-casting dates vary greatly. In a study performed by Dr. Harry Jacobson and Bob Griffin of the Department of Wildlife and Fisheries of Mississippi State University, it was found that antlers were shed over a *three month* period.

"This very possibly shows that bucks have a pre-programmed rhythm that causes them to cast their antlers," said Dr. Jacobson. "Say that Deer No. 1 casts his antlers on December 22 and Deer No. 2 casts his on January 31. If these deer are kept under identical conditons from year to year, the evidence is great that they will cast their antlers *on almost the same date every year.*"

"Casting is truly amazing," concludes Dr. Brown. "One day you can't knock a buck's antlers off, and then the next day they'll just fall off. The buck's testosterone drops below the level needed to maintain antlers and the pedicel then demineralizes. Casting soon follows."

After shedding, the pedicel looks like an open sore, but it heals quickly.

Someday soon, scientists will probably know all the answers to the antler questions. But even then, the antler will be no less marvelous. A structure like an antler will always be . . . amazing!

PART 2

HUNTING WHITETAIL DEER

More Land To Hunt Deer

By John O. Cartier

My partner and I were executing one-man drives through small woodlots in western Michigan's farm country. It was my turn to take a stand along the north end of some brier thickets near a gravel road. I had walked within 50 yards of my destination when I glimpsed four whitetails sneaking through the brush. I was sure that Charlie had jumped the deer, but the vegetation was too thick to see if any of the animals wore antlers.

The dilemma was over in seconds. The whitetails bounded out of the briers and onto the road, in clear view. The largest one wore a six-point rack that glistened in the late-afternoon sun. The last deer in line was a fine spike buck. I had no time to shoot, though—the deer no more than hesitated before they began running. I'm sure that they were unaware of me because none had looked in my direction. I watched them run across a clearing, then melt from view in another woodlot 300 yards to the north.

"They didn't even notice me," I said when Charlie arrived on the scene. "I saw all four white flags clearly as they reached the edge of the woods, then they just disappeared. I think those deer stopped as soon as they hit cover. I'd bet they're standing there watching us."

Charlie didn't even bother answering me. He turned and began trotting toward his truck. I knew exactly what was going through his mind. First, we didn't have permission to hunt the property where the deer were. Second, we had less than two hours to get that permission, make another drive, and shoot a buck before it got too dark to hunt.

There wasn't a farmhouse in sight, but there was a quick and easy way for us to find out who owned the property. We checked our plat book, which we always carry in the truck. In moments, we found

that the woodlot we wanted to drive was part of 116 acres owned by Ralph Berndt. The book also told us that there were buildings on the north side of the property, and we surmised that one of the buildings would likely be the house where Berndt resided.

Within 15 minutes, our assumptions proved correct. As soon as we introduced ourselves, we got good news.

"Yeah, you guys can try for those bucks," he said. "Partly because you had enough courtesy to ask before charging into those woods, and partly because I'm getting too much crop damage from deer. I see deer coming out this end of those woods all the time, and they almost always walk out through the same gully. I'll show you right where to stand."

About 40 minutes later, I was making my zigzag drive through the woodlot when I heard the crack of Charlie's .243. I walked toward the sound and came upon Charlie field-dressing the six-pointer.

He looked up, grinned, and said, "Thank the Lord for plat books."

Plat books (sometimes called land atlas books) are books of maps. Each full-page map covers one township, and a full book covers all the townships in any given county. My plat book covers Mason County, Michigan. It has detailed plat maps for the county's 16 townships. In effect, my plat book gives me land-ownership details on more than 100 square miles of potential hunting country.

Plat books have various uses. A county extension agent told me: "I use my plat book all the time while

working out problems with farmers. When a landowner calls me, I can immediately check to see where his land is and how many acres he owns."

Oil companies use plat books when working on lease arrangements. Any business that is involved with particulars of land ownership has use for plat books.

All plat books detail and depict specifics relating to many factors besides land ownership. All data in the books is gathered from official public records at county court houses and elsewhere. An index map in each book shows the geographical location of each township. Numerals on each township indicate the page on which particular maps appear in detail.

Each parcel of land in a plat book map shows the name of the owner or owners, the exact location, the area and shape of the parcel, and its size in acres. Towns and villages, rivers and lakes, locations of buildings on each parcel, all roads and highways (including their names), railroads, section numbers, and section lines are also shown on each map. A list of landowners is included in each book, as well. This index is an alphabetical listing of every landowner in each county whose name appears on the book's township maps.

Here's how the alphabetical listing can help you. Suppose somebody mentions that he heard there are a lot of deer on Fred Johnson's property in Branch Township, but he doesn't know where the Johnson property is. Just get out your plat book and look up Fred Johnson in the index listing. Following the

Plat books are the key to a deer hunter's treasure chest. A little research with these landowner maps can put you onto prime deer territory that the average hunter doesn't even know about.

Photo by Dan Brockman

name, you will find the section and page number of his land.

Typically, a plat book is useful for those times when you see a piece of property that you want to hunt, but it can be used in other ways, too. Strange as it may seem, we used my plat book twice last fall to get hunting permission for lands that we had already hunted for many years.

In the first instance, we had decided to work our one-man drive in a wooded area that always held a lot of deer. When we drove up to the place, we noticed that it had been freshly posted with "No Trespassing" signs. The land had been sold, so the hunting permission granted from the previous owner was obviously worthless.

Fortunately, our plat book for this area was a brand new, updated issue. It did indeed show that the land had a new owner, but there were no farm buildings on the property. We drove to a country store, looked up the landowner's phone number in a directory, and called him. We got permission to hunt the whole 120 acres.

Another instance concerned a new gate across a two-track road on property that had never been posted. We had been hunting the lowlands for so many years that we couldn't remember the owner's name, but we did recall that he taught school in a nearby village. Our plat book immediately revealed the landowner's name. It took only minutes to call the school and get in touch with him.

"I put that gate there because I'm getting too much traffic on the two-track," the landowner told me.

"But if you fellows want to walk in, go right ahead. You can still hunt my land."

Our most surprising access to hunting lands through use of our plat books came one fall several years ago, when we had found two well-traveled deer runways during our preseason scouting. We suspected that they very likely merged on property that we didn't have permission to hunt. We tracked down the landowner and didn't have any trouble getting hunting permission.

One evening several days later, we were studying a plat book when we came across the same landowner's name on a different piece of property. Then we found that the same man owned two more 80-acre parcels in the same area. Over the weekend, we visited him again.

"All told, I own almost 400 acres and rent another 200," Brad told us. "You fellows can hunt on all the land I control."

That's still not the end of the story. It turned out that Brad did quite a bit of hunting himself, and he happened to mention that the cost of ammunition was getting so high that hunting was becoming too expensive. Well, Charlie handloads all of our shells and cartridges so, the next time we visited Brad, we left enough .30/06 and 12-gauge loads to last our new friend for years.

He thanked Charlie and said. "My uncle owns a lot of land in this area, too. His name is Robert Lundberg, and I'll tell him that I've given you two permission to hunt it. Feel free to hunt any Bob Lundberg land you can find on your maps."

In that instance, our use of a plat book gained us hunting access to almost 1,000 acres of land.

Another similar experience occurred when Charlie and I were going grouse and woodcock hunting one day before the firearms deer season opened. We always leave home about dawn so we can look for deer feeding in crop fields on our way to bird hunting spots. It's not unusual to see one buck in a picked cornfield and, sometimes, we see two together. Rarely do we see more than two, though, so you can imagine our astonishment when we spotted five mature bucks in one bunch.

We naturally figured that we had chanced upon a great place to hunt deer. So we forgot about gunning birds and decided to try to get deer hunting permission. Out came the plat book. We discovered that the bucks had been standing on property owned by Charles Holden. There were no buildings on the 80-acre parcel, so we resorted to a trick that we often use when we're in a hurry. We check names on mailboxes in the immediate area while driving slowly down nearby roads. The stunt worked that day. Within minutes, we found a roadside mailbox bearing the landowner's name.

Holden turned out to be another one of an increasing number of farmers who are suffering too much crop damage by deer. Not only did we get permission to hunt his land, but we got the OK to hunt his brother's adjoining 80 acres. Further, we received permission to hunt the Holden family homestead, which covers 120 acres in the same area.

Although plat books can be a tremendous help in getting hunting permission, they're certainly no guarantee of positive results of any kind. Some landowners will consider giving permission; others won't. The most negative response I ever got occurred several years ago when Charlie and I came upon a farm-country pond that was loaded with ducks.

I found the owner's name in my plat book, got his phone number from a telephone directory, and called him. The conversation was very short.

"Hello," said the friendly voice.

"Hi," I responded. "My name is John Cartier. My buddy and I do a lot of duck hunting, and we were wondering. . ."

"Absolutely not," the now-hostile voice roared. "I don't want anybody shooting those ducks. Leave 'em alone and don't bother me again."

On the other hand, one of the most positive approaches led to some top-notch farm-country mallard hunting last fall. The first morning of the season found me trying to decoy ducks on a friendly farmer's pond. Flock after flock bypassed me, heading east. Because I wasn't getting any shooting, I decided to try find out where those ducks were going.

After only a few miles of driving while watching other east-flying flocks, I hit pay dirt. The ducks were going down in what appeared to be an unbroken field of standing corn. I knew that there had to be one or more ponds out there, but what was more important was the total lack of shooting. If I could get permission to hunt that place, I'd have the fabulous action all to myself. That's just the way it worked out.

After my plat book led me to the farmer, he told me, "Sure, go ahead and hunt those ducks. A lot of them have been there all summer. There's three ponds out there, and there's two ways of getting to them. C'mon, get in my truck and I'll show you the lay of the land."

You can't do much better than that. But keep in mind that some parcels of land that you may not have thought of, or may not have even realized existed, are open to public hunting.

In many states, public utilities own rights-of-way for their power lines. Often, these routes are about 200 yards wide by hundreds of miles long (watch for private holdings on either side, though). I hunted lots of those rights-of-way last fall. They're clearly marked in my plat book.

Other top bets are paper company lands. In many cases, they're open to hunting and, of course, they're clearly mapped in plat books. Still another possibility is tax-advantage land. This is privately owned land, but its owner gets tax breaks if he or she opens them to public hunting and fishing. Check to find out if your state offers these property-tax advantages.

Everything said so far will help you only if plat books are available for the counties in which you want to hunt. There is one sure way to find out. All privately owned lands in every state are taxed, and

tax assessors must have totally accurate land descriptions. Such descriptions are always kept in county courthouses. Any one of three sources, in any county courthouse in the nation, will have information on whether or not a plat book (or county land atlas) is available for the county you're interested in. Visit or phone the county clerk, registrar of deeds, or treasurer.

Plat books are compiled by private concerns—usually map publishers. I know of only three, but there are probably more. Of the three publishers that I'm aware of (one each in Colorado, Indiana, and Illinois), the largest is Rockford Map Publishers, 4525 Forest View Ave., Box 6126, Rockford, IL 61125 (815-399-4614). This concern publishes county plat books for at least some counties in 18 states. It has maps for more than 100 counties in Illinois. The picture is similar for Indiana, Iowa, Michigan, Minnesota, and Wisconsin.

Ron Baxter of Rockford Map Publishers had the following to tell me: "We start from scratch on every plat map we produce. We begin with the aerial surveys and regular highway maps. We have our own crews check out all important facts about land descriptions, then they draw our maps. There often is little uniformity from state to state on how land parcels may be mapped for tax purposes. But the bottom line is that plat maps always show who owns what and precisely where it is. I doubt if there is a better tool for a sportsman who is serious about finding new lands to hunt on."

Plat maps are no more difficult to read than standard highway maps. A few of the legends are a bit unusual, but the explanations for them are found on a general information page in the beginning of each plat book. Most of Rockford's plat books sell for $17 each. Some are more expensive because they cover more than the average number of townships.

If a plat book isn't available for the county that you live in, there probably is another route to some of the same information. In every county courthouse, there is a department that keeps totally accurate land descriptions. In my county, it's called the Equalization Department. It may be called something else in other states, but its purpose is to keep accurate land descriptions for tax purposes. The information in these records is available to the public.

Suppose, for instance, I want to hunt some property that's located at the corner of Dewey and Hanson roads. I can go to the Equalization Department in my county courthouse and ask about the property. I can then learn who owns the property and how many acres it covers. At this point, I know if the property is large enough to warrant hunting, and I have the name of the person to contact. The problem with this approach is that you must have a reasonable description of where the property is before the county employee can find it in the tax roll records. The point is that somebody in every county courthouse can tell you who owns a specific piece of property that you want to hunt, whether or not there's a plat book that covers the county.

Plot Your Buck: How To Forecast The Rut

By Jerald Bullis

The merest mention of the rut in the company of whitetail enthusiasts is enough to start a discussion that only the onset of deer season may conclude. And no wonder. Of all North American game species, probably none is as much surrounded by homespun beliefs as the whitetail. In my Ozark youth, I once listened to two old-timers argue for an hour about which side of a tree to hang a saltbait on.

Of all the myths that have evolved, though, few are as ingrained as those concerning the breeding season. It seems to be a rule of human nature that, where mystery most abounds, opinions set the hardest. But if you believe that a warm fall blunts the sex drive in bucks, that the rut peaks after three or four hard frosts, or that the breeding season occurs earlier the farther north you are, you may just as well be telling deer stories around the fire.

Anyone who has ever bagged a spikehorn within hollering distance of a ground scrape or a buck rub has an opinion on this subject. In recent decades, however, the whitetail rut has increasingly been the subject of scientific investigation. Thanks to the work of wildlife researchers, we now know a lot more about the ritual mating behavior of deer than our precursors afield could possibly have known. But the mass of information—often conflicting—is itself bewildering. And if you don't sort it and interpret it like a detective, it may do more harm than good for your self-image as the natural heir of Boone and Crockett.

It is no secret that whitetail bucks, especially tro-

phy bucks, are a little easier to hunt during the rut. But you can't hunt the rut effectively if you don't know when it occurs, what is its duration, how it proceeds, and what phases of it are most productive from a hunter's standpoint.

From 1961 through 1968, Lawrence Jackson and William Hesselton, who were both then senior wildlife biologists with the New York Department of Environmental Conservation, headed a study to determine the breeding dates of whitetails in New York. The graph of *Breeding Dates of Whitetailed Deer in New York State,* which accompanied their published research, remains one of the most valuable summaries of such data that a whitetail hunter can possibly find.

Using the embryos from 864 dog- and road-killed does of various ages, and assuming an average gestation period of 202 days, Jackson and Hesselton determined the ages of the embryos and then, by backdating, were able to pinpoint the times of conception for does in the sample. Their work confirmed studies conducted in other Northern states, which indicated that breeding in this range occurs primarily from mid to late November.

"Fine," says the veteran hunter of Northern whitetails. "Now tell me something that I didn't already know."

That was my reaction when I first saw the graph. But the more I thought about it, the more I became intrigued by the peak-and-valley motion of the rut's progress. All experienced deer hunters are aware of this surge-and-lull characteristic of whitetails during

With the help of the graphs and chart included in this chapter, you can actually calculate and plan on the days when a buck will return to an active scrape. Photo by Leonard Rue III

the rut. One day, you can't buy a buck scrape; the next, the woods and field edges are polka-dotted with them and whitetails are seemingly everywhere. Then the scrapes dry up, leaf over, and the species appears to be nearly extinct. Suddenly, the scrapes are scuffed clear again and big bucks are charging through the woods once more.

The reason for this on-again/off-again behavior is well known. The bucks, especially prime-age bucks, are both physically and psychically ready for action long before actual breeding takes place. The timing of the rut is determined by when does come into heat. But such activity all too often appears completely haywire from a human perspective. The Jackson and Hesselton graph describes a pattern of breeding behavior that—regardless of when the peak of rut occurs—is remarkably consistent throughout the temperate zones of the whitetail's range.

But if you don't know how to interpret this information, it isn't going to help much. According to the graph, the peak New York breeding date is November 15, and the major secondary peaks are on November 20 and 22. Most hunters would assume

that these are the prime times to scrape-watch for a buster buck. Actually, though, these are the *worst* dates for hunting a key scrape, particularly if you are trophy hunting.

The hunter should focus on the graph's valleys, not the peaks. The peaks indicate those 24-hour periods when a substantial number of does are bred. Necessarily, then, these peaks represent those brief times when a larger than usual number of does are in heat.

The slopes and valleys represent the lulls in *actual breeding*. This is an all-important distinction for the scrape hunter, because the lulls in actual breeding are the peak times for bucks to be in the vicinity of the key scrapes. From the hunter's point of view, the valleys *are* the peaks.

At the peak breeding times, the dominant bucks and most of the lesser bucks will be off the scrapes and on the does. After each peak, scraping action will increase as actual breeding diminishes. This pattern makes perfectly good sense from the bucks' point of view, and they seem to know what they are doing. Various researchers have estimated that 95

HUNTING THE RUT: NOEL FEATHER

Noel Feather has taken three Boone and Crockett whitetails, two of them with a bow, and a number of other bucks that qualify for the Pope and Young bowhunter's record book. He's well known as a hunter who has successfully rattled in bucks to within bow range. I decided to ask him how he hunts the rut in his home state of Illinois.

"Rattling did not work as well during the peak week of the rut. The reason," he said, "is that the bucks most always have a doe with them. If she is in heat or he knows that she is soon coming in heat, he will not leave her at this peak time to respond to horns in order to steal another doe.

"Rattling works the best during the two weeks prior to this peak week and two weeks after the peak week. After that, it still works for the remainder of the hunting season, but tends to taper off somewhat."

Is hunting undisturbed deer important to his success?

"Most of my hunting is done during the bow season. At this time, there is not as much competition. In Illinois, 95 percent of the land is privately owned. Therefore, you need permission to hunt, and most landowners will only give a few people permission to hunt on their land. As a rule, you don't have enough people in the field at one time to disturb the deer."

to 98 percent of mature does are successfully bred every year throughout the whitetail's range, regardless of weather or hunting pressure.

After running with a doe or does from, say, November 14 to 16, the mature buck will immediately resume making and checking scrapes when those deer are no longer in heat. But now the number of does coming into heat is falling off, and the competition among all antlered bucks is much keener, so the buck may not find a receptive doe in his first circuit of the scrapes. If this is the case, he simply starts making the rounds all over again until he is successful.

The mature buck's pattern of monitoring prime scrapes during the valley periods of the rut is of special significance for the hunter during the month immediately preceding the actual peak of breeding. Both Gene Wensel and Noel Feather, who hunt in western Montana and northern Illinois, respectively, agree that this prepeak period is when the most dramatic ritual rutting activity takes place. The observations of these two phenomenally successful whitetail hunters have been decisively confirmed by a recently published study conducted in Upper Michigan, *Comparative Breeding Behavior and Performance of Yearling vs. Prime-Age Whitetailed Bucks* (Ozoga and Verme, 1985).

According to this six-year study of breeding behavior, ground scraping for both prime-age and yearling bucks peaked from November 3 to 9. But the peak breeding time for all bucks was November 17 to 23. Hence, ritual rutting activity—sparring, fighting, scrape-making, and scrape-checking—be-

gan to peak two weeks before actual breeding reached its high point. The other significant finding is that bucks in the 3- to 8-year-old category begin scraping long before yearling bucks do. Among the study animals, yearling bucks did not commence scraping until October 13. The older bucks began in late August, though their scraping did not increase sharply until October 27. (Note that October 27, on the New York graph, is the first significant valley date following the mini–breeding peak that takes place on October 23.)

So what does all of this mean to the hunter? Simply that the actual peak scrape-hunting times, according to the graph, are October 16 to 20 (when primary scrapes are opened by dominant bucks—approximately 28 days before the breeding peak); October 30 and 31 (the time immediately preceding the first plateau of breeding on November 1 and 2); the major valley breaks during the two weeks before actual breeding peaks, namely, November 3, 11, and 14; and the chief valley periods within the November 15 to December 6 span (November 16 to 19, November 21, November 23 to 27, November 29 to December 1, and December 3 and 6).

I do not mean to suggest that you should forget about hunting on opening day and begin marking the calendar for November 21, November 23 to 27, and so on. The graph is simply another means of coordinating your strategy with the movement patterns of deer.

I've heard that, if you watch a fresh primary scrape for five days, you'll see the buck that made it. The graph supports that theory insofar as there is not a five-day span without a major valley break. But do you want to spend five days in a tree not knowing which day the buck is going to show up? Or would you want to enter and leave a prime scrape area that many times, thereby increasing the chance of spooking your quarry out of the area entirely? Scrape-watching is a tricky undertaking at best, and every hunter who has had success this way agrees that you are better off spending 10 hours in the right place on the right day, instead of two hours there on five successive days.

How accurate is the graph? You would think that variables such as weather, herd size, number of fawn does in the herd, buck/doe ratios, and other factors would cause drastic annual fluctuations in the pattern of the rut. Neither my New York records nor studies of whitetail breeding seasons elsewhere in the United States confirm yearly fluctuations.

Take the presence of many fawn does in the herd, for example. Research by fetal examination has established that fawn does normally are bred later than adult does in all parts of the country. The presence of fawn does in a research sample to determine breeding dates will typically increase the length of the breeding season—say, from October into March instead of October through mid-December. But the fawn does have no effect on the central breeding pattern. A Massachusetts study is representative (Shaw and McLaughlin, 1951). All does in the sample

SAMPLE GRAPH (New York)

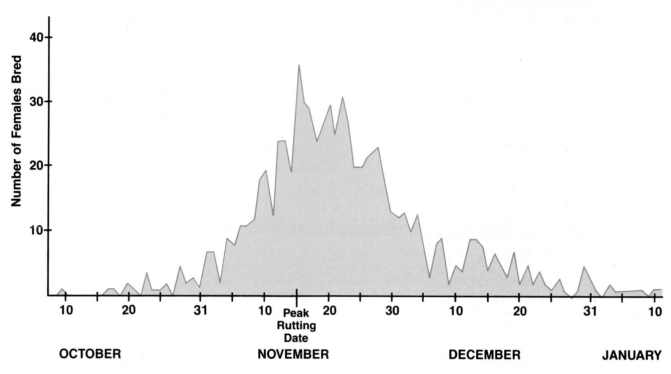

The top graph, taken from BREEDING DATES OF WHITETAIL DEER IN NEW YORK STATE, shows that the peak breeding date is November 15. The best times to watch a scrape for a buck fall on the corresponding valley dates: November 11, 14, 18, 21, 24, and 30. Valley dates for the months of October and December are also productive.

Check the Known Rutting Dates table on page 38 to find the peak breeding date or dates in your state. Write that date at the bottom of the graph below, on the line that marks the highest peak. Fill in the dates before and after accordingly. Many of the states in the table list several days as the peak, while others have a range but no peak. Simply pick the median date from either and plot it below the high peak. When completed, the valley dates will denote the best times to hunt.

PLOTTING GRAPH

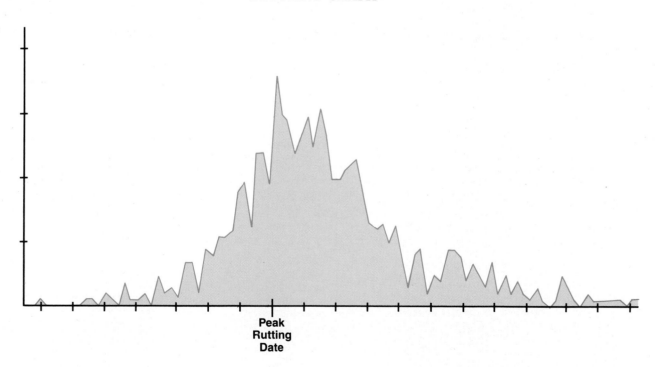

bred between October 31 and January 29. The peak breeding date was November 15, and 45 percent of adult does bred between November 15 and 21. All but one adult doe bred by December 6. The late breeders were all fawns, and the principle breeding pattern conformed to the Jackson and Hesselton model.

Noel Feather lives in Sterling, Illinois, and has taken three Boone and Crockett whitetails in that northern portion of the state. He says that the peak breeding week where he hunts is November 15 to 22 and that significant rutting activity begins during the week of October 25 to November 1. These dates are in precise accord with the New York graph and are generally supported by a study conducted at Crab Orchard National Wildlife Refuge in Illinois (Nelson and Woolf, 1985).

His first Boone and Crockett buck was killed with a gun on November 12, 1977. No scrape was near or in the immediate area. The 12th is the first day of a two-day breeding peak. A hunter watching a primary scrape in the buck's territory probably wouldn't have seen him that day, even if Feather hadn't been in the woods.

His second Boone and Crockett buck was bow killed on December 3, 1977. This date is a valley on the graph. Again, no scrape was close by, but the dominant buck was called in with rattling antlers, a sure sign that he wasn't with a doe in breeding condition.

"My third Boone and Crockett was a bow kill on November 25, 1982," Feather said. "There was an active scrape within 30 yards of where the buck was taken."

As the graph shows, November 25 is smack at the bottom of the most extreme drop-off in actual breeding following the November 15 to 22 peak span. This buck was rattled into a scrape area during a prime period of ritual rutting activity after a period of intense breeding.

My own experience also confirms the accuracy of the graph. During bow season some years back, I rattled in what looked like an excellent buck, but he wouldn't come all the way to a bow shot. The next day, November 3, I rattled from the same spot at 8 A.M. The stand was situated about 70 yards from an active primary scrape and 25 yards off a scrape line. In the 45 minutes after I rattled, four antlered bucks and two button bucks passed within bow range of my stand. One of the antlered bucks came in with his rack swinging and was trying to rake one of the buttons when I killed him. I caught those bucks back in the scrape area right after the first important breeding peak of the season.

Known Rutting Dates

State	Range	Peak	State	Range	Peak
Alabama	Oct. 25–Feb. 21	Jan. 24–31	Michigan	NA	Nov. 1–15
Arizona	NA	Feb. 1–15	Michigan (U.P.)	Oct. 28–Jan. 27	Nov. 17–23
Arkansas (north)	Oct. 21–Dec. 17	Nov. 5	Minnesota	Sept. 15–Feb.	NA
Arkansas (central)	Nov. 2–Jan. 1	Dec. 1	Mississippi (north)	Dec. 5–Jan. 28	Dec. 18–31
Arkansas (south)	Oct. 25–Feb. 6	Nov. 27	Mississippi (south)	Dec. 5–Feb. 24	Jan. 29–Feb. 11
Colorado	Oct. 1–Dec. 15	NA	Missouri (south)	Oct. 1–Dec. 7	NA
Connecticut	Sept. 24–Jan. 7	NA	Montana (northcentral)	Nov. 7–Dec. 10	NA
Delaware	NA	NA	Montana (southwest)	NA	Nov. 17–23
Florida (Palm Beach area)	Aug. 1–Sept. 27	NA	Nebraska	Oct. 21–Mar. 1	NA
Florida (Keys)	Aug.–June	NA	New Hampshire	NA	Nov. 15
Georgia (northeast)	Nov. 5–Nov. 30	NA	New Jersey	Oct. 20–Jan. 4	NA
Georgia (mid-east)	Oct. 10–Nov. 25	NA	New Mexico (north)	Jan.–Feb.	NA
Georgia (central)	Nov. 1–Nov. 30	NA	New Mexico (central)	Dec.–Jan.	NA
Georgia (midwest)	Oct. 20–Nov. 20	NA	New Mexico (south)	Dec.–Jan. 15	NA
Georgia (southeast)	Sept. 5–Oct. 30	NA	New York	Oct. 1–Feb. 9	Nov. 15
Georgia (southwest)	Dec. 1–Jan. 15	NA	North Carolina	Oct. 1–Nov. 10	NA
Idaho (Hatter's Creek area)	Nov. 18–Dec. 11	NA	North Dakota	Sept.–Mar.	NA
Illinois (north)	NA	Nov. 15–22	Ohio	Oct. 22–Dec. 9	NA
Illinois (Crab Orchard NWR)	NA	Nov. 16–27	Oklahoma	NA	Nov. 2–26
Indiana	NA	NA	Pennsylvania	Sept. 24–Feb. 14	NA
Iowa	NA	Nov.	Rhode Island	Oct.–Dec.	NA
Kansas	Nov. 8–Dec. 20	NA	South Carolina (west-central)	Sept. 30–Dec. 25	Oct. 28–Nov. 2
Kentucky	Oct.–Jan.	NA			
Louisiana (Jackson-Bienville-GMA)	Dec. 2–Jan. 26	Dec. 2–15	Tennessee (Cumberland Plateau)	Oct. 29–Feb. 9	NA
Louisiana (Tensas Parish)	Dec. 10–Feb. 26	Jan. 1–15	Texas (central)	Sept. 1–Dec.	Nov. 1–15
Louisiana (New Iberia)	Sept. 26–Dec. 9	Oct. 1–31	Texas (south)	Nov. 16–Mar. 15	Dec. 16–31
Louisiana (Red Dirt GMA)	Oct. 22–Jan. 25	Nov. 1–15	Vermont	Nov. 1–Dec. 15	NA
Louisiana (Delta NWR)	Nov. 15–Jan. 18	Dec. 14–29	Virginia	Oct. 1–Nov. 30	NA
Louisiana (W. Bay GMA)	Sept. 27–Dec. 9	Oct. 16–31	Washington	Oct. 1–Dec. 15	NA
Maine	Oct. 20–Dec. 28	NA	West Virginia	Oct. 13–Jan. 18	NA
Maryland	Oct. 1–Dec. 31	NA	Wisconsin	Late Sept.–Jan. 8	NA
Massachusetts	Oct. 31–Jan. 29	Nov. 15	Wyoming	NA	NA

The next fall, I was hunting grouse and woodcock one afternoon during the bowhunting season when I found a freshly worked-over key scrape area. I hurried home, stashed the shotgun, and hung a stand ten yards off a scrape line heading into the big scrape. I spend the next two days there and saw one doe—she was blatting all out through the brush about 100 yards off.

I decided to try it again the next morning anyway. I watched a pushing match between a spikehorn and a six-pointer that began about 8 A.M. At 9:30 A.M., an eight-point buck came by and, when he crossed the scrape line 10 yards out, I put an arrow through his lungs.

The date was November 11. The interesting thing to me about this situation—which occurred before I had laid eyes on the graph—is that I found the scrape cluster on November 8, as the rut was moving toward its first real peak. I hunted the area without success on November 9 and 10 when, according to the graph, the first high point of the 20-day peak breeding span occurs. Then I saw the bucks start sidling back in the next day, as the graph took its biggest dip of the season to that date.

One morning in 1985, I climbed into a stand that I had placed near a hedgerow a few days earlier. I was 150 yards from the nearest woodlot and nowhere near a primary scrape. I had a fine view of cut corn and winter wheat all around, though, and figured that I might learn something about the dawn movement of deer before the shotgun season opened.

I hung my bow on a limb and started to get the binoculars out when I heard a *chunk-chunking* in the frost. It was coming along the hedgerow toward me. A doe went by and, by then, I had an arrow on the string.

A few seconds behind her came a nice buck with another doe. He didn't look as if he was going to stop and pose, but he wasn't moving all out. The arrow angled forward from left to right, a complete pass-through that caught liver, diaphragm, and right lung.

The date was November 15, the breeding peak. That buck wasn't anywhere near a hot scrape, and neither was I.

So what does all this mean for the hunter who doesn't live in New York state? Quite a bit, I believe, because the evidence so far strongly indicates that the New York graph portrays the core model of the rut for whitetail deer anywhere in the United States. I call it a core model because, regardless of how compressed or stretched out the rut may be in a specific habitat, the central breeding span seems to follow the pattern outlined by the graph.

For example, say some researchers perform fetal examinations on a herd sample and find that the first breeding day was September 22 and the last breeding day was March 1. They find that the rut peaked on November 10. It's likely that the very early breeders were older does and the the very late breeders were fawn does. Nevertheless, they find that 95 percent

of all does bred between October 23 and December 23. To use the New York graph for this hypothetical herd, you should simply move the peak date from November 15 to November 10 and adjust the other dates accordingly.

I'm going to go out on a high but fairly sturdy speculative limb and say that, if you know when the peak of the rut occurs where you hunt, you can construct your own whitetail breeding graph by using New York's as the model. Just slide the peak forward or back, and let the rest of the dates distribute themselves correspondingly.

Much of this data has been compiled from charts and other sources used by Robert D. McDowell in *Photoperiodism Among Breeding Eastern Whitetailed Deer* (1970). McDowell's work is the most comprehensive study of this subject to date. I have also surveyed research published since 1970 and, whenever possible, either the peak-of-rut date or the peak span is indicated. For states in which research has arrived at different dates for various geographical regions, I've given the dates for each region.

It isn't always clear how researchers have arrived

HUNTING THE RUT: GENE WENSEL

Dr. Gene Wensel of Hamilton, Montana, and his brother Barry have each taken several Boone and Crockett and Pope and Young whitetails. They hunt exclusively with the bow.

"The best time to hunt trophy bucks is the buildup before the rut peaks," said Gene. "At that time, the bucks are ready. They can smell it, they can feel it, but the does aren't quite ready yet. So the bucks are very frustrated and move a lot. They're almost frantically overanxious, looking for a hot doe. Deer 3½ to 4½ years old really start feeling their oats.

"Out here, the scrapes are usually opened around the first week of October. They're primed about the middle of October. The majority of the mature does come into heat from November 17 to 23. And the best time to kill the biggest buck is just before the peak—let's say, November 12 to 17.

"In 1983, the difference between November 16 and November 17 was classic. Up to the 16th, there was a lot of buck activity. Then I was on stand the morning of the 17th and saw six button bucks go by without an adult doe anywhere. So the greatest increase of rutting activity hit the night of November 16.

"Interestingly enough, the 1984 season followed the same pattern. Between November 11 and 16, my brother and two other guys were videotaping while I rattled in bucks, and we had a dramatic increase in rattling results during that period. On November 13, I missed a huge buck. I killed a big one on November 16. The greatest increase in breeding activity, for both 1983 and '84, hit the night of November 16.

"The first does usually come into estrus around the middle of October, and you'll get quite a bit of scrape activity. There'll be a slight flurry, say, approximately from October 15 to 20, then it drops off for about two weeks and then picks up dramatically for about two weeks. When I define the peak of our rut, I'm talking about a four- or five-day period. Usually, a big percentage of the mature does will come in within a week."

at their peak-week dates so, where the published data has not been precise enough, I've used my own judgement, along with the New York graph as a touchstone. For instance, my South Carolina dates are from a study that placed the peak as November 17 to December 13. That struck me as a pretty long peak, especially because the only significant cluster of breeding dates in the sample occurred from October 28 to November 2. So that time span is listed as the rut's peak until researchers do fetal exams on a few hundred more does in South Carolina.

For some regions, the available data just isn't very long on hard scientific fact. If you live in one of these states and want to play this game, I guess that you'll just have to get out in the brush, like Gene Wensel in Montana, and start counting motherless fawns.

One oft-repeated "fact" of the whitetail rut is clearly put in question by the dates on the national map. The McDowell report and more recent research blow gaping holes in the belief that the farther north you hunt, the earlier breeding will occur. In north Arkansas, the rut peaks nearly a month sooner than in central or southern Arkansas, but it peaks later all over the northern tier of states than it does in north Arkansas! According to a Texas study, conception dates for central-Texas whitetails are strikingly similar to those for whitetails in New York (Harwell and Barron, 1975). Ninety-five percent of does are bred in New York between October 28 and December 28. In central Texas, 96 percent are bred between October 16 and December 15.

While it is true that in the whitetail's extreme southern range (latitude 28° to 32°) the breeding season begins much earlier and ends much later than in the mid-latitude ranges, the same is also true of whitetails in their extreme northern range (latitude 44° to 48°). And, as the map clearly shows, the breeding season in the temperate zones can vary greatly even within a state.

As more research is completed on this subject, the latitudinal-band notion looks increasingly flimsy. Why? There are number of factors that haven't been considered fully yet. Heredity is a major one and may, in part, explain why the primary rutting patterns in New York, central Texas, Michigan's Upper Peninsula, and Illinois are nearly identical. Whitetails were close to extinction in much of their present range by 1930, and herds were reestablished from remnant seed deer found in places such as upper Michigan and New York.

Geography may also be an important determining factor in breeding dates. A Louisiana study (Roberson and Dennett, 1966) states that the only common factor among its late-breeding herds of Delta Refuge and Tensas Parish "is the annual flooding of the Mississippi River, which normally occurs in the spring. While flooding does not still occur in Tensas Parish, it did when the herd was started." Early-breeding does would lose their fawns to the spring flood; the fawns of late-breeding does would have a better chance to survive. So we have a clear case of natural selection for late-breeding deer.

Nutrition is undoubtedly a factor. Research has shown that deer with poor diets breed significantly later than healthy deer, no matter when the rut is supposed to occur.

But the chief reason for the apparent confusion of breeding dates is that the breeding season is determined by light, not by latitude. A hormone released from the pituitary gland triggers breeding activity, and the hormonal release is directly related to a decrease in the amount of daylight. The confusion has arisen because we have assumed that daylight varies proportionally in strict latitudinal bands, so that the autumn stays brighter a little longer in Pennsylvania than in Vermont, and a little longer in Virginia than in Pennsylvania. But this is not the case.

The autumnal equinox occurs at the same time for all whitetails, about September 22, regardless of latitude. McDowell writes that "breeding begins approximately with the autumnal equinox." Only 27 of 4,663 adult does in his 19-state survey of Eastern states were bred prior to September 22. The greatest disparity in hours of daylight throughout his study area does not occur until after mid-December.

An early study (Bissonette, 1941) found that the fall breeding season for goats was hastened by keeping them in dim light. When you consider the local effects on daylight that oceans, the Great Lakes, swamps, and mountain ranges can have, it isn't so surprising to learn that some whitetails in Louisiana breed earlier than whitetails in Northern states.

My faith in the Jackson and Hesselton graph is based upon personal field experience. But the exact dependence on light gradations of the whitetail breeding season establishes why the graph is magically reliable—no matter whether the fall is rainy or dry, cold or hot.

If a hunter is watching the wrong scrape from the wrong place at the wrong time in November, and it happens to be 70 degrees in the shade, the excuse for not having any action is very likely to be that "the hot weather has stalled the rut." If it is 10 degrees below zero and snow has made a whiteout out of the woods, this is the reason why the bucks aren't moving.

A couple of years ago, I stayed home on one of those ten-degree-below-zero snow-blowing days in November and, while I was watching our orchard at about midday, from indoors upstairs, an exceptionally fine buck trotted into view out by the wood stacks. He crossed over to the orchard, passing under the transformer pole in the west yard, dogged southward, nose to the ground, until he came to the paved road; then he turned back toward the house and stopped under the old maple out by the road (which would have been a good stand location). The last I saw of him, he was headed back north right into the teeth of the storm.

The plain fact of the matter is that our "modern" whitetails have been breeding in North America for 15 or 20 million years, year after year, regardless of the weather.

And that's one heck of a rut to get out of.

Whitetails On The Map

By John H. Williams

On opening day the year before, I'd taken a fat six-pointer from this same hillside. He had walked alone out of the swale at the base of the hill and moved slowly along the runway, each step bringing him closer to my position. Now, I was sitting in the exact same location and hoping for a repeat performance.

Shots rang out behind me around 9 A.M. Within seconds, I could hear the sound of deer approaching—fast. I spun off my seat and pivoted to my right, hoping to be camouflaged by the pine tree directly in front of me, but it was too late. Two large does braked to a halt not 30 feet away. I could see the legs and part of the body of a third animal in the brush behind them. They weren't directly in front of me as I'd anticipated, though. They were on my left and, by moving, I'd completely exposed myself. I had forgotten that the runway behind me forked, and the deer had taken one avenue of escape when I'd planned on something different.

Deer hunting errors such as this happen to us all, and they cost us precious opportunities. It's entirely possible that the deer concealed in the brush on that day years ago was another doe but, because the deer wheeled around and exited without ever exposing itself, I'll never know.

The year after the above incident, I was hunting the same general area when three deer jumped out of a thicket in front of me. At least two of them were large animals, but all I could see were hindquarters and flags. I couldn't identify their sex. Without a moment's hesitation, I was able to interpret from their action and direction what their next move would be.

I immediately turned to my right and ran down a cut for about 400 yards, then turned east when I reached the edge of a woodlot. I followed an old tractor path for another 200 yards to the edge of a ravine. I laid down on the lip of the ravine with my gun ready and my eyes glued to the thicket in front of me. About five minutes later, a large doe approached the end of the thicket, hesitated, and stepped into the clearing ahead of me. Another doe followed the first, and a third, smaller animal brought up the rear. It was the same trio that I'd jumped just minutes before.

All three were does, but it was satisfying to me that I'd anticipated their actions so precisely. The actual kill in deer hunting, as in any other type of hunting, as far as I'm concerned, is incidental; it's the correct analysis of a situation that's exciting. The games within the total sport of hunting lend satisfaction and a sense of accomplishment.

Successful deer hunters learn how to minimize their errors. There are, of course, various causes for deer hunting errors, but many of them stem from the hunter's lack of knowledge about the environment that he is in. The deer that you pursue know what their escape routes are. In normal travel, they know the best way to get from one point to another. How, then, can a hunter minimize his errors? The answer is by thoroughly mapping out his deer hunting area *in detail*.

After the incident with the hidden deer, I began searching for better ways to learn the area that I hunt. I'm a great believer in the benefits of preseason scouting and was already devoting all my spare time to this activity, yet there remained voids in my knowledge of the area. Because increasing my time afield was out of the question, I had to come up with another way to help fill in the gaps.

At home one evening, I decided to see just how

Illustration by George Buctel

well I did know my hunting area. I started with generalities. What crops are growing in which fields? How large are those fields and how do they lie in relation to all the others? Where are the fence rows and where are there holes in them for ready passage? Where does the creek run? Where are the hardwoods that produce mast? The answers to these questions were easy.

But then I started asking myself more detailed questions, and I began having problems. I knew vaguely where the deer runs were but, when I actually tried drawing them onto the map, I couldn't. Does the run cross the creek there, or is it down farther? I was amazed at just how imprecise my knowledge was when I forced myself to put it onto paper. I soon realized that my knowledge of an area that I swore I knew very well was actually incomplete. I couldn't make an accurate hunting habitat map.

Over the next two weeks, I revised my map. I'd sketch in a run, for instance, then I'd actually go out and walk it. I found that I was soon concentrating on particulars that I'd overlooked before. Crossing points, thickets, and openings all seemed more obvious than they had before. Spatial relationships between various features became much more obvious. As a result of this simple exercise, I was truly learning the area. By spending three to five hours a day for two weeks on my exercise, I knew the particulars much more thoroughly.

Ever since I started making maps, I've done much better in my deer hunting efforts. I feel more comfortable and confident in my ability to predict the deer's actions and movements. Now, when I begin my scouting activities each year, I start a new map from scratch. I first draw in the obvious particulars: fields, woodlots, swamps, creeks, lakes, and so on. Then I begin work on the more detailed aspects and the specifics for that particular year: which crops are in which fields, the locations of any mast, the course of the runways, and so on. All the while, I make actual field inspections to check my accuracy.

About five years ago, I began adding buck sign locations to my maps, along with the dates on which they were found. Because I scout just about every day from October 1 up to the opening of deer season, I soon have a very detailed account of all buck activity in the area. Rub and scrape patterns soon begin to emerge on my maps—patterns that I'd probably never notice or fully comprehend otherwise.

The first year I recorded buck sign, for instance, I found that most of the activity began on the night of October 16. Before that date, there was nothing; but on the night of the 16th, the bucks went berserk. On the 17th, there was buck sign, in the form of rubs, everywhere I went. Over the next four or five

⭕ Rub	⌂ Hunting Stand
⭕ Sparring Rub	—·—·— Major Run
✕ Scrape	----- Minor Run

43

days, it began to create a definite pattern and, although there was some sign everywhere, it was mostly concentrated in two core areas. One of these areas was a small section of perhaps 30 acres inside a dense woodlot roughly one-quarter mile square. The other was an area roughly 500 yards long by 50 yards wide inside an alder thicket a half mile long by 1,000 feet wide.

On November 4, I found my first scrape of the year inside the core area in the alders. By November 7, I'd found three more active scrapes, all on a straight line from this thicket. On opening day, which was the 15th, I took a stand on the edge of this area as I'd mapped it out. I got to my stand well before daylight because I figured that the buck was using this spot as his bedding area and I did not want him to arrive before I got there. At about 8 A.M., following a run that cut just south of the line of scrapes, along came my buck.

I'm convinced that, if I had just been scouting but not keeping a written record of my findings prior to the season, I'd have never diagnosed that situation so easily. When you attempt to commit everything to memory, much of it will be lost. When you record it on a map, you have it right there in front of you, whether it's one week or one month later.

Because there are no maps of any area as detailed as what you'll want and need—and the entire purpose of the map is its usefulness as a self-teaching tool—I feel that it is essential to make a new map each year. I'm as careful as possible to draw in every detail, no matter how small or insignificant.

My experiences this past fall were even more demonstrative of the map's benefits. From October 1 to 27, I found nothing in terms of buck sign, and I was becoming concerned. There was a lot of deer sign and some of the tracks that I was finding were huge, but there was no definite evidence of bucks. Then, on October 28, I found several rubs. On October 29, I found several more. In the days following, I found a great many more, and a definite pattern again began to emerge on my map. Three areas were being thoroughly worked by the bucks.

I keep a written journal in which I record weather, hours spent afield, unusual events, sightings, and other notes, in addition to my maps. On November 11, I wrote in my journal: "Have made up my mind to hunt the cedars west of the creek, north of corn, unless something new shows up before the 15th."

Then, on November 13, something did show up. An area west of the other three began showing buck sign for the first time, while the other areas languished. A scrape appeared in this new area, while scrapes in the other areas went untouched. Rubs appeared in the new area, while none appeared elsewhere. If I hadn't been out each day and recording my findings along with corresponding dates, I doubt that I'd have noticed the change. But by looking at my map it really hit me: The deer had changed locations. Obviously, the does had shifted their feeding areas and, naturally because of the rut, the bucks had followed.

I quickly decided on a new stand within this latest area of activity. On opening morning, I collected the biggest buck I've taken in Michigan to date. A big eight-pointer, which field-dressed at 202 pounds, came gliding out of the fog between two pockets of cover within 30 yards of my stand.

This all leads to what I feel is the most powerful use of map making: trophy hunting. Based upon my experiences of making such maps over the last eight years, I'm convinced that any hunter will benefit from them. But for the hunter seeking better-than-average bucks, the map's advantages are absolutely essential. Any hunter can, "just by chance," bag a super whitetail but, for the hunter who wants to minimize the odds, the additional insight that such a hunting habitat map will provide is crucial.

You can make your hunting habitat map as simple or as complex as you desire. Hand-tailor it to your needs and your time constraints. The hunter who has limited preseason time may want to make such a map simply to help himself to learn his hunting area more thoroughly. Start with a large sheet of paper. I prefer a 36 × 36-inch sheet for each square mile that I draw. A sheet this large allows the recording of all particulars, no matter how detailed you get, and it will help you to keep the map from becoming cluttered.

Using a pencil, try to draw your hunting area, from memory, in as much detail as possible. I'm sure that you'll be amazed at just how quickly you'll become confused and unsure of yourself. Is that thicket north or south of the fence row? Do those poplars extend right up to the alders, or is there a slight opening between them? Regardless of how sure you feel, check the map by actual field observation once you've finished that stage. You'll be amazed at how you pick up details that would have gone unnoticed before.

For the hunter who has more time, the hunting habitat map is a much more powerful tool. Begin your operation the same way that I've described above. Once the physical layout is complete, record your scouting data as it's found. In order to conserve on space and to aid in reading my maps, I use the following symbols for recording all sign:

⬭ = rub		⌂ = hunting stand
⬯ = sparring rub		‐‐‐ = major run
✗ = scrape		‐ ‐ ‐ = minor run

Obviously, recording data on the map is not an end in itself. Once the date is there, you must be able to interpret its meaning. This process is best explained by analyzing the map on the facing page, which I drew in 1979.

The bucks began creating sign on October 28. All the initial sign fell into three basic areas, labelled I, II, and III. Sometime between October 31 and November 11, I'd almost made up my mind to hunt Area III. I based this decision, not on the number of rubs and scrapes I found in the area but, rather, on the size and quality of the sign. In 1978, I'd taken

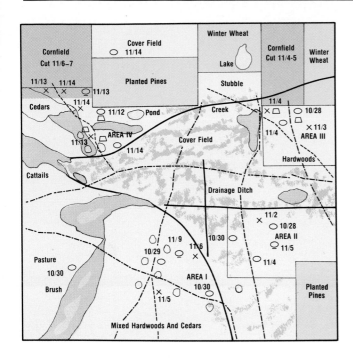

a large eight-point buck from Area I. In the fall of '79, the rubs that I found there were all made on small saplings and trees. This indicated to me that a buck had taken over the area vacated by the eight-pointer I'd harvested the fall before, but he was a young, small buck—not the type I had in mind.

Area II showed better rubs, but they again indicated a smaller buck, as did the scrapes within that area. As a general rule, the larger the buck, the larger and more vicious his rubs, and he'll generally make them a little earlier than his smaller brethren.

Rubs and scrapes are made by all bucks during the autumn months, and they are basically of two kinds. One is a cleaning rub made by the buck as his velvet begins to dry and wither. The animal will gently rub his antlers against small trees and brush in order to remove the clinging velvet and to polish his antlers. These rubs are the first to appear each fall and can be found anytime after late August in the North or September farther south.

Sparring rubs occur later in the fall, and they constitute a part of rutting activities by the bucks. As the breeding season draws near, bucks get cross and belligerent with all the other deer. Generally, these initial aggressive feelings do not lead to fights among the bucks but, rather, to the creation of sparring rubs.

A buck will gently, almost lovingly, rub and polish his antlers when creating a cleaning rub. When he creates a sparring rub, however, his intent is to destroy the object of his attack. He'll run at it, shake it violently, and trample it into the ground. This not only abates his aggressive mood but serves notice to the other bucks that he is forced to reckon with. All this activity is a nondangerous way of establishing a hierarchy among the bucks.

Scrapes are generally made along the edge of cover and under the limbs of an overhanging tree. The ground is pawed and raked by both hooves and antlers, and the limbs of the tree are thrashed, as well. Scrapes range from one square foot to more than one square yard in size and generally appear from early November in the Northern states to early December in the South.

You can see on the map that Area III had both the first rubs and the first scrape, and they were larger. Some of the poplars that were rubbed in this area were three to four inches in diameter. Because of all this data, I was planning to hunt where the hunting-stand symbols are in Area III—the selection depending upon the wind and overall weather conditions on any given day. Because the deer were actively feeding in the winter wheat and stubble fields north of Area III, I had an excellent idea of which way my buck would be traveling in the mornings and in the evenings. Further—again depending upon the weather—either of the two sites that I'd selected would have been perfect should the buck wander about within the cover during midday, as deer so often do.

Remember that bucks, especially larger, undisturbed bucks, follow a minor or seldom-used runway to get into cover far more frequently than they'll use a major run. Once in cover, they'll often amble off the runway entirely and slowly pick their way through cover to their beds.

Further, at some point during midday, bucks will get up off their beds to stretch and feed within cover for an hour or two. They will then lie back down until just before dusk. When they leave cover in the evening, they are less likely than other deer to follow a runway at all. They'll begin moving to the edge of cover very slowly, picking their way and feeding cautiously.

Now look over at Area IV on the map. The cornfield north and west of this area had been cut on November 6 and 7, and the deer had shifted their location in order to feed on the spilled grain. Throughout most of the year, a big, dominant buck is not going to forsake his normal core range just because of such a change by the other deer but, during the rut, he often will. As you can see, all sign making by bucks ceased outside of Area IV after November 9, yet sign making within this area was intense.

Another rule of thumb is that big bucks like thick cover to bed in, and this buck was no exception. A line of scrapes that appeared over the nights of November 12, 13, and 14 led directly to the densest stand of cedars in the entire area. My stand, on the right side of Area IV, was positioned so that I'd intercept him at the edge of his sanctuary.

That buck's head now adorns my front room wall. A hunter who puts the time into creating a hunting habitat map will find it of immeasurable assistance. It isn't a replacement for scouting, hard work, knowledge of deer habits, and good deer hunting skills, but it is a very powerful adjunct to all the other assets a hunter brings to his sport.

Places Without Faces For Whitetails

By Jeff Murray

There's an old North Woods adage that says, "You can't eat deer sign." What it means, of course, is that you've got to see deer to score.

It sounds simple but, if today's hunter is going to see more deer, he has to look in some offbeat places. There's a ton of competition in areas where hunters abound, and the deer in there wise up quickly.

Over the years, I've discovered five honest-to-goodness hotspots where you'll see more deer than hunters. Guaranteed. And you won't have to travel great distances to find them—in fact, they may be in your own backyard, where you've driven by them for years. Not neccessarily in order of importance or frequency, they are swamp islands, river routes, highway corridors, pockets of private holdings amidst large public tracts, and small public tracts surrounded by large private holdings.

Each is unique, but they all share two characteristics: They concentrate deer, and they are generally avoided by hunters. To fully appreciate this precious union, let's go back to last fall.

Chances are good that you, like most serious deer hunters, did your homework in the field prior to the firearms season. If you are a bowhunter, you did some double duty. Deer sign—primarily trails, beds, and scrapes—were noted and carefully evaluated, and soon a pattern or two emerged. Then you built or selected your stand and, for better or worse, stood your ground for that season.

If you were lucky, the deer continued in their daily habits and you had your moment of truth. Just as often, however, those patterns became interrupted, and the buck never materialized.

Why? Every circumstance is slightly different, but the interrupting agent is usually the same culprit—another hunter. So the end result of all your diligent scouting and scheming is the selection of an area where deer will either spend their evenings or, more likely, an area where they used to be.

That situation leaves only two options: Take hunter pressure into account, or totally avoid it. The former is risky business, unless you are intimately familiar with a given geographic area, as well as with the deer and the hunters who occupy it. Even then, there are variables to contend with, such as new faces or old ones doing different things.

On the other hand, what if another hunter never entered your area: At the very least, preseason scouting could tell you where deer could expect to be sighted later on during the season. That's the exciting thing about finding places without faces.

But is it really practical for the average hunter in an increasingly urbanized society to totally avoid hunter pressure? At first, I thought the concept was limited in application only to those states with lots of public lands and widely scattered population centers. Lately, I've come to realize that the solution is far from simply putting distance between myself and the nearest road. Deep-woods deer, with their enigmatic movement patterns and thin numbers, can

Photo by Michael H. Francis

If your last deer season consisted of contemplating tree trunks and counting orange hats, try hunting an area that most hunters avoid. You'll find that the deer don't!

make for tough hunting conditions. So I'm not out to get lost; rather, I'm looking to make a find: a patch of real estate with deer and no people.

Finding them boils down to understanding a little bit about human nature as well as wildlife behavior.

Take the first area, a swamp island. I'll never forget the day I made that discovery. I had been invited to

accompany an old college friend on one of central Wisconsin's special refuge hunts, where the state would open certain sections to the hunting public when deer populations reached explosive levels. The previous year had provided some fabulous results with a very high success rate and many good bucks registered. The only thing I did not like about it was the regulation restricting all scouting on the refuge before the season.

Indeed, there were plenty of deer (I saw 50 in two days) but the woods were also crawling with red coats: apparently the word had gotten out. Consequently, I spent most of my time just looking for some cover that lacked red or Blaze Orange jackets. In the process, I bumped into an old-timer who was dragging a ten-point buck through the woods. He wore a fatigued face and he was drenched with sweat, so I offered him a hand in getting his trophy back to his pickup.

He thanked me and, as he was about to leave, he gave me a strange look.

"I owe you one," he said in a raspy voice. "If you can keep a secret, I'll show you where I got that buck. There's more where he came from."

"You don't have to do that," I responded. Then I began to hedge a bit. "Did you really see other bucks besides that big one?"

"Are you kidding?" he snapped. "I let a bunch of scrawny spikes and forkhorns go by—and a six-pointer."

It took us only 45 minutes to get to the spot; it woud have taken even less time, but the tag alder thickets made for slow going. The old man had found a real gold mine all right. Those deer had a perfect fortress that was well buttressed on all sides. It was a small knoll surrounded by a tangled alder swamp. The knoll couldn't have been more than three acres, and the swamp was 20 or 30 acres.

Swamp islands often serve many needs of a buck: a reprieve from four and two-legged predators; solitude, which seems to be a socially ingrained preference among mature bucks in a given environment; food and shelter from the elements; and a good bedding and breeding site. And remember, these little patches are often the only places where a deer can avoid standing in water without traveling great distances. Thus, they can be a natural attractor of big game from that standpoint alone.

Prospects are good that you'll find a number of them to choose from locally. Just purchase the proper quadrangle contour map of your area and look up the marsh symbol. A potential knoll will reveal itself as an isolated ring or doughnut in a sea of marsh symbols. The final step is simply checking out their "face value" in the field to make sure that bucks are using them and hunters aren't. I do this by covering them during the deer season, looking for human tracks as well as buck tracks. I want to be certain that I'll have the spot all to myself. Then, the following summer, I'll set up my ambush by building my stand and cutting sight lines well in advance of the season. Each year, I keep on the lookout for new areas to consider for the following year.

Since I first learned about this hotspot, when the old man brought me to his coveted little knoll, I've found enough new ones to convince me that this pattern is reliable and repeats itself wherever whitetails and swamps can be found. Not all produce, but those that do will yield venison for years to come.

A brother to the swamp island—and just as productive in certain situations—is an island splitting a river or one that's close to the mainland of a lake or pothole. Wounded deer often seek out these areas when hotly pursued—a point worth remembering when the situation arises.

If hunting swamp islands sounds too rigorous, in spite of the prospects of seeing more deer than hunters, there's another untapped area with easy travel available: canoe routes. This is evidence of yet another hunter neurosis. For some reasons, some hunters just don't or won't engage in certain activities: Duck hunters don't like to portage, pheasant gunners won't camp out, and deer hunters are gun-shy of canoes.

With the advent of a plethora of canoe routes being charted and mapped across the country (due, in part, to legislation such as the Wild and Scenic Rivers Act), finding a canoe route with miles of decent whitetail habitat all to yourself is entirely possible. Begin your search with your local Department of Natural Resources agency, then contact chambers of commerce in areas with a river or two (some may promote only summer tubing, so be alert), and local canoe clubs.

Your chief concern is a relatively accurate map with put-ins and take-outs, rapids, dams, and campsites carefully marked to scale. Using two cars—one parked at the take-out point before putting-in—will save on backtracking upstream, giving you more time to hunt.

Canoes allow effortless and silent travel, as well as versatility. Don't like the deer sign along one stretch? Paddle downstream until you find fresher sign. And don't be caught off guard by deer working the riverbed right along the banks.

Rivers are also a natural in providing good deer habitat for a number of reasons. Vegetation is usually denser and lusher along bottomland, yielding both feed and cover for game. Water is obviously available in abundance but at safe locations (deer are excellent swimmers and not the least bit intimidated by most white water). And deer like to evade their enemies by doubling back on their trail and losing their scent in the river—a ploy often used by pressured bucks.

Waterways can also provide easy hunting because game trails often parallel the contours of the river banks, providing good tracking and easy walking. Noise is also muffled by gurgling waters, so you can step on more than your allotment of twigs and probably get away with it.

Swamp islands and river routes work for the enterprising hunter because there is a basic weakness in the mettle of many modern hunters: They take the paths of least resistance, involving the least amount of hassle. That's easy to understand. But there's another psychological trap that manifests itself among the hunting community that defies definition. For lack of a better term, I call it the Farthest Armchair Route (FAR) syndrome.

This malady can also be used to the advantage of any deer hunter, once the condition is properly diagnosed. It usually goes something like this. We

Water will hinder hunters, but it won't stop deer from traveling. Small farm areas near public land are havens for pressured deer.

Photo by Michael H. Francis.   *Photo by Richard P. Smith*

head out the door and drive the expressway or highway toward a county road, turn off another road, keep turning, take another fork, take the dirt road, swing off onto the forest road and then to the tote road, trail, powerline, railroad, or what have you. The major point is that we keep looking for lesser traveled roads, staying in that car or truck as long as we can. In the process, however, we pass up bucks . . . especially along the highway.

I have a friend who's a game warden, and one of his least favorite tasks is tending to road kills.

"I wish hunters would throw away all those crazy manuals," he said out of the blue one fall day.

"What manuals?" I asked.

"The ones that say that the best hunting is only found along dirt roads," he replied.

He did raise an interesting point. And what about road kills? We all know the keen interest that various states take in lowering traffic fatalities. One of the tedious records that they keep is the location of all reported car/deer collisions. With a short letter, any hunter can shortcut a lot of field work by requesting such information in a given area. In general, the agency to contact is the transportation or highway department for the state in which you will be hunting.

Lands adjacent to major highways are good bets, not only because of the FAR syndrome, but also because highways are a natural barrier that serve to somewhat constrict daytime lateral movements of deer. Again, topographical maps can further refine and pinpoint a local hotspot. A neighbor of my butcher used to bring in a bragging-size buck for processing each fall for many years. The only information about his hotspot that I could get out of him was the name of the nearest city and the fact that he could "hear car tires" from his stand. When I found out that he switched cars with his uncle during the deer season, I knew what to look for and, a year later I saw it: a blue pickup parked off the right-of-way of the interstate highway that leads out of town.

When I confronted him, he admitted that there "was a certain area that deer traveled parallel to a certain highway because of a certain creekbed that meandered nearby." He found the area by checking a topo map after he narrowly missed hitting a big buck with his car on the interstate one Halloween night. He saw a grand total of two people in those woods during a 10-year period, and one of them was looking for a lost hubcap.

The many warning signs posted along highways, alerting motorists to deer crossings, can also be an indication of roadside deer concentrations. They aren't put up without reason, so pay attention to their locations next time you're driving through deer country on a major thoroughfare.

Perhaps the best antidote for the FAR syndrome is a conversation with frequent highway travelers—truckers, salesmen, or highway patrolmen—followed up by a stroll along suggested corridors during the deer season. You'll be amazed at what you've been passing up.

The best opening-day stand that I've ever seen, bar none, belongs to a friend of mine named John who lives and hunts in Ohio. At first glance (and probably at second and third), the little wooded fence row looks like a good hunting spot for cottontails, maybe, but certainly not for bucks—especially the huge ones that my friend bags almost every year. And the setup is not unique across the country where private farms are scattered within transitional woodlands.

Wherever you find national, state, or county forests near small tracts of cultivated fields, you've found great potential for a similar surprise attack. On the forest lands, deer invariably get pressured—often from all sides—toward creek bottoms, swales, and isolated woodlots on nearby private holdings. All you have to do is to determine the most likely routes that bucks will take from the forest to the farmland, and to obtain permission in advance.

Photo by Tom Huggler

Riverbottom vegetation is generally thick—tough access for hunters but good cover for deer.

For the most part, bucks will take the most direct route available where cover can break up their outline against otherwise open fields. Brushy fence rows are ideal.

"I felt downright silly when I first set up at the T of two fence lines," John confessed to me. "I thought that no self-respecting buck would expose himself in this dangerous bottleneck."

But John stuck it out for a whole 20 minutes and had his mind changed in a hurry.

"It sounded like World War III over in the woods as soon as the sun came up," he said. "Then, all of a sudden, this big buck just popped out of nowhere, heading right for me. It was as easy a shot as a guy could ask for."

Two more things stand out about his spot. First, the farmer, who doesn't hunt, was glad to have John help him out by thinning crop-eating deer that "trespassed" on his farm. Second, John always sees big bucks—no spikes or forkhorns—in areas like that. But I guess that's OK.

The final hotspot is one that's especially common to the Midwest, and it's not *under*hunted . . . it's *un*-hunted! I learned firsthand about these areas while pheasant hunting more than 10 years ago.

Scattered across the nation's midriff in prime pheasant habitat is a myriad of state and federal tracts that are managed for wildlife, obstensibly waterfowl and upland birds. Wildlife management areas and public shooting grounds also provide the perfect sanctuary for pressured bucks in midseason.

As a bowhunter, it was easy to settle into a WMA and wait for bird hunters to push through the tanlged thatches and swamp thickets. Eventually, deer would be driven toward me along fairly predictable travel lanes. Lately, however, I've found that WMAs, especially the smaller ones, can conceal a mighty-fine buck without most hunters giving it a second thought.

While pheasant hunting one fall, I found a large set of deer tracks that led into a half-acre swale that was part of just such a public tract, but it was bisected from the rest of the area by a ditch bank. I walked the entire perimeter of that patch and quickly learned that no tracks came out, in spite of the fact that the deer had to have winded me. Somewhat puzzled yet confident, I entered the swale. Suddenly, no more than ten feet away, a heavy-necked, wide-racked buck sprung to his feet as if he had been bedded on a trampoline. I must have been the first hunter to have pressed that buck in a long time. Apparently, even other pheasant hunters considered the patch unworthy of a going over.

That was one startled buck, and I was one surprised rooster hunter. But, in hindsight, I should have known that it was just another one of those places without faces that deer seek out and hunters avoid. Next time, I won't be so surprised.

The Wiliest Of Whitetails

By John H. Williams

Mid-morning on November 19 found me alertly slinking between a cedar swamp and a standing cornfield. I moved along a step at a time, looking for sign and hoping to find deer. During the previous two hours I'd seen plenty of sign, but nary a deer. Finally, I worked my way up a long incline; here, the corn had been cut and the cedars gradually gave way, first to a dense alder thicket, then to a thick stand of hardwoods.

A couple of scrapes, which I'd found a week earlier along the wood's edge, were still evident, but no longer fresh. The rut was obviously over. When I reached the crest of the hill, the ground fell suddenly away in front of me and I sat down to rest. Because stillhunting, properly done, is mentally but not physically taxing, I sat down more to rest my mind than my body.

Nestled at the base of the hill was a farmhouse and its adjacent outbuildings. A couple of hundred yards beyond the barn was a patch of standing corn, and adjoining its western end was a 20-acre woodlot. I had told my friends at the farmhouse that I'd probably drop in and help them drive the area late that morning, but, as I sat there watching, I could see a bustle of activity as the house quickly emptied and the drive began. I decided it would be more fun just to watch. Besides, I thought, they have plenty of hunters already.

From what I could see through my binoculars during the next hour, plus what my buddies told me later, this is what transpired.

Eleven hunters took part in the drive. It was in-tended to roust deer out of the woodlot on the west, pushing them past blockers as the deer moved to the east on their way to another woodlot, several hundred yards distant. From past experience, the hunters (mostly local farmhands) knew that the deer normally left the woodlot via the standing corn; they'd then traverse the corn to a fence row on the east, and follow the fence row to the next woodlot to the south.

Eight drivers started through the woodlot, coming from the west. Two blockers were posted at the northeast corner of the woodlot, each slightly back in from the corner itself. A third blocker was posted at the southeast corner of the standing corn. As the drivers neared the woodlot's eastern edge, three deer, two does and a moderate-size buck, escaped into the corn too quickly for anyone to fire a shot, although three of the hunters saw them. The men posted on the woodlot said the deer never came out of the corn. The hunter posted on the corn said they never came out. I was sitting high enough on the hill to know that no deer ever came out of the east, north, or south sides of the corn.

Quickly, two hunters were posted at the eastern end of the corn. The cornfield appeared no more than 100×200 yards in size. Nine drivers went abreast through the standing corn. When they were roughly halfway through the lot, two does broke cover, running down the fence row, as planned, to the next woodlot. The buck was never seen!

I think that the buck had somehow slipped back through the advancing hunters—despite the fact that

The craftiest whitetail on four legs can be found within sight and sound of human activity—if you know where to look.

each man could see the two men adjacent to him at all times during the drive—and retreated back to the original woodlot from where he'd come. Regardless of how he did it, that buck escaped without so much as a shot being fired in his direction. I venture that practically any other whitetail, in practically any other location than a farmland, would have panicked in such a situation and been tagged, yet such experiences are not uncommon for whitetail hunters hunting farmlands.

I believe the overwhelming reason for this seemingly phenomenal escape savvy in farmland whitetails is their familiarity with humans. Farmland deer are exposed to humans every day. In large measure, deer live in a fishbowllike environment; they are continually bombarded by the smell, sight, and sounds of humans. They cannot afford to panic every time a human gets too close—so they simply don't. The farmland whitetail's armor, then, is his escape cover, but it is not without flaw. A farm deer, more than any other whitetail, is inexorably tied to the farm. This is true because cover, in a farmland situation, includes only a small percentage of the available land area.

For the farmland whitetail hunter, cover is a two-edged sword: for those who are not prepared to work it correctly and do not know its nuances, it's their nemesis; for those who understand its uses and the whitetail's ways, it's their staunchest ally. It matters little where you happen to hunt in farm country— it may be on southern Michigan's smaller block farms, on Wisconsin's larger dairy operations, or in southwestern Minnesota's corn belt—the whitetail's habits are basically the same. These deer are masters at utilizing the available cover to their optimum benefit. Just as that buck did to my friends, they'll often confound the hunter who pursues them. Those same deer who feed brazenly in the open fields throughout the early fall seem to vaporize when hunters appear.

As opposed to their Western cousins, the mule deer, whitetails are essentially creatures of the forest. Whenever pressured in any way, cover is what they seek and, especially for bigger whitetail bucks, the thicker the cover the better. Once these deer get into cover they're comfortable with, they're extremely reluctant to leave it.

I've had this demonstrated to me more times than I care to remember, but one time stands out in my mind as being particularly memorable. Six or seven years ago, I was hunting a large farm that had an essentially undeveloped north side. On the east of this area, there was a 200-acre woodlot of mixed hardwoods and brushy bottoms. On the west was an equally large area of brushy bottoms and thorn apple filled hills. Two weeks earlier, I'd found three lage scrapes amongst the thorn apple trees. The scrapes were now abandoned. The rut was over, but I was convinced that the buck who had made those scrapes was still around. I knew from the size of the scrapes, and the damage that the buck had inflicted upon some nearby hardwoods, that the deer was huge. I also knew that he hadn't yet been tagged, because, in such a small community, word would have spread quickly and I'd have heard about it if he had been.

The third or fourth afternoon of the season, I took a stand overlooking a brushy draw which led from the woodlot into the thorn apples. A well-worn run, which traversed the draw, led to within 50 yards or so of the first scrape in the series. While I knew the buck wouldn't check his scrapes, I believed the reason he'd originally planted them was because he and the rest of the herd routinely used that corridor as their gateway between the woodlot, the thorn apples, and an abandoned orchard still farther west. From evidence I'd seen, the deer were feeding heavily in the orchard.

I'd been on my stand for roughly two hours when another hunter ambled over a rise and headed my way. When he reached me, we stood and talked quietly for at least ten minutes, then he continued on. The whole time I'd posted, the wind was in my face, and now the other hunter walked downwind away from me. When he was about 40 yards away, from out of a dense tangle, which covered all of 100 square feet, came the biggest buck I'd ever seen in the area—not 20 feet from the other hunter. By the time I heard the commotion and turned, all I saw was the buck broad jumping a four-foot-high fence.

I never had a chance to shoot, and my comrade in arms was as flustered as I was; he never got his gun out of port position. That wily old buck had, I'm sure, winded me long before, but it was equally obvious that he was content to stay in his bed so long as he knew where I was. Had the other hunter not wandered along, that buck would have either slipped out the back door or waited until I left. Bucks like that one are hard to tag—but they're not impossible.

Three or four years ago, about six weeks before the season opened, I found signs of what appeared to be an enormous buck roaming about between two farms which I routinely hunt. I spent the next six weeks trying, anyway I could, to pinpoint his activities. I found some massive buck rubs in a thicket of tag alders and willows, growing along the southern edge of the area. In addition, I also found enormous tracks in the crop fields, to the north deer this thicket, and on the runways in between. Without

giving away any of my information, or my fondest hopes, I discreetly questioned the farmers and their sons about the various bucks they'd seen in the area. No buck, such as the one I envisioned, had been seen—yet I was convinced that he existed.

When the rut came in early November, I found a great many scrapes in the area. Along the edges of the woodlots to the north, I found scrapes two to three feet in diameter and sparring rubs where the bushes and trees had been bent and broken. In the thicket to the south, I found scrapes four feet or more in diameter, and bushes and trees that had been completely destroyed. Now, more convinced than ever that a big buck lived there, I began to formulate a life pattern for this critter.

The "Boss," as I was beginning to think of him, lived in his thicket year-round; it was his core range. The thicket was extremely dense, and covered perhaps 80 acres. He hid and slept there during the daylight hours, venturing north, into the nearby crop fields and adjacent woodlots, only under the protective cover of total darkness. He was clearly the dominant buck in the area, and he seldom, if ever, left his daytime retreat during daylight hours. I decided the only realistic hope of tagging this fellow was to go into the thicket each morning, before daylight, and stay there until dark.

During the first four days of the season, little happened. I'd seen a few deer, including one small buck, and on several occasions I had heard others, but the cover always prevented me from seeing them. From all the shooting, the sounds of all the traffic in the background, and the occasional yelling, I knew that the surrounding areas had intense hunting pressure, yet I saw no other hunters. Mid-morning of the fifth day I saw the Boss, and my season was complete. A massive eight-point rack, with a 19-inch inside spread, was my reward for seven intense weeks of activity; but the key to the entire hunt was the cover, and how both the buck and I had used it.

Before someone tells me how all that scouting and tramping, prior to the season, will spook the deer, let me explain why that's not always so. Too much scouting, or too much activity of any kind—logging, for example—will, in most cases, severely affect a deer herd and its behavior, but not so with farmland deer. Dubious? Here is a good example of what I mean.

The department of natural resources in southern Michigan has a program known as the hunter access program, in which the state leases hunting rights on certain farmlands. The farmer is paid so much per acre, per year, to enroll his land in the program. He, in turn, allows so many hunters per day access to his lands. Only a relatively small percentage of lands are enrolled in this program and most are quite heavily hunted.

Last fall, I hunted two farms adjacent to each other which were in the access program. For at least five weeks prior to the general deer season, partridge and woodcock hunters, myself included, had hit the woodlots, planted pines, and tag elders hard; waterfowlers had worked the marshes and the fields; and the farmers had brought in their crops. Squirrel hunters had thoroughly worked the hardwoods for weeks, and rabbit hunters and their attendant hounds had punished the brush. Even the nights had been busy, as coon hunters worked the corn and adjacent woodlots.

Two days before our deer season, I cruised through a woodlot to check on some scrapes I'd found earlier. I then cut to the edge, intent on checking one more place before dark. As I broke cover, I looked to the far end of the harvested bean field and there stood three deer. Even though they were more than 500 yards away, I did not need field glasses. There was no mistaking that glinting sunlight; one of those deer had one heck of a rack! I hunkered down in the fence row to watch the show.

Intent on sexual matters, every few minutes that big bruiser would lower his head, almost to the ground, sway it from side to side, then give chase. The two does would run a short way, stop, and then, in a few minutes, the process would be repeated. At 4 P.M., with the sun still high in the sky, that buck couldn't have cared less about the three rabbit hunters working the brushy field immediately to the north. It was only the does disappearing into the woodlot that finally took him into cover.

Opening morning of the deer season, I ran into three young men about a half-hour before daylight. They explained how they'd been hunting rabbits a couple of days before and how they had seen a monster of a buck out in the open. They told me they were going to hunt the perimeter of the bean field. I moved off into a nearby woodlot and took a stand. At daybreak, three shots rang out from the bean field, then total silence. That night, I discovered that one of the young hunters had taken a nice little eight-point early, but that no more deer had been seen. I'd seen seven deer, but no horns.

Off and on through the remainder of the season, I kept encountering two of the young hunters I'd seen earlier. Falsely believing that if their friend had taken one buck from that open field that others were to follow, they hunted the field exclusively. When I last saw them, near the very tag end of the season, they'd only seen two other deer, both does, despite 12 days of hunting between them. In the meantime, from my vantage point in the thick cover, I'd seen in excess of 70 deer, including two small bucks and many more I couldn't identify with certainty.

The point to all this is simple. Although I'm not sure how they know, it's obvious that deer do know when they're the object of a hunter's pursuit. Hunt birds and/or scout for deer in farm country, and the deer will pretty much ignore you. Hunt deer in farm country, and you'll drive them into cover every time.

Farmland cover does not have to be thick to hold deer, it simply has to provide them with the needed relief from hunting pressure, the escape routes they demand, and, therefore, a sense of security.

What all this translates to, however, is that, be-

cause of the whitetail's natural tendency to seek cover, large expanses of farmland can be safely ignored by hunters. With the possible exception of opening day, it is highly unlikely that a mature whitetail buck anywhere in farm country is going to be taken in the open (unless forcibly driven from cover). Therefore, concentrate on hunting the available cover, not on hunting its perimeter or in the open areas.

Whitetails everywhere depend upon their senses to guide them, particularly their sense of smell. What triggers one reaction in a wilderness whitetail, however, will generally trigger a completely different response from a farmland deer. For example, let a wilderness whitetail wind you and you can almost wave goodbye. Not so with a farmland buck. Farmland whitetails have learned to separate the man's activities into at least two categories: neutral or malevolent.

A farmer pursuing his fields, or mending his fences, walks and behaves in a completely different manner than a hunter cruising along the same course. To the whitetail, the farmer doing his work signals no danger or fear, while the hunter is a definite threat. The difference in deer is that the farmland whitetail will not react to the sight, smell, or sound of a human until it has made that differentiation; the wilderness whitetail will. A wilderness whitetail never encounters that many humans, so it's safer for him to assume that *all* people threaten his well-being than to attempt any distinctions.

Often, the farmland hunter can use this behavior to his advantage. One way in which this can be done, especially in lightly hunted areas, is to intentionally move deer, then cut them off or outmaneuver them. A couple of years ago, I was hunting some heavy brush a quarter of a mile or so north of an active farm. I knew that some relatives of the landowner had been intensively hunting the crop fields and nearby thickets, but they hadn't ventured into my area. While changing stands in midday, I jumped five or six deer. I heard them crash off, but all I could distinguish were a few flags flying as they bounded away. Stopping only briefly, I heard them run for 50 yards or so, and then silence. Figuring that they wouldn't go far, I thought that if I moved steadily on, they'd then slowly circle back into the same area they'd just vacated. I moved steadily for 100 yards, making plenty of noise as I went. Then I began to quietly but quickly circle back, downwind from where I had originally come.

About 40 yards from the spot where I'd first seen them, I stopped and leaned against a tree. Twenty minutes went by and I heard brush popping. Moments later, I heard more brush, then leaves rustling. Four does and a nice six-pointer ambled into view as they slowly fed on their way back to their beds.

By continuing to move steadily away—not showing any interest whatsoever—the deer had felt secure that I'd simply passed them by, just as the farmer does every day while doing his chores. Ambushes, such as this, can be routinely effective for the farm-land hunter who is familiar with the land and the deer.

Whitetails, at times, seem to have an almost cavalier attitude about their proximity to man, his home, domestic animals, and so on.

A couple of years ago, I dropped a nice little eight-point buck in the latter part of the Michigan season. Each morning, as I was hiking in to my various stands, I'd see hunters walking in front of me, or I'd have them pass me by after I'd reached my spot. Then it dawned on me that no one was hunting the little thicket immediately west of the barn that was used for storage.

That afternoon, I cruised the area. It really wasn't much; a four- or five-acre area separated from a much larger woodlot by a 100-yard swath of cover field. Everyone had been walking around it, heading for the woodlot or the crop fields farther beyond. Next morning, I arrived a little earlier than usual and was on a stand less than 100 feet from the barn before anyone else had arrived.

Soon, a parade of hunters drifted past, through the field behind me, heading for their more distant stands. Shortly after daylight, I heard something moving in front and upwind of me, but saw nothing; then, for a time, everything was still. Just before 11 A.M., I again heard faint rustlings, then I saw a deer's flank as my little buck complacently fed not 50 yards from the roadway! Don't overlook the obvious—sometimes the best hunting is right under your nose.

Hunting tactics in farmland areas should depend on your preference and on an honest and realistic appraisal of your hunting abilities. Hunting possibilities are usually excellent, provided that you have the patience and skills required. *Slow* is the key ingredient to this deer hunting approach. You must learn to let your eyes, much more than your feet, explore the cover. Try to anticipate where the deer are most likely to be. To a certain extent, this is the result of years of experience, but, as I've mentioned, an important and often overlooked element is in knowing where most hunters are not. Cover that is too thick, wet, far off, or near the road—cover that demands either too much effort or is too obvious—is exactly where you should be. Often, something as simple as a pair of hip boots will get you into areas where other hunters seldom go. Even in the most heavily hunted farm areas there are at least a few places, for whatever reasons, that few, if any, hunters violate. Search these out to increase your odds, and keep in mind that the majority of farmland hunters hunt the open areas almost exclusively.

Stand hunting is another productive tactic. Choose stand locations with great care, and do so well in advance of the season. Always get to your stand at least a half hour before daylight. Whenever possible, plan on spending the entire day on the same stand. Farmland cover generally is in small blocks and, if you're moving from one stand to another, the deer will detect your presence and slip away unnoticed.

Do not use the same stand more than once or twice a week because human odors will build up and the deer will avoid the area.

Prior to opening day, you should have at least a half dozen, and preferably more, stand sites already selected. Concentrate on bedding areas instead of fedding sites; farmland whitetails quickly revert to nighttime feeding schedules during the deer season. Recheck your stands' usefulness, as the season progresses, on the basis of fresh sign present or absent.

You'll probably find that as the season progresses, especially if there's been heavy hunting pressure, the deer will be farther back in the cover than they were earlier. You should be, too. The deer will be getting into these areas earlier and staying later. Because of their light-gathering capabilities, a good quality scope, even if you hunt with a shotgun—will give you a few additional minutes of effective hunting time at both ends of the day.

Farmland areas provide unequaled opportunities for deer drives, and in some areas it's the only approach that works.

Deer drives can operate productively with as few as two hunters, but probably should never include more than 10 or 12, and then only if the hunters are highly experienced. Safety is the top priority.

A drive master should always be in complete control. The drive master will assign positions, direct the tempo of the drive, choose the routes taken by the various members, coordinate timing, and so on.

The drive master must be intimately familiar with the areas to be hunted and, in addition, he must have a detailed homemade map of each area. No commercial maps will have the essential details. Every major feature of the area must be included: crop fields, favored fence crossings, major and minor deer runs, stand sites, creek and river crossings, everything important to influencing the deer and their possible movements. With the aid of such maps, members of the drive will recognize their assigned locations and readily understand what is expected of them.

All participants, drivers and standers alike, should wear as much Blaze Orange as possible. Blaze Orange snowmobile suits are probably the best choice, but, at the very least, Blaze Orange coats, hats, and gloves are essential for everyone involved. It is important that everyone on stand have some sort of concealment as well. Break up your silhouette by employing blinds, brush, trees, and so on. Remember that a drive's success or failure can hinge on your actions. Your hunting partners, and especially the drive master, have put a lot of time and effort into this operation—so follow directions and stay alert at all times.

Any whitetail, in any environment, is an admirable and worthy quarry, but to my mind, the farmland whitetail is the most challenging. They have nerves of steel, and they possess the senses and instincts that are perfectly suited to duping the best woodsman on any given day.

Web-Footed Whitetails

By Ben Conger

The first whitetail buck I ever shot was more the result of luck than skill. I was on my first deer hunt with New Jersey hunting club in the Mount Misery area of Lebanon State Forest. After three days of fruitless driving and standing, I was finally out on my own for an afternoon of stillhunting. Most of the older hunters had jobs and, after hunting the first two days of the season, they left us kids to mind the camp until they returned Friday night to hunt the last day.

After wandering for two hours, taking compass readings at every turn, I knew that if I cut through a small cedar swamp, camp would be no more than half-mile away.

I entered the cedars and began jumping from one dry hummock to the next. Stopping for a moment, I decided to try picking my way through the wall of trees on several dry spots that I noticed up ahead. I leaned against a tree, with my single-barrel 12 gauge under my arm and took a compass reading. I was searching up ahead for my fourth or fifth dry spot to alight on, when the chosen dry spot slipped away into the darkness.

As I stood staring in disbelief, another dry spot slid into view, replacing the first one—only this one was different. It had black eyes, a black button on the end of its nose, and two very widely set ears, pointing my way.

It was as if someone had dumped ice cubes down my back. I knew what I was looking at, but wasn't sure whether it was real or not. Then a parade of deer began moving through the water as easily as ducks in a pond.

With aching eyes, I examined each head as it appeared among the trees, searching for any sign of antlers. Often it was impossible to tell whether I was looking at the head or tail-end of a deer; there were so many in that small stretch of swamp with me, and they kept changing positions. Finally, I eased the shotgun to my shoulder and searched diligently for antlers.

Suddenly, I saw a head with antlers on it. They were only spikes, but big enough to be legal, and I was afraid if I took too long to make my shot that they, too, would disappear. With all the precision I could muster, I sighted down the barrel and squeezed off the single load of 00 buck shot. Tree bark filled the air, and the sound of snapping twigs and many feet splashing in the ankle-deep water surrounded me.

My right cheek ached from having been pressed down too tightly on the gun stock during recoil. My feet were getting soaked as I raced to where the deer had been standing when I shot.

There was nothing there. My deer was gone. I looked around, wild-eyed, and then saw a tan heap, just five yards away in the tea-colored cedar water. I had my first buck.

The drag out of the swamp was uneventful, except for the sound of crinkling skim ice and the splashing of water, as deer moved around me within the swamp every time I paused for a rest. Back at camp, everyone congratulated me. When I told them we could all get our bucks in that swamp, they sniffed a little deeper of the swampy aroma emanating from my drying socks and pants near the wood stove, and

A whitetail's greatest protection may well be the fact that most hunters aren't willing to look in the right places.

Photo by Murray O'Neill

said they knew of dryer areas where deer were. My buck was the only deer taken in camp that year.

The part that water plays in a whitetail's life is debatable. Observers of deer behavior, and many biologists, say that deer sometimes drink water after eating, but insist that the need for water is not the driving, dependable force that their need for food is. These same people also claim that deer get the bulk of the liquids their bodies need from the succulent foods they eat.

Maybe so, but I have never found whitetails far from water. Perhaps they don't need to consume the water directly, as many insist, but the plants containing an excess of liquid, which they eat, do need an abundant water supply. That may explain why whitetails are always found near water.

A friend of mine, Fred Buckley from Huntley, Montana, sends an annual Christmas card inviting me to come to his in-laws' ranch to hunt. We originally became acquainted while hunting whitetails in Wyoming.

"The whitetails on the ranch are concentrated down in the river bottoms," Fred wrote to me one year, "like they were in the Devil's Tower area of Wyoming."

Fred, Reggie Lingle, Paul Bruun, and I had been deer hunting the Black Hills, located on the Wyoming-South Dakota border. Although we hunted the Bear Lodge area, often we drove to Devil's Tower to observe the whitetails. It was not unusual to see as many as 100 in a herd, drifting up from the brush-lined banks of the Belle Fourche River and feeding in the open ranchland every evening.

Our camp was situated within 100 yards of a small creek that emptied into the Belle Fourche. One morning, while sitting on a stump overlooking the creek, I saw three deer crossing it. The range was about 70 yards. At the sound of my shot, two deer

ran off, and the third thrashed a few seconds in the autumn leaves before laying still.

Paul was standing over my deer when I got to it. He had been seated on the other side of the creek and was waiting for the deer to move a few yards so he could get a shot. Paul got his deer the next day, 200 yards further down the creek.

The deer in this area are typical of Western whitetails—they're never more than a few hundred yards from an abundant water supply. Again, this may not be because of any need to drink heartily two or three times a day, but rather because creek and river bottoms are the only places they can find suitable cover for concealment, and the lush, moisture-laden foods they need.

On the other hand, I know of very few Eastern, Southern, or Midwestern swamps of more than a few acres in size that don't have whitetails in or near them. Also, I have never found a high mountain with whitetails living on it that does not have a flow of water somewhere near its crest.

It needn't be a big stream; any flowing water will do. I learned this while turkey hunting one spring near my home in Vermont. Close by is a high ridge that looks like good game country, but doesn't have an obvious swamp or stream on it. I rarely hunted this mountain, except to occasionally prowl the lower slopes when squirrels were gorging on acorns.

At dusk one May evening, I was driving on a road near the ridge. I'd stop once in a while and squawk on a raspy crow call, hoping to get a gobbler from the valley to respond. At one stop, from far up on the mountain, I heard a gobbler answer me. Assuming it was an older bird that was dethroned and chased from his original territory, I planned to return to the mountain early the next morning and try to capitalize on his misfortune.

The gobbler was responsive to my calling at dawn.

I was elated when he stepped into a woodland trail 90 yards away and looked in my direction. But then he turned directly away from me and walked off. He ignored my most seductive calls. As I sat staring after the now-departed gobbler, a deer stepped out into the same trail and walked up the mountain, following the turkey.

Shortly after the deer disappeared, and while I was debating about walking up that trail to see what was so popular up there, I was startled to see the gobbler walking back down the trail toward me. He had remembered exactly where my calls were coming from and walked to within 20 yards of me, pausing to strut every few steps.

I left my gobbler hanging in a tree and walked up the trail to see what was so interesting. What I found was a spring seep.

Water percolated up out of the ground and seeped downhill for perhaps 50 yards before being completely swallowed up by the dry mountainside again. This 50-yard swath had low, lush brush growing along it, the edges of which were showing the first green grasses of the year.

When I later mentioned the spring seep to a game biologist, he said that many states were looking for a way to effectively manage and encourage growth around such watering places. It seems that these seeps remain open and have lush growth surrounding them, even in the bitterest of winter weather. Often, in a dry autumn, they may be the only reliable water supply that game has for a mile in any direction. Now, when the wild apple crop is not abundant—which usually occurs during a dry year—I use a tree stand overlooking a spring seep high up on a ridge among the beechnuts and oaks.

My observations of spring seeps from tree stands have revealed some interesting hunter habits. Every hunter I saw moved only a short distance up or down the seep, until he found an easy place to cross. Even hunters in thigh-high rubber boots avoided getting their soles wet. They all crossed at a 90-degree angle.

Yet, the area within five to ten yards on each side of a seep is where many whitetails exist. Any stalker's odds are greatly increased if he hunts up and down spring seeps, rather than across them.

Available water not only provides the moisture and food that deer need throughout the year, it also provides protection from predators and hunters. The deer in that New Jersey cedar swamp were not there for the food—the closest edible leaf was 30 feet off the ground. They were hiding from hunters, and I just happened to stumble onto them.

I stumbled onto a similar situation when hunting the farm country of northern New Jersey.

I had been bowhunting from a tree stand where a well-used deer trail exited a cornfield and entered a patch of woods. Seventy yards into the woods, a 20-foot wide, ankle-deep creek flowed. For more miles than I cared to walk, the creek banks were lined with big oaks, beechnuts, and maples from 20 feet to 100 yards out from the water. The occasional patch of evergreens or honeysuckle was interspersed along the field edges, between the various cropfields and the woodland strip.

While basking in the early-morning sun and observing the cornfield, I heard splashing water behind me. I looked back and saw two bucks, an eight-pointer and a six-pointer, exiting the creek. They moved about 20 yards from the creek bank into the brush and, after staring at their backtrail, bedded down. Ten minutes later, a bowhunter walked down to the water. He stared at the tracks entering the stream. He was evidently trailing the two bucks.

The hunter looked upstream, then downstream. Not seeing any stepping stones to facilitate a dry crossing, he walked off. All that separated him from two beautiful bucks was a pair of wet feet.

I tried stalking the two bucks, but they recrossed the stream and eluded me, even though I did get my feet wet. That afternoon, I moved my tree stand. The next time they tried this evasive maneuver, I was ready. Unfortunately, my marksmanship was not.

But I learned that even if whitetails don't need a drink every day, they are never far from water. And, they are masters at using water to their advantage.

In New York's Catskill Mountains, a strip of lush greenery separated a highway from the shores of a man-made lake. My hunting partners and I knew deer were there. After several failures, because of insufficient manpower to drive them into a waiting hunter, we decided to try a squeezing operation.

The three-eighths-mile forested strip was about 200 yards wide at one end, tapering down to only 30 yards at the other end. With the wind in our faces, my brother and I began moving slowly and silently through the ever-narrowing strip—he up top by the highway, me on the lake side.

The plan was simple. The deer would be squeezed down into the narrow neck and, rather than break out across the highway, they would turn and try to come back through the other, now closely-spaced, hunters. It seemed almost foolproof.

"Did they cross the highway?" I asked my brother.

"No," he answered, looking down on us from the roadway 50 feet above. "But what's that out there?"

I looked where he pointed and saw seven deer, one with a rack of antlers visible above the water from 250 yards away, swimming to the far shore. Two days later, we pushed through the same area, and the buck was dropped on the shore as the deer tried their water escape trick again.

The secret to scoring on these deer is a willingness to get your feet wet. Just wearing waterproof shoes or boots is not enough—you must be able to wade swampy areas and follow the marshy course of spring seeps and small streams.

And if a biologist tells me that he has discovered whitetails that have developed webs between their split hoofes to take better advantage of their watery environment, I'll believe it.

Float A River, Tag A Buck

By Tom Huggler

Morning fog curled above the river like campfire smoke as Al Davis, in the stern of his 16-foot canoe, kept us on course with deft flicks of the paddle. From my bow-end advantage. I drank in the early-October beauty along the southern-Michigan river. Changing leaves offered a panorama of autumn colors. We were only 15 minutes downstream from our launch site, and I had already seen a great blue heron, beavers, muskrats, and several fox squirrels.

My partner silently negotiated a pretzel bend. There in the brush, not 20 feet away, stood a fat forkhorn whitetail. The buck watched us for a long moment with ever-widening eyes, then swapped ends and melted into the woods.

"Too bad we're hunting ducks and not bucks," said Davis, a veteran waterfowl float hunter, "I always see deer on these rivers."

Three weeks later, on another float, he proved that point. The firearms deer season was open, and I had exchanged my over/under for a slug-barrel shotgun. Had I possessed a doe permit that day, I could have filled it in the first half mile of our drift. Those trips motivated me to think about how deadly effective float hunting for deer could be.

The practice is probably as old as North American hunting. For hundreds—maybe thousands—of years, Indians canoed the continent's waterways in quest of game, including deer. Beginning with Lewis and Clark, early white hunters also relied on float hunts to keep fresh meat in camp. Floating was highly popular with New York state hunters who drifted Adirondack Mountain streams in specialized guide boats. An 1892 Winslow Homer painting, *Hound and Hunter*, shows a young man in such a boat, reaching for a huge buck that his dog had driven to him.

Floating is an excellent deer hunting tactic, yet—with the exception of moose hunters—few sportsmen try it. Nowhere is this more evident than in my native state of Michigan where, if hunters do turn to rivers, they invariably are after ducks or squirrels—rarely are they after deer. On a Sunday afternoon last November, during the statewide firearms deer season, I took a little survey from an I-75 bridge overpass near Flint. Of the first 100 vehicles containing what I figured were hunters, 37 also carried whitetails tied to hoods, roofs, or trunks. Only one vehicle toted a canoe, though, and one other pulled a boat.

Float-hunting opportunities exist across the country. All of the Lower 48 states have huntable populations of deer, and many host intricate river systems ideally suited to this sport. Michigan, for instance, contains more than 36,000 miles of streams and more than 9 million acres of public land open to hunting. Is float hunting legal, you ask? Well, according to the game law regulations of 15 states that I spot-checked, shooting deer from watercraft *not under power* is generally allowed. One state, Kansas, technically prohibits the killing of game from any vehicle (including unpowered boats). According to Mike Cox, the fish and game commission information and education supervisor, however, that reg-

Photo by Jim Henry, Courtesy of Mad River Canoe

Float hunting can give you the drop on the biggest, smartest bucks—and you don't even have to own a boat!

ulation might well have been relaxed by the time you read this. Even if it is not, there is no law prohibiting Kansas hunters from using boats as a means of access to hunting areas, nor does it stop them from transporting game in the same manner. Be sure to check your state game law digest or to ask a conservation officer, however, before you go afloat.

Why should you consider float hunting? I know of five important reasons:

- Deer naturally frequent waterways in their travels, using these protective covers enroute to crossing spots, winter yards, sources of drinking water, and food.
- Hunting pressure drives the biggest, smartest bucks to riverbottom cover. Here, they hide out along brush-choked banks, in mature lowland hardwoods that are often strangled with grapevines, throughout conifer swamps, and on dry pods in cattail marshes. Heavy snowfall also tends to concentrate deer in thick cover. This is especially true in the cover that I call green stuff— lowland conifers that are usually interlaced with water pockets.

- Rivers permit float hunters the opportunity to get close to unsuspecting deer. My hunting partners and I have jumped bedded whitetails from as close as 20 feet. Perhaps because most deer are used to movement on the river, they do not expect danger in the form of hunters there.
- Rivers allow hunters to cover a tremendous amount of prime deer habitat in a short period of time. Other than road hunting or aircraft reconnaissance—both of which are illegal in many states—there is no better way to scout territory nor to hunt it effectively.
- Waterways greatly increase accessibility to remote areas that are low in hunter pressure and, in some states, to public land that is landlocked by areas that are privately owned. Further, in addition to stalking deer by watercraft, rivers also open the door to other successful tactics such as stillhunting, trail watching, rattling, hunting over scents or baits, and driving.

So how come more deer hunters don't do it? Chances are many never gave float hunting a second thought. Then again, some may not be willing to do the homework involved. This includes scouting a river for floatability, deer habitat, put-in and take-out access, and who owns the land enroute. It also involves using two vehicles or making pickup arrangements with another party, and it could mean knocking on a door or two if the stand of oaks that you wish to hunt is privately owned.

Carl Salling, a professional guide who is president of In Season Adventures Inc. of Mesick, Michigan, began float hunting for deer when he was a college student 20 years ago. To date, Salling has killed 108 bucks in four states and British Columbia. Fifteen or 20 of these deer came via float-hunting tactics. He has guided others to river hunting success, too, including three clients who each tagged a buck in a single day. Salling picks rivers such as Michigan's Big Manistee, which has large tracts of public ownership and meanders slowly through good deer habitat.

"You have to know local terrain and pressure conditions," Salling said. "For instance, opening-day pressure on high ground such as ridges often drives deer to lowland cover. A hunter sitting in a canoe can connect if he is in the right place at the right time."

Salling said that deer have regular river-crossing spots, which are typically found in brushy or wooded areas abutting straight, shallow river sections. A proven hunting method is to anchor upstream of such a trail, then wait for other hunters to move deer along it. A second effective tactic, especially when bowhunting, is to beach the canoe downwind from the trail, then take a stand in heavy cover where you can watch the runway. Salling has shot a buck each of the past seven years during Michigan's gun season by posting the same trail from his blind. On two occasions, he shot deer moving down the trail toward

him after he had seen them cross the river.

Driving is another effective technique that has worked for Salling, his friends, and clients. Pressured deer often seek refuge on points and islands covered with brush or thick timber. Salling's driving method involves dropping one or two drivers off at an upstream point. The remaining hunters (a three- or four-hunter party is ideal) quietly drift downstream to the head of the island or point. Depending upon cover size, a variation of this plan also works. For instance, on a long and wide point, Hunter No. 1 might get out at the beginning, Hunter No. 2 at the point, and Hunter No. 3 at the other side of the base. Once an agreed-upon length of time has lapsed, hunters 1 and 3 move toward Hunter 2, who acts as a poster. The best location to post is one that gives a clear view of both sides of the cover. Sometimes deer will break out on top of a waiting hunter; on other occasions, they will spurt from cover halfway along the drive. Extra hunters could act as blockers to intercept these deer. Drivers, incidentally, should move quietly and zigzag slowly to discourage bucks from sidestepping the drive.

Forested ridges can also provide ideal drive conditions. A poster or posters are dropped off far upstream, then skirt lowland cover on their way to hilltop stands. Drivers get out at strategic spots along the lowland cover and, at a prescribed time zigzag their way up the slope. All driving/posting tactics require an intimate knowledge of the terrain. Topographic maps are extremely helpful. If the land is state or federal property, hunters can check with area foresters or game biologists to see if cover-type maps are available. A county plat book will aid in identifying landowners. These books are usually available for about $10 at most courthouses and from many chambers of commerce. Hunters seeking permission to enter private lands then know who to call or visit.

Brothers Jim and Jeff Redmon of Higgins Lake, Michigan, have used plat books to find suitable stretches of public land on a dozen northern state streams. Like several others I interviewed, the Redmons, who also guide deer hunters, got into this sport through floating rivers for ducks.

"But there were days when we saw more deer than waterfowl," Jim told me. "So five years ago, we switched our deer hunting methods to floating. Now that's all we do."

During those five years, Jim Redmon, who's 29, and his brother Jeff, 32, have tagged eight deer between them. Interestingly, the Redmons are bowhunters and their average shots are only about 20 yards from canoe to deer.

"You can get so close to deer in a canoe because you can be quiet," Jim explained. "Besides, deer are used to objects moving along the river, and it is difficult for them to wind you."

Another advantage is that Michigan's bow season begins October 1 and runs six weeks until the firearms opener in mid-November.

"The rivers we run during bow season are always

open," Jim said, "but sometimes they freeze up during gun season or later in the year."

Michigan, like many other states, offers special December-only muzzleloader and bow deer seasons.

Redmon cites lack of hunting pressure in the early season, particularly along rivers, as another reason for his and Jeff's ability to get close to deer.

"Sometimes, they'll just stand there and look at you," Jim said.

Seconding that experience is Jim Henry, the president of Mad River Canoes and an expert deer hunter from Waitsfield, Vermont. While float hunting, Henry has shot mule deer along Wyoming rivers, tagged whitetails from the bottomlands of Minnesota's Vermilion River, and taken deer along the tributaries of Maine's Penobscot River. Most of these experiences were wilderness hunting expeditions in unpressured areas that are inaccessible by car or truck. In Maine, during the past two Novembers, Henry and his friends used a 21-foot freighter canoe to transport their wall tent, stove, and other gear; then they buddied up in 16- or 17-foot Explorer canoes to drift streams flowing into Chesuncook Lake. Their method involves relying upon paddle power to cover large areas of prime deer habitat, and they keep an eye out for crossing areas.

Mornings and evenings are best because deer are moving along waterway edges, looking for food and mating partners. Two falls ago, the Henry party of four hunters tagged an eight-point, a four-point, and two does. All were shot from canoes.

Getting close to deer and away from other hunters are two key advantages to float hunting. Access to prime habitat and the ability to cover it in a short period of time are other pluses. Although I know of no one who does it, rattling from a canoe at ten-minute intervals every mile or so could be a dynamic hunting tactic. A good-size canoe or inflatable also allows hunters to carry plenty of gear, including bait where legal, and affords a means of transporting game.

Depending upon stream type and flow rate, johnboats, rowboats, canoes, and inflatable rafts can be ideal for float hunting deer. Canoes, though, are the most popular choice. Those constructed of aluminum are light and easy to transport, plus they handle easily and can be propelled quite rapidly by muscle power. Aluminum, however, is noisy. To deaden sound, some hunters line canoe bottoms with carpeting and place slit flexible hose over the gunnels. Others opt for wood or fiberglass boats but then lose the lightweight advantage. On the other hand, the space age offers durable, lightweight synthetics such as Kevlar, polypropylene, and hypalon, all of which are now popular materials in boat construction.

The Achilles Inflatable Corporation, for instance, produces several inflatable rafts, each made with a four-layer fabric of heavy-duty nylon reinforced with hypalon and neoprene, both man-made elastomers. The result is a tough, snag-free fabric that is also surprisingly light. An SPD-4DX Sport Dinghy model that I used to float down a Michigan river weighed just 93 pounds. With its 990-pound capacity, however, it can transport two hunters and a whitetail buck. The raft can also handle a 10-hp motor.

Kevlar is the new rage in canoe construction. The Sawyer Company is building 17-foot-long canoes made of closed-cell, foam-core Kevlar for a total weight of less than 50 pounds. Mad River's Explorer, a 16-foot, six-inch-long canoe, is also made of Kevlar. It weighs 57 pounds. A 12-foot Porta-Bote, constructed of polypropylene and featuring a cargo capacity of 600 pounds, weighs only 59 pounds. The Porta-Bote is actually a rowboat that folds into surfboard shape only four inches high, and it comes with oars. Your choice of boat for float hunting deer is purely personal. You should know, though, that there are excellent products to choose from.

Actually you don't even have to own a boat. Many canoe liveries are open late into the fall. Kevin Hughes, a friend of mine, rents canoes to drift Michigan's Betsie and Chippewa rivers for deer during the firearms season. I have also heard about a small handful of innovative hunters who drift brush-choked streams in float tubes that are normally used for pond bass fishing. I can believe the stories that tell of these hunters being able to approach deer almost within touching distance. A Madison, Wisconsin, hunter I know of stillhunts by wading trout streams that wander through tag alder swamps skirted by hardwood ridges. This hunter has shot bucks by posting logging roads and fence lines— natural travel routes for deer—that he encounters in his stream travels. He claims that firm-sand stream bottoms aid in walking and that his low vantage point is a big help in picking out deer in heavy cover.

From a boat, you can hunt alone or with a partner. If you're hunting with a friend, only the hunter at the boat's front end should be armed for safety reasons. Hunters can swap positions halfway through the float. Another safety precaution is to add sponsons to the canoe if the stream you plan to drift is wide and slick running. Another idea is to wear a life preserver, especially the vest type. They are comfortable, don't impede shooting, and actually help to keep you warm. Pack matches, tinder, and a dry change of clothes in a waterproof bag and tie it to a boat seat or thwart. Tipping over in an ice-cold stream is not my idea of fun. Neither is flirting with hypothermia, the No. 1 outdoor killer.

If floating rivers for deer is a new sport for you, start with friendly streams that you can easily negotiate. They are often the best waterways for deer anyway, because they meander through lowland cover, allowing hunters plenty of time to check banks for deer activity and sign. One or two practice drifts will help you to become familiar with both the river and its habitat. It will also give you an idea as to the travel time required.

This fall, I'm hoping to float a river and tag a buck in heavily hunted northern Michigan, as well as in wilderness Maine. In both places, I don't expect competition from another float hunter.

Common Scents For Deer

By Harlan Kaden

It was the last day of the first segment of the bow season. I was anxious to fill my tag before the gun season opened and put all the deer on orange alert. After an unsuccessful morning on stand, the first snowstorm of the year began driving huge wet flakes into the woods—perfect conditions for slow and silent stillhunting. The wind was stiff and constant from the northeast, giving me the opportunity to quarter into the wind toward the brushy pockets north of my stand where I expected the deer to be bedded down.

I was moving extra slowly and carefully because I wanted to see the terrific ten-pointer that I knew had made this ridge his home territory. I hadn't been very successful at stillhunting during past bow seasons—I killed only one deer with that method—so the red squirrel perched on a log some 70 yards ahead of me provided the perfect prospect for practicing the stalking game.

Every time he gnawed on the walnut in his front paws, I took a step and stopped. When he stopped to look around, I remained stock-still. When he resumed his nut-chewing chore, I resumed my sneaky approach. When I got within 20 feet, I was beginning to feel proud of how I was catching on to this still-hunting/stalking method.

Finally, the squirrel caught a slight movement and skittered off the log and up a tree for a better look. Instantly, a doe and the monster buck that I wanted rose from their beds 40 yards away in thick brush. They were still unalarmed, but curious about the squirrel's behavior. After ogling the rack that wanted to hold my attention, I forced myself to avoid making eye contact with the big buck and began concentrating on his rib cage. I was waiting for him to move closer or lay back down. After three minutes short of eternity, the doe laid down.

"Come on big boy, lay down with her," I silently pleaded. But ten points don't grow on the heads of bucks that relax and take life easy. He decided to check things out a little better before settling down again. I smiled behind my camo mask as the buck started circling to get downwind of where the squirrel had been.

"Nice try," I thought to myself, "but it'll never work. I've got on about $5 worth of the best doe scent on the market."

I confidently waited for him to circle into a little opening only 25 yards downwind of me. The wind was still strong and steady and, when he hit the airstream directly downwind—still two steps short of the opening—he acted as if he had walked into the muzzle of a cannon. I never did see whether he turned around on his feet or just turned himself inside out as he shot out of the timber over the hill. The doe followed.

Several days later, I vowed to find a better way to control my odor, and I swore off bottled scents. I had already taken all the normal precautions, washing my hunting clothes in clear water with no soap and even hanging them outside to air dry. Showering without scented soap or shampoo before every hunt was already a habit for me.

I had also experimented with various kinds of scents. Doe-in-rut lures, skunk essence, fox urine, and other cover scents were all able to accomplish one thing: They made my clothes stink! Don't get me wrong—I'm just as ready as the next hunter to go to any length and suffer any indignity to bag a trophy whitetail. But if it doesn't work, I can't see any sense in coming home to my wife smelling as if a fox used me for the woodland equivalent of a fire hydrant.

I felt that I had eliminated all the odors of my hunting attire, except for the smell that my body was manufacturing to warn every deer in the county that I wasn't at home behind my desk where I belonged. There had to be something more I could do. When the bow season reopened, I continued hunting and looking for a new solution to the scent problem.

One evening, I decided to sit downwind of a fresh scrape for a while. Because I had no tree stand in the vicinity and there were no suitable trees to climb and sit in the limbs, I simply selected a broad tree about 20 yards from the scrape and started digging the light snow away from its base. When I got to the leaves and forest litter, I kept digging until I had an area free of all sticks, leaves, and crunchy ma-

Does this buck detect a familiar or foreign scent? It it's the latter, he'll bolt.   *Photo by Tom Edwards*

terial. I wanted to make sure that I could move freely and quietly when it was time to draw my bow. As I dug down into the leaf mold, I was surprised at how strong and how pleasant the earth smelled. I could still smell it even after sitting on the bare ground for several hours. Later, the wind calmed and the evening thermal drift started sliding downhill *toward* the scrape. I could feel the cool air on the back of my neck.

Shortly before dusk, a fat six-pointer headed down the trail. I was fully prepared for him to bolt and run when he got below me, where my scent—carried by the thermal airstream—would reach him. But, to my surprise, he stopped to freshen the scrape. It was only the movement of my draw that put him on the alert. The arrow was headed straight and true toward his chest when the only oak branch between us reached out and grabbed my broadhead inches from the deer.

Even though I didn't get that particular deer, I did get an idea that has helped me to kill deer consistently since then. Now I not only camouflage my body with clothing that blends with woodland foliage, but I also camouflage my odor with scents that naturally occur in the terrain I hunt.

I started experimenting with just the leaf mold from the ground. I gathered several inches of the ground litter in a large garbage bag, placed all my hunting gear on top of the litter in the bag, and sealed the bag. Over a period of several days, my clothes took on the clean odor of this natural woods compost. I continued trying different types of vegetation. Whenever I was out hunting, I always sniffed here and there to find out what deer constantly smell within their natural habitat.

I finally settled on a combination of background scents that I use effectively: walnut hulls (not the shells, but the outside covering that turns black and mushy), leaf litter (especially oak), and cedar branches. It gives me a lot of satisfaction and confidence to open my scent bag every couple of days and discover that my hunting clothes smell as if they were part of the woods.

Now, deer don't pay any more attention to me than they do to the trees in the woods. And the colder it gets, the better it works. The extra layers of clothing help to hold my own body scent in an envelope of woods smells. As long as I don't physically overexert myself and work up a sweat in the process, my odor seems to be effectively contained and camouflaged.

To make this method of scent camouflage work for you, it's important that you try to blend into the background odors of the woods where you hunt. You can start during scouting trips by finding out what the most common trees and plants are in your hunting area. Note which ones are the most aromatic. Crushing the leaves or breaking the twigs often releases more scent.

I have hunted primarily in the Midwest, from western Pennsylvania to Missouri, and I now live and hunt in eastern Kansas. The best scent sources I have discovered so far include walnut or hickory hulls; cedar, pine, or hemlock needles; sassafras leaves; hedge balls (osage oranges); leaf litter from the ground; and acorns. Use your nose to find out what all those plants smell like. There are many others indigenous to your particular hunting area that would be ideal for camouflaging your body odor.

I try to use odors that are of no interest to deer, and so I avoid food and sex scents. When a deer gets wind of me, I want to elicit no reaction at all.

There are two exceptions to this rule, however. One would be food scents that are so prevalent that they would not really qualify as attractors but are actually background odors. In the predominantly oak woods that I hunt, acorns are a good choice. Their odor is not as strong as some other sources, however. Apple scent is very aromatic and pleasant, but I won't use it unless I am actually hunting in or on the edge of an apple orchard.

The second exception would be using commercial doe-in-heat lures on trails or scrapes. You can even use it to create mock scrapes. But I no longer use it on my shoes or clothing. I want the deer's attention focused on anything but me.

When you have selected the mixture of scent sources common to your hunting spot, place it in the bottom of a large plastic garbage bag. I put my shoes and boots in next because they come into contact with the woods floor and will deposit a scent trail. When they smell like the woods I walk in, they leave no distinguishable trail. By placing them directly on top of the walnut hulls, the scent permeates the leather of the soles and uppers. The boots also make a good platform to stack the rest of my clothing on, to prevent the scent material from staining my gear. (Walnut hulls can darken a camouflage suit.)

Your clothing should remain in the bag for at least two weeks to be fully scented. You may even wish to freshen the scent material periodically if you find that it weakens.

Watch out for allergic reactions as well as skin irritations from some plants. Poison ivy, sumac, and stinging nettles are obviously poor choices for scent sources.

I've used natural outdoor odors to camouflage my scent for five years, and I've seen many more unalarmed deer than before I used them. My hunting success has improved from taking an occasional deer to regularly filling my tag. Plus I save money by not buying expensive bottled scents; I come home to my wife with a natural, earthy, clean outdoor scent instead of smelling like a walking wildlife outhouse.

The first buck I took after switching to natural scents was feeding on acorns under a large oak tree. Because I was stillhunting toward my car at the time, the wind was at my back and was blowing toward the buck. But I was still able to slowly stalk within 30 yards of him before putting my arrow cleanly through his rib cage.

So sniff around a little yourself. Camouflaging your odor—in addition to your body—may work for you, too.

Good Deer Hunting On Bad Days

By Coy F. Hollis

A buck is not the only creature in the woods who gets into a "rut" during hunting season. Many hunters adopt a particular method of hunting and never consider changing it, even though the weather and, therefore, the hunting conditions change. For instance, many hunters automatically take to their tree stand and wait. To them, there is simply no other way to hunt. However, on very windy, cold days preceding and during the passage of a cold front, you can sit in a tree stand until you wear the brads off your britches and never see a deer. On the other hand, there are also hunters who would never climb a tree and who insist on stillhunting. But on those days when the woods are extremely dry, you can walk to the next county without spotting anything.

The point is, if you wish to improve your hunting success, you must be adaptable and let prevailing conditions, rather than past practices, determine your hunting methods. While there is much to be said for hunting hard and putting in a good effort, flexibility, rather than fortitude, is the key to good hunting on bad days.

Before devising hunting strategies based upon the weather, it will prove helpful to examine the effects of weather on deer behavior.

As a rule, deer follow their normal routine of bedding, feeding, and moving throughout a wide range of climatic conditions. It is not unusual to see them feeding normally during rain or moving on breezy days. In general, scientists and observers agree about how deer act in relation to weather.

According to Al Berner, a biologist with the Minnesota Department of Natural Resources, "Under typical rainy conditions, there is minimal effect on deer—they will continue to move about normally—but during a freezing rain, they will seek shelter."

He also reported that deer continue their normal movements during windy days, but are careful to move into the wind so that they can more easily detect danger.

Dean Murphy, chief of the wildlife division of the Missouri Department of Conservation, said deer increase their activity somewhat during normal rainy days. This is largely because light is reduced to a level nearer the diurnal range. The amount of daylight on overcast days closely resembles light in the early morning or late afternoon, which is when deer normally move.

A study recently completed by Scott Hygnstrom, a graduate student at the University of Wisconsin at Stevens Point, revealed some interesting data on buck movements in relation to the wind. The study was conducted with the assistance of members of the Stump Sitters, an organization that studies deer behavior. The results of the study showed that, under perfectly calm wind conditions, there were fewer sightings of bucks than expected. However, under light wind conditions, there were more buck sightings than expected. As wind increased in velocity, buck sightings decreased proportionately.

Upon reflection, it seems reasonable that bucks would be more active in a light wind. The wind would make it possible for them to detect danger more easily by catching the scent. At the same time, their ability to hear would not be as diminished as it would be in a strong wind.

Francis X. Leuth, formerly a biologist with the Alabama Department of Conservation and Natural Resources, discovered that the same holds true for whitetails in the Southern United States. Deer continue normal movements in rain and wind unless it becomes very strong or very cold. During such times, deer will hold in cover—sometimes for as long as several days.

All researchers agreed that deer tend to hole up during very heavy weather, whether it be cold rain, wind, sleet, or snow. Most of them also reported increased movement 12 to 36 hours before an advancing front and immediately after its passage.

These authorities also agreed on another point: If hunters continued to hunt during bad weather instead of looking for a warm dry place to wait it out, they would be much more successful.

Before examining various weather conditions and the hunting methods best suited to coping with them, it is important to define the three types of hunting that will be recommended.

The first of these, stand hunting, involves taking a position—either up in a tree or in ground cover—and watching one area for the duration of the hunt. While stand hunting has many advantages, its primary disadvantage is that you are limited in the territory that you can cover. If deer are not moving in the area that you are watching, the hunt is over!

Walk-and-stand hunting means finding concealment on the ground and watching an area for a period of time, then moving on to a new area. The idea is to watch different kinds of areas to determine where the deer are located. It is somewhat like a bass fisherman trying to establish a pattern by fishing in different kinds of structure, depths, and locations.

Stillhunting involves intermittently moving and stopping in a slow, deliberate pattern as you move through the woods. It offers you the opportunity to cover more territory, but it also provides deer with an opportunity to spot you.

Some of the conditions that indicate a need to change hunting routines are sudden changes in the weather, days of heavy rain, windy days, and extremely dry conditions. Let's look at them in detail and see which hunting method best fits each one.

A sudden change in the weather is usually associated with an approaching low-pressure system. For some reason that is not fully understood, all wildlife seem to be more active under these conditions. It is not known for certain whether they know that bad weather is coming and are moving to areas that offer better protection, or whether they are eating an extra portion to hold them over for a while. For these reasons, or for some other unexplained reason, their movements increase during these few short hours.

Regardless of the reason, this type of behavior carries certain implications for hunting techniques. During an approaching front, the walk-and-stand hunter may have a slight advantage. The stand hunter usually places his stand along known trails leading to and from feeding and bedding areas. He also tends to hunt in the morning and the afternoon in order to take advantage of the early/late movement pattern. Because of frequent variations in their movement patterns during an approaching front, deer may not follow their established routines, thus lessening the chance that one will pass by when the stand hunter expects.

The stillhunter is also at a disadvantage because, although the deer are more active, they are also more alert. Because they are more exposed to danger, they exercise greater caution.

Walk-and-stand hunting offers the best combination of stand and stalk hunting, especially if you stay in the woods all day. The best pattern is to pick a location that offers an open area—not necessarily an open field—and to watch for movement near the edges of cover. If you can find, say, an open hardwood hollow bordered by pine thickets or honeysuckle, you may find some crossing action or movement along the borders of the thick cover.

After watching an area for an hour or so, move to another location and repeat the pattern. This allows you to cover a lot of territory during a day, and you are then likely to find an area in which the deer are moving.

The most uncomfortable condition to hunt under is rain. If you are going to hunt in the rain, still-hunting offers some advantages. First, you can move very quietly when the ground is wet. Secondly, you can cover more territory. This is often required during rain because you have to go to the deer if they are not moving.

During periods of light rain, the deer's behavior is hardly affected at all and there would be little need to change a preferred method of hunting under these conditions. However, if you are not skilled at stillhunting and wish to learn more about it, this would be an ideal time to give it a try.

If you are not an experienced stillhunter, it is a very awkward and difficult method in which to develop confidence. You feel exposed and think that everything in the woods is hiding and watching you. In turn, the temptation is to try to hide behind trees, rocks and bushes. The problem is that you always see a better place in front of you and you keep moving from one hiding place to another. Soon, you have

During most inclement weather, deer are more active than usual. Are you? Photo by Tim Irwin

gone through the area that you were supposed to be hunting and have come out convinced either that nothing was there or that stillhunting is a waste of time. The problem is, you were concentrating on hiding instead of on hunting.

A few points may prove helpful in learning this highly productive method of hunting. First, move as slowly as possible. Deer see movement more easily than they recognize objects. Second, when you stop, kneel down to blend into the ground cover or lean against a tree so that you are not silhouetted. And third, move less and look more. Study every area of cover and *use binoculars!* Look for parts of a deer such as an ear, a leg, and especially for the horizontal lines of a back or a belly among the vertical lines of trees or bushes. Many hunters think that binoculars are used primarily to see great distances, but their best use is to find small pieces of a deer in thick cover.

Probably the only thing worse than hunting in the rain is hunting when the woods are bone dry. It is more comfortable to the hunter, but it means more difficult hunting. Every movement and crunch of leaves is a signal to the deer to clear out.

Stillhunting and walk-and-stand hunting are difficult, if not impossible, during dry weather, leaving stand hunting as the most logical choice. You may want to choose a ground blind for convenience sake but, where it is legal, hunting from a stand in a tree enlarges the area that you can hunt effectively.

Even with the advantage of being able to see better from a tree stand, remember that you cannot see everything at all times. You can only see about one-third of the area at any time and many opportunities for a shot can be missed if you are not alert.

If you want to prove this to yourself, think about how many times you have suddenly noticed a deer standing in the open, 15 or 20 yards from the nearest cover. It did not simply appear on that spot. The deer walked there while you were looking somewhere else. It hurts to think how many bucks go by unnoticed.

The principal way in which dry weather helps the stand hunter is that it cuts down on the area that you have to watch. You patrol the area with both your eyes and your ears. A deer can move more quietly than you can but, when it is dry, even deer will give away their positions. On windy days or when the woods are wet, however, deer can slip by without a sound.

One effective technique is to locate your stand on the edge of a field or an open woodland area. You can then hunt the open area with your eyes and the thick woods with your ears, thus covering your hunting area more thoroughly.

If it is not too wet or too dry, it can always be too windy. Wind has probably saved hunters more ammunition than any other weather condition. I'm not referring to those days when there is a steady breeze blowing—this can be beneficial to the hunter—but rather to those days when it is bitter cold and the wind seems to come from all directions at the same time. On these days, deer will either hold in thick cover and not expose themselves or they will pick up your scent and slip away without you ever knowing that they were there.

Using a buddy system to move deer into the open offers an opportunity to get a shot at a good buck on such days, but the plan must be carefully thought out in advance. Preplanning not only places hunters in the most opportune positions to get the best shot, but also provides a safety measure in that they know where *not* to shoot.

For the purpose of illustration, consider a hunting situation in an agricultural area with woods dispersed between fields. The driver should start on the downwind side of the thickest cover in the hope of moving the deer down the hollow into more open areas or across the field into the adjoining woods. If there are fingers of the land protruding out into the fields, they provide natural escape routes. Bucks in particular will cross an open area at its narrowest point. Hunters should position themselves to cover these routes, but it is better if they take a stand across the field in the adjacent woods, rather than in the same area of woods.

When a deer is jumped and makes its escape across an open area, it will likely slow down once it is out of the immediate area of danger. Often, it you take a stand along an escape route away from the jump area, this will mean a standing or walking shot rather than a quick glimpse of a white flag. Contrary to appearances, deer do not leave the state when disturbed. They leave the area of disturbance quickly, but soon resume their normal activity at a much slower pace. Hunters should be stationed at other escape points and farther down the hollow in case a jumped deer chooses to move on down the wood line rather than cross the open field.

When attempting to move deer out of cover, it is better to stop occasionally than to walk continuously. Often, a deer will watch from cover and let a hunter walk on by. If you have ever observed deer while driving, you may have seen a similar reaction. If you keep moving, they stand and watch but, if you stop, they move out. The same thing is often true of a continuously moving versus a moving-and-stopping technique of hunting.

A buddy system of moving deer can be devised for any type of terrain you hunt. The important points to remember are to use the system in an area that everyone is familiar with, to identify the stand placements carefully, and, for safety's sake, to coordinate the time and the direction of movements of each person.

Occasionally, even for those of us who are willing to modify our hunting techniques and to learn new ways to hunt on bad days, there are those times when it is neither too wet, too dry, nor too windy. And on those days, even if you don't happen to see a single deer, you can always think, *What a great day to be hunting!*

Whitetails In The Wind

By Bill McRae

When I first saw the buck, he was coming directly toward my stand, but I shifted my weight, which caused the tree to sway slightly, and the movement caught his eye. I froze. He stared for several minutes and, though he didn't seem greatly alarmed, he altered his course and entered the brush 100 yards to my right.

It was a bitter October morning, with four inches of new snow, and deathly still—far too cold to be motionless in a tree for long. Figuring I had seen the last of the deer for that day, I was about to climb down when I spotted another bowhunter approaching from the opposite side of the five-acre thicket where the buck had holed up along with several does. My hopes soared.

To enter the thicket where he, no doubt, intended to stillhunt, the hunter had to cross a barbed-wire fence. He was obviously trying to be quiet, but as he depressed the top strand of wire, the fence made a loud squeaking sound.

In less than a minute, the deer were on the run, heading straight for me. The tree had been chosen for a stand because it was surrounded by thick brush; the kind of place, I figured, where whitetails would stop to reconnoiter when spooked. I was right. Soon there were deer under me, some so close that I could have dropped an arrow on them, but the buck typically lagged behind. I could see him coming, a dark shadow slipping through the brush on a course that would bring him through a narrow shooting lane at about 15 yards.

Struggling to stay calm, I weighed the situation. The buck was walking fast and, since I use a bowsight, it takes me a bit longer to shoot than it would if I shot instinctively. If I waited and drew my bow when he was in the opening, the buck would be across it before I could shoot. I decided to draw just before he entered the lane. That was a mistake. Perhaps it was the swish of my clothing, the sound of the arrow sliding over the rest, or a slight creak in the tree stand, but the buck heard something and stopped instantly.

There I was, holding the 70-pound Hoyt/Easton bow at full-draw while the buck, his computer running, stood motionless behind a thick clump of diamond willow. Instead of stepping into the open, he turned, paralleled the shooting lane, and stopped at 25 yards, still screened by brush. It was less thick, and I could see his form clearly, including his heavy 5×6 rack. I had counted the points earlier with binoculars. Deciding there might be enough open space to get an arrow through, I shot. The arrow clipped a half-inch-diameter sapling and settled harmlessly to the ground, two feet short of the buck.

I've relived that morning many times and, considering all the might-have-beens, I've decided that what others consider rotten luck was really the result of the stillness that allowed the deer's senses to function at their very best.

Let me tell you about another day on that same stand. A 10- to 15-mile-per-hour wind, with 30-mile-per-hour gusts, was blowing. I approached the stand, none too carefully, and climbed the tree. While I was pulling my bow up, a doe and fawn bounded out of the brush, a short distance away, and disappeared. Minutes later, another doe and fawn came out of a small round brush patch about 50 yards away. Apparently, the swirling wind had carried my scent to them but, instead of running off, they came toward me and lay down not ten yards from my tree. In the next half hour, I moved a good bit while glassing the surrounding area, but the doe and fawn never saw, heard, or smelled me.

Much as had happened on the calm day, a hunter spooked deer my way, although they came from different directions. As they came into my brush patch, the doe and fawn got up and all the deer milled around nervously.

A spike buck was standing about five yards from the tree and, since I didn't want him, I decided to have some fun. Taking from my pocket a small rock originally intended for use as slingshot ammunition on a drive the day before, I tried to drop it on his back. Naturally I missed and when the rock hit the ground, the buck jumped sideways and moved off a few yards.

Then I did what I should have been doing all along—I looked around. Standing at the edge of the brush, 30 yards away, in yet another direction, were two bucks. They hadn't come with the other deer. I suspect that they had been bedded somewhere near all that while, and had gotten up to check the new arrivals.

Before I could shoot, I had to nock an arrow, turn around, and squat to clear an intruding limb. The smaller of the bucks, a fat forkhorn, caught my movement and bounded into the cover. The larger buck, a respectable 4×4, confused by his companion's actions, took a few steps and stopped. Lightning reflexes being what they are, at the snap of the string he wheeled to run. Consequently, what should have been a good broadside hit put the Easton aluminum arrow, tipped with a Razorbak 4 broadhead, behind the rib cage. It passed through the liver and exited through the far lung. The buck went 125 yards.

While all this was happening, the wind was blowing like Hades. This was significant to me because I had recently read the following statement in an authoritative book about deer: "To attempt to hunt deer in high wind is a waste of time." The authors—both of whom I respect—gave the same reasons for not hunting in windy weather that I am about to give as reasons for doing so. This was their logic: the wind, which causes erratic air currents, noise, and the movement of vegetation, hampers the otherwise acute senses of smell, hearing, and sight of deer, and makes them extremely nervous, and, presumably, unhuntable.

I disagree. In the first place, a strong wind doesn't cause whitetails to panic. Where I live in central Montana, if deer panicked every time the wind blew, they would go crazy. Second, while wind does make deer nervous, it doesn't cause them to evaporate. They are still there, and they are, if anything, easier to hunt. To understand why, let's look at the whitetail's primary defensive senses—smell, hearing, and sight—and see how each is affected by the wind.

Every year I see things that increase my respect for the whitetail's marvelous nose. On the advice of the experts, I always wear rubber boots so as not to leave a scent trail when I approach my stand.

Nevertheless, in this past season alone, deer stopped to sniff my tracks on six different occasions. A doe, loping along with head high, bolted when she crossed my trail, which was on dry grass. Then she stopped, put her nose to the ground, followed the trail for a few yards—no doubt to see which way I had gone—and then went off in a different direction.

Another time, I laid out a dead branch 30 yards from my stand, as a range marker. Five days later, I watched in amazement as a fawn cautiously approached the branch with neck extended. Its nose almost touched the spot where my gloved hand had been, when its head snapped back as though the branch were a coiled snake. I had seen similar things happen before with recently handled items, but five days later! We humans cannot begin to comprehend the whitetail's sense of smell. Imagine, if you can, sniffing a few tracks, made less than a second apart and half an hour earlier, and being able to tell, by their relative freshness, in which direction their maker was going.

Deer not only detect the faintest odor, but they also have an uncanny ability to tell where it is coming from. Here's how I think they do it. Whitetails have relatively small home ranges, which they know intimately. That intimacy, no doubt, includes a thorough knowledge of how local air currents move under varying weather and atmospheric conditions. It is also likely that they can tell the point of origin of a foreign odor by known smells that accompany it.

In any event, deer have very accurate scent pictures of their surroundings, and they rely on them. Strong winds, because they rapidly disperse and dissipate odors, and because they eddy and swirl endlessly, confuse deer's scent pictures. Consequently, they are less able to tell where a hunter is located on a windy day.

A whitetail's hearing is almost as discerning as its sense of smell. As with smell, we can only begin to imagine what a deer's hearing is like.

In his book *The Deer of North America*, Leonard Lee Rue points out that a whitetail's outer ear, which funnels sound into the inner ear, has approximately 24 square inches of reflective surface, while a man's ear has only about 3½ square inches of reflective surface. Rue also notes that deer can swivel and turn their ears to effectively gather sounds from any direction. This gives them the ability to pinpoint the location and distance of sound sources.

Does having ears roughly seven times larger than a man's mean that whitetails have hearing seven times more acute? The correlation may not be exact, but I believe that deer hear at least that much better than we do.

At times, I have also suspected that deer have a sixth sense that warns them of danger, something

Photo by Wyman P. Meinzer

Windy weather brings the greatly superior senses of deer down to a level where they are more evenly matched with those of man.

like telepathy. It could be, but, more likely, it is the extreme sharpness of the animal's senses that alert it. Remember the big buck that stopped just out of bow range, reconnoitered for a few seconds, and then headed away as though he knew you were there? He could have picked up thought waves from your conniving mind, but, more likely, the buck heard your labored breathing, or even the pounding of your heart.

For example, take a whitetail buck bedded in a patch of thick cover. He rests, ruminates, and perhaps dreams of the coming rut, but, all the while, he is listening, his big ears swiveling to zero in on the faintest sound. He hears doors slamming, people's voices, vehicles starting and stopping— hundreds of sounds. If the sounds are familiar, he pays little heed, but strange sounds get his attention and he records their locations. This is why chances of taking a bedded buck are slim indeed.

What effect might a strong wind have on this same buck? Instead of the pervasive stillness, which makes it possible to give clear meaning to every sound, the woods are full of noises —the swishing, howling, and moaning of the wind; trees creaking, groaning, cracking, and popping—a cacophony that must be almost deafening to a deer. It isn't a cinch, but you just might get him.

I am tempted to say that humans have better eyesight than whitetails, but, if that is true, it is only in certain ways. A deer's vision differs greatly from ours. Incidentally, I'm convinced that mule deer see much better than whitetails. Most noticeable is the deer's inability to distinguish and identify stationary objects. On a wilderness elk hunt this past fall, a whitetail doe and fawn caught me in the open. We saw each other at the same instant and I froze. They looked me over carefully from about 50 yards, and then walked past. They came as close as 30 yards, where they stopped and stared again. Then they continued on their way and did not spook until they were about 150 yards away, where they caught my scent.

I have also had whitetails stand directly under my tree stand, not 20 feet away, and stare up at me. As long as I remained motionless, they didn't spook, but they did sometimes stamp their feet, as if trying to startle the strange creature in the tree into moving.

After a few experiences like that, one begins to think whitetails are nearly blind, but then they spook half a mile away when they see you moving. They seem unable to distinguish between motionless objects, but are incredibly quick to see the slightest movement.

There are other differences. Man has stereoscopic vision. Because their eyes are on the sides of their heads, deer very frequently employ monocular vision. That is, they often cannot focus both eyes on an object at the same time. They therefore lack precise depth perception. Their eye placement does, however, give them an extremely wide field of vision. The only place a deer can't see is directly behind

its head. They also have much better night vision than humans.

It is widely believed that whitetails don't look up. Experienced tree-stand hunters know better. True, deer don't look up a great deal, but the only animals that do so are those that are often preyed upon from above, usually by predatory birds. Also, I've found that other hunters are just as likely to walk under my stand, without seeing me, as whitetails are. Tree stands work primarily because deer almost never smell the hunter and, if you're quiet and don't move, they won't hear or see you.

I don't mean to imply that windy weather renders deer blind, deaf, and unable to smell—it doesn't. But it does bring their greatly superior senses down to a level where they are more evenly matched with our own.

On still days, when their senses give them a clear picture of what's going on around them, deer act with greater confidence. During a drive, they either move out, well ahead of the drivers, or, because they can hear every footstep, the deer easily circle back around the drivers. On quiet days, the action usually goes to the standers, provided they have taken their positions without being detected.

On windy days, whitetails must rely heavily on their weakest sense—sight. They seldom move until they can visually identify the hunter, which is made harder by the fact that vegetation is constantly in motion. If the deer can see the hunter, the hunter can see the deer. Because the wind deprives them of sound/scent knowledge, deer tend to hold tight when it's windy. On windy days, therefore, drivers are more likely to get shots than standers.

We have covered the reasons why deer are less likely to detect a tree-stand hunter on windy days. Now let's take a look at some of the problems. It is hard to shoot well in a strong wind, especially when you are perched in a swaying tree. The wind once blew one of my arrows right off the arrow rest. A strong wind could even cause the hunter to loose his balance and fall. Wear a safety belt or rig a safety line. A few times, I have actually gotten out of a tree because I was afraid it was going to blow over.

Windchill is also a problem. It's hard to stay in a tree when the temperature drops, and wind makes it all the colder. For example, a 20-mile-per-hour wind at 20 degrees yields a windchill factor of minus nine degrees. All things considered, I still prefer some wind over a still day when I'm in a tree.

Stillhunting is pussyfooting through the woods looking for game; stalking is trying to sneak up on game when you already know its location. In either case, the goal is to get close enough for a shot. It is here that wind benefits the hunter most of all. It whisks his scent away and masks his movements and the sounds he makes.

At the McRae house, the alarm goes off at 5 A.M. most mornings during whitetail season. Nothing gets me out of bed quicker nor raises my hopes higher than the sound of the wind.

Lessons From The Stalkers

By Peter Miller

Where are we? I don't know. The Benoits won't let me tell.

"You write where we are and every fool dear hunter in New England will be up here! You know where you are—somewhere in northern Maine!"

The country is gently rolling. Logging roads criss-cross the area and, every so often, a loaded truck comes barreling down at you and you're in trouble if you don't pull over, because the drivers don't swerve, don't slow down, don't wave, and don't smile. After all, it's their road. Where they've cut the pulp, it looks like a battlefield—clear-cut patches of slash and stumps, surrounded by woods of pine, spruce, cedar, some hardwood. The trees look dark and forbidding, standing like specters on the edge of the clear-cut. Where are we? Let's just say that most of the lumberjacks speak French Canadian.

"Those big bucks, those hoosiers," Larry said, looking at a deer track on the side of a road. "They're swamp bucks. Wide-beamed bucks. Gray faced. Some of those swamps are so thick you can't see only a couple of feet. Mister, you head north," and he pointed his carbine toward the leaden sky, "and you can walk to infinity."

He looked down at the track and let loose with tobacco juice. All the Benoits chew. They don't smoke. They don't drink at all in deer camp.

"This is just an itty-bitty-buck, maybe 150 to 160 pounds. Let's go."

We jumped back into Larry's Blazer. We were on a scouting trip, on a gray morning when the clouds, swollen with snow, hung like a canopy over the treetops. We were searching for the tracks of a big buck that might have crossed the road during the night. Larry was driving. He is a short man who walks lightly. He has brown eyes that do a lot of quiet looking. Larry likes to be neat when he is deer hunting, so he is clean shaven. Sometimes feisty, sometimes sentimental, he has a gift for storytelling, but there is no storytelling about the way he hunts. He gets on a buck track and the buck doesn't know it, but he's a dead buck, nine times out of ten.

Sitting next to him was Shane, his youngest son and his father's closest hunting companion. He is quiet, almost gentle, like a wild animal. Shane is the artist of the Benoit family; he drew some of the oil paintings of bucks that decorate the stocks of the Model 760 and the Model 7600 Remington carbines that the Benoits use.

In the back seat was Lane. Larry—his children call him Pop—is as neat as Lane is, well, sort of wild looking. His beard is full and makes him look like a woodsman who had been in the woods too long. His eyes have a glint to them, humorous, mad, full of life. His nickname is Slam.

Lanny, the oldest of the Benoit boys, is with his friend Alfie, scouting out a ridge above a swamp that is cut by an old tote road. Lanny has blond hair, blue eyes, blond beard. In real life, he runs a sheet rocking business. In the woods, he is an animal, the best of the Benoit deer hunters; he learned his lessons well from his Pop. He has wicked reflexes, uncanny eyesight, and a way of moving very quickly through the woods. He shoots a good game of Skeet, sometimes from the hip, sometimes by holding the gun through his legs. Don't ever get uppity with him. He is very, very fast in whatever he does.

Then there is me, more of an observer than a hunter. You might call me a foreign correspondent out in the field, reporting on how the top deer hunting family in America snakes out those big bucks from country so thick with timber that most hunters spend more time reading their compasses than following deer. Or you could call me Tanglefoot. That's what the Benoits call me. Whenever I am with a Benoit, and a buck is close by, my feet get sort of tangled, the buck takes off, and I get these looks that would wither an oak tree.

I hate to add up how many trophy bucks—bucks weighing more than 200 pounds—Larry and his three sons, Lanny, Lane, and Shane, have downed. Let's just look at the first five deer seasons in the '80s. Larry won't tell what he's shot—you can read that statistic in the revised edition of his book, *How to Bag the Biggest Buck of Your Life.* But his sons don't mind telling what damage they have wrought on the deer herds in Vermont and Maine. Over the past five years, they have knocked down 15 bucks that averaged out at 220 pounds, each decorated with an eight-point rack.

I have been with a Benoit only once when a buck was downed in front of me. That's because I'm a tanglefoot. But I have been there shortly after, and I have followed the tracks of a Benoit on the track of a trophy buck.

Larry downed the buck that I witnessed. It was near Rangeley, Maine, in an area where they no longer hunt. It was a leaden day with six inches of fresh snow on the ground, soft, slightly wet snow, the best type for tracking. This is what the Benoits are best at—tracking and unraveling deer sign while on the track.

We cut this track on a logging road. This is a favorite trick of the Benoits—ride along a logging road or walk an old tote road in the morning and look for tracks that say, "Lookit me, I'm a huge buck and I'm lookin' for does." When they find such a track, they go after it. If the track is old, they follow it and unravel where that buck's stomping ground is.

Larry squatted down and studied the track. He brushed away the snow and looked at it, stood up, and then he stared in the direction that the track was heading.

"He'll go more than 200 pounds and he's not an hour ahead." Larry said. "Stay behind, and don't make any noise. When I slow down, that buck is nearby. You slow down."

I followed about 50 yards behind Larry, tracking him as he tracked the buck. He walked quickly at the start. Within five minutes, I caught up to him. He motioned me to slow down and I noticed his body was taut, the rifle held at the ready. He began to pussyfoot. Larry scarcely looked at the track as he squatted, then stood up and swiveled his head left and right, looking for a piece of that buck.

Larry reads a track like a map that gives instructions along the route. A buck track, I have found, is staggered—two prints left, two prints right. The bigger the buck, the bigger the stagger. They walk that way because of the way they are built: "Wide haunched" is an apt description of a 200-pound buck track.

"Petey," said Lanny to me when we were looking at a big track during another hunt. (At times he is very patient.) "Now, you know a big buck leaves a big track. So does a small deer with a big hoof. A heavy deer has a track that sinks evenly in the ground, from front to back. A light deer with a big foot has the weight forward and only the front of the hooves sink in. Look at the tips. Are they uneven? An old buck wears down his feet. The tips are uneven. An old buck is usually a big buck. I can spot that track and tell that buck a week from now."

When a buck gets to settling down to take a snooze, he begins to feed, to nip at buds, paw in the leaves to uncover ferns, and nibble at mushrooms growing on dead trees. They meander and amble, stop, and keep heading toward a safe bed—on a ridge, in a swamp, or near a blowdown. A buck always beds down with an easy-access escape route. This much the Benoits had already taught me. The way Larry was hunting in front of me, I knew he thought that the deer was close by. He knew it was a buck and he was scanning the woods for a patch of gray, a tail, an eye. Spotting a buck in the woods is like putting together a jig-saw puzzle.

"Most hunters look too high," said Larry. "A deer ain't that tall. Look down lower to the ground. Don't look for antlers. If you have to look for antlers, you haven't done your homework."

I was with Lanny once, on the track of a buck, when he pointed out where the buck had left a nose print in the snow as it was feeding. It had also left tine marks.

"An eight-pointer," Lanny whispered to me.

I was skeptical until I stepped on a twig that snapped like a firecracker and the buck took off out of his bed. Lanny, after giving me a look that should have turned me into a pillar of salt, showed me the bed and had me count the tine marks in the snow.

I was about 35 yards behind Larry and trying to be as quiet as a resting buck. One foot up, one foot down. Position one foot, then raise the other foot, twist the body to avoid those dead branches—break one and I've got another firecracker underfoot. Feel for dead twigs under the sole of the boot, and put the weight down where there will be no snap, crackle, or pop. The Benoits wear very light, uninsulated boots. They wear one pair of socks. That's like wearing surgeon's gloves. Now a stumpsitter dressed this way would feel like his feet were soaked in permafrost. But the Benoits are always on the move, so they dress very light. Even lunch—brownies, a small can of tomato juice, a peanut butter and jelly sandwich, and small chocolate bars—is eaten as they track. I sat down once for lunch, dressed like the Benoits, and started to freeze. They dress lightly—

light pair of long johns under the wool pants, light T-shirt, and light flannel shirt under the black-and-green wool jacket—that's all. Sometimes, if it's warm out, they change to lighter dress—dungarees or corduroy—but never heavier. I have been hunting with them when the temperature was down about ten degrees and have never been cold. A tracker puts in a lot of miles, and you don't get cold when you are always moving, expending energy.

The buck that Larry was following was going to bed down in the swamp, about 300 yards from the edge of a beech grove that swept uphill. Then I put the wrong foot down. *Snap!* Larry whirled and shook his fist at me. If I had been right behind him I think he would have punched me. The buck took off and Larry loped behind him for 100 yards, then stopped. The buck was going for high ground—bucks on the run either go deep into a swamp or head for the ridges. The buck stopped making 30-foot leaps and began leaving the tracks of a fast-walking deer. He

wasn't that startled. Or perhaps he was curious. Larry walked out into the hardwoods 50 yards and stopped, looking uphill. Then he raised the rifle.

The muzzle blast, in contrast to the silence that I was trying to preserve, scared me so much I almost fell backwards. For some reason, I didn't think that he was going to shoot. The deer should have been long gone.

"Up there in the beeches, about 120 yards," Larry said when I ran up to him.

We climbed the hill and stopped where the deer was when Larry had shot. I saw nothing.

"You must have missed him."

"Missed him! What's that there?" and he pointed the barrel of the rifle about six feet on the other side of the track. There were two deer hairs. "He's hit, bullet went through him."

Larry turned to follow the deer and we both saw the buck at the same time. He was moving into some spruce. I saw his rump, his head, and a gosh-awful set of antlers. Larry shot again and then the deer disappeared.

All the Benoits use Remington pump carbines. The gun is then equipped with a sling and new sights, a Williams front sight that rides on a high ramp so it is easy to center in the woods, and a Williams rear peep sight. The ivory on the front sight and the eye side of the peep sight are painted with fluorescent orange. The color stands out like a neon sign when the woods are dark, and it makes sighting in on a deer much, much easier. Larry uses a .30/06 with 180-grain bullets; so do Lane and Shane. Lanny prefers the .270 with 150-grain slugs. All have the same sights except Shane, who prefers a Williams open sight rather than the peep. Shane sights in for 100 yards and uses Kentucky elevation for shots over that range. Larry, Lanny, and Lane sight in so that they can hold on their target for up to 300 yards. However, most of their bucks are shot in under 100 yards.

The buck led us for about a mile. It was late in the day, a gloom had settled into the woods as dusk approached. I saw Larry kneel and steady his rifle on a tree. Flame scorched out of the barrel. The buck was laying down, head up, his antlers silhouetted against the snow. Then the head went down. The hunt was over and the saddest ritual of big-game hunting began. We made our peace with proud deer before the hard work of dragging it out began.

It dressed out at 209 pounds. The antlers were well spread into an awesome rack with ten points. Larry seemed noncommittal, but I think that he was secretly pleased. His dream, of course, is the 300-pound buck. The closest he has come was a couple of years ago in Maine, but a blizzard caught him as he was going for help to drag it out, and he spent the night in the woods. So much snow fell that he could not find the buck the next day, or the day after. The heavy snowfall had turned the woods into a stretch of land as anonymous as the sea.

Each of the Benoits has developed his own style of hunting. You can divide them into two camps—the Larry way of hunting and the Lanny style.

Larry and Shane hunt pretty much in the same style, slow, careful, easy. One day, I was with Larry when he was scouting for a good buck track. It hadn't been the best year for Larry. He and his youngest son had been in Maine for a month, first scouting, then looking for the biggest buck of all buckdom. Larry found one that was up in the 230- to 240-pound range. He had a wonderful shot at it, from about 40 yards. This buck had stopped to peek at him.

Larry took me to the spot and pointed out where he shot—very thick spruces, dead and alive, stood between him and the deer. He couldn't see all of the buck and somehow this dead tree popped right up in front of the deer as Larry shot. He nailed the dead tree dead center and the buck made a hasty retreat and was never seen again.

Larry hunts slowly and usually doesn't make a mistake in shooting. He prefers to sneak up on the

The Deer Stalkers (from left) are Shane, Lane, Larry, and Lanny shown in the Maine woods.

deer and make a clean kill with one shot. It used to be that he would run after a buck, but age has slowed him down and he now relies almost solely on his deer sense to ambush his quarry. He can sense when a deer is a rambler—a sex-mad maniac looking for does and going in a straight line, deviating only long enough to meet the does that he comes across. Most bucks range in a circle. In Vermont, that circle often has a ten-mile radius. In Maine, Larry has found that the bucks make up to a 20-mile swing. He likes to find their swing lines and, if he doesn't get the buck on the first day, he comes back for it again, cuts the track, and dogs the buck for the day.

In Vermont, he would spend almost the whole day on the track. But not in Maine where it is easy to get lost.

"Some people go in these woods and are never seen again," Larry said. Although he used to scoff at compasses because, as he said, "I have one built in my head," he found that this built-in compass was not in perfect working condition in Maine, "where you climb a ridge and don't know that you climbed it, because the woods are so thick, or there is a fog or it is snowing out. You're also in trouble when you cross a brook in the morning, then cross it again and find, to your utter dismay, that that brook is climbing uphill in the wrong direction. You can make circles awful easy in these woods."

Larry now keeps a compass pinned to his jacket.

Shane has more patience than his father. I trailed behind him during a day when he tracked a doe in the hope that the doe would lead to a buck. She eventually did, but it was a small buck not worth shooting. Shane pointed out the holes in the snow, where the doe urinated.

"A buck now, he struts along and dribbles as he moves, or urinates on a sapling," he said. "That's part of his calling card. A buck's urine is strong. Smell it, then smell a doe's urine.''

We came across where a doe in heat had urinated and colored the snow pinkish yellow.

"Go on, smell it," Shane cajoled me. "It's almost perfumy."

He was right. Later, I smelled a bed that a buck had been laying in. The scent was almost acrid, yet softened, like a mixture of urine, sweat, hemlock, and stump water. It was raunchy.

Most hunters do their best to hide their scent when in the woods. I never once heard the Benoits talk about ''upwind'' or ''downwind.''

"You get on the trail of a buck," Larry told me, "and you think he's going to worry about your scent?'' If he scents you, then he just might get curious enough to backtrack and take a look at what makes such a stench. Deer are curious, you know.''

Shane hunts as slowly as his Pop, maybe even slower. He walks softly and picks a good line through the woods. I tailed him as he pussyfooted behind a feeding buck (yeah, I scared it but it was a small buck anyway). Shane took five minutes to go 30 yards and, as I watched, his head never moved up or down; his body took up his motions as he went over deadfalls, skirted trees, and walked on logs without making any noise. The Benoits have trained themselves to walk in the woods. They trained themselves to walk on logs and even to shoot accurately from them.

Larry and Shane take small steps. Larry has a keen sense of what path to follow. He is not a slave to a deer track. He will glance at the track, figure where the buck is headed, and take a short cut. Or, if he is close to the buck, he'll take the path with the least amount of booby traps. I have followed Larry's tracks and he always manages to pick a path that is quieter than the one I would normally take. All of the Benoits, when they walk, use body English to sidestep dead branches, saplings, and deadfalls. Their prime purpose is to walk smoothly and quietly. Quiet. That is a key word. They wear wool because it is noiseless when it scrapes on branches. They use a cartridge belt so the shells don't clink in their pockets. They don't carry small change. All their gear is streamlined to be light and quiet.

Lanny is the eldest of the Benoit sons and he is a natural. He is awesome to watch in the woods. I have walked directly behind all the Benoits and looked at their tracks. Larry takes neat little steps, carefully placed. The left foot goes out a bit. Shane takes bigger steps but more in a straight line. Lane sort of lopes and Lanny walks somewhat like a duck, with the toes of the boot splayed out.

He used to run his bucks down. Lanny once followed a buck that he estimated went about 15 miles, up and down 4,000-foot mountains.

"He sure didn't like me behind him, now did he?" Lanny questioned no one in particular. "But it didn't make much of any difference at all, now did it?''

Even after all that exercise, the buck weighed more than 200 pounds. Now Lanny is pushing 40 and he doesn't jog his bucks to death, but he still moves awful fast. When he is on the track, he sort of hunches over. His eyes are focused up and to the side, only occasionally on the track. The rifle is tucked under his arm. It almost looks like he scuttles through the woods, using a sideways motion like a crab. This is because he angles his body so fluidly around trees and saplings without slowing down. He's swift and silent, like a trout moving upstream.

"You know, Petey, a buck with a big rack walks around the spots in the woods that would hang up his antlers. And so do I.''

Lanny is a strange mixture. He is very impatient and fast. He races snowmobiles and drag-races cars and, too often, he wins. But when he gets close to a buck, he has lots of patience—until he starts shooting. Then he often empties his carbine.

"I sort of like to get rattlin'," he said.

Lanny's eyesight in the woods in phenomenal. All the Benoits appear to have Superman vision when they are hunting. Lanny once picked out a rabbit sitting in front of us in a maze of ground cover, and all he saw was the ear. He once spotted a buck taking a peek at him through a thicket of brush by noticing the nose with the ring of white around it.

I've seen Lanny walk into a swampy mix of alders and spruce where it looked like a war had been fought. Saplings were shredded, and the ground was pawed and torn up something awful where bucks had fought, then mated with some does. The area was littered with tracks.

The trick here is to unravel those tracks and get behind the biggest buck, the one that did all the punishing in there. The Benoit method is to make circles, ever widening circles, around the tracks until they pinpoint the direction in which the largest set of buck tracks is headed.

Lanny found three buck tracks and went after the largest. It was what he calls ''an awesome track.'' It led to a 217-pound eight-pointer. Did Lanny shoot it? No, he coaxed the deer up the ridge to where Lane was, and he downed it.

Lane is all strength and energy, except in the morning, when he shouldn't be bothered. He moves quickly through the woods, has quick eyes, and is just a tad below Shane and Lanny in the weight of his bucks. However, he did come through with the largest buck the Benoits have taken in the '80s, a 248-pounder that he knocked down in 1981. Lanny downed the biggest Benoit buck in 1979—a 271-pound 13-pointer.

Do the Benoits miss? Sure. Each of them misses about once every seven years. As they say about those bucks, ''they're still runnin','' and then they shrug their shoulders. They are always looking ahead. That 300-pound 12-pointer is just over the hill, maybe down at Dale Pond, maybe up on the border of Maine somewhere, maybe in northern Vermont, New Hampshire or the Adirondacks—someplace where the trees grow scrambled, the woods are dark, deep, and mysterious, and all the bucks are big, strong, and wary as all get out.

PART 3

HUNTING MULE DEER

Crazy Places To Find Muleys

By Jim Zumbo

You're going to hunt deer *here?''* the amazed man asked me.

He had seen me carrying a rifle in the seemingly barren Utah desert and had stopped to ask what I was doing. I nodded and told him that I was going to give it a try. He shrugged and gave me some advice.

"Ain't nothin' here but coyotes and jackrabbits," he said. "I don't believe that there's a deer within 20 miles of this place. Good luck!"

At that, the man drove off in his pickup truck, leaving a big cloud of dust in his wake.

I continued walking down the road and turned into a wash that held a hidden water hole. I had discovered the oasis several weeks before while hunting antelope. When I noted dozens of doves flying up the wash, I investigated and spotted the water hole. Further surveillance turned up a modest three-point buck deer and several does. I was surprised because, like the man in the pickup truck, I didn't think that muleys inhabited such dry, desolate regions as this.

My desert hunt had a happy ending. Late the second afternoon, I tied my tag to the three-point buck. I ambushed him as he came in to water. I even saw a bigger buck in my headlights while driving out that same night.

Mule deer live in a wide range of environments— from lowland deserts to alpine tundra. While it's true that there are habitats that offer prime deer hunting, because they have what muleys prefer, there are many spots off the beaten track that hold deer, too. Furthermore, those out-of-the-way places are ig-

Photo by Larry Ditto

nored by other hunters, and you won't have to compete with other people when you go hunting.

A recent Wyoming hunt with *Outdoor Life* Executive Editor Vin Sparano, Editor-at-Large Pat McManus, and several other writers illustrates how you can take advantage of places ignored by hunters. We were on a combination antelope and deer hunt, and had decided to take our antelope first. With that done, we turned our attention to muleys.

Camped next to a road in the lowlands leading up to high country, we noted heavy traffic each day as hunters drove into the mountains. According to several people we talked with, hunting was poor. Apparently, few deer were even spotted because of the severe winter, which caused heavy big-game mortality not in only Wyoming but in other states as well.

We decided to hunt in a rocky outcrop area just adjacent to the well-traveled road. The spot covered several hundred acres and had a maze of small washes tucked between sharp ridges that resembled a dinosaur's backbone.

Though we weren't successful, we saw a decent buck and several does. The buck managed to give us the slip because we spooked a small herd of does that alerted him.

The important point was the fact that no other human tracks appeared in the soft earth where we hunted, even though the season had been open for almost ten days and the area was next to an accessible road. Hunters had simply ignored the spot in favor of the higher country, which is the traditional deer range.

That wasn't the first time that I'd discovered mule deer in unusual places—far from it. In fact, I make it a habit to pursue muleys where other people don't. It's become an annual challenge, and I like the solitude. To be sure, I see more deer in the traditional places where everyone else hunts, but there's something satisfying about taking a deer in a spot that's overlooked by other hunters. I've found most of these unusual spots by accident, usually when I'm hunting for something else.

Several years ago, I was hunting ducks in a swale along a river. As I walked through trails in the cattails made by livestock, I noted deer tracks. Deer season was closed, and I wondered if any bucks used the area. As far as I knew, no one hunted deer along this stretch of river. There were too many houses in the area, and most hunters headed up to the mountains for their venison.

A half-hour later, I jumped a small flock of mallards. After I shot, I heard a commotion in the cattails less than 50 yards away. I looked to see a nice four-point buck bounding through the brush. No doubt he was just as startled as I was.

I looked the area over thoroughly and found that the deer obviously had been using the cattails as a bed. The following year, I told a friend of mine about the buck. I wasn't able to hunt because of my schedule, but my buddy killed a nice buck in the swale on opening day of deer season.

Another time, I was setting out goose decoys on an island that I'd floated to, and I jumped a nice buck in the willows. The deer ran to the edge of the water, jumped in, and swam across the river to the safety of heavy brush. I saw the buck three more times that year on the island. I swore that I'd hunt him the following fall, but I wasn't able to find him when the season started. I flushed several does and fawns on the island, but the buck never showed. Nonetheless, the spot was a perfect refuge for deer because they weren't disturbed. I'm sure that the island will be home to another buck in the future, and I'll visit it again during deer season.

Mule deer are seldom thought to be the farmland deer that whitetails are, but many muleys commonly live their lives out within sight of a farmhouse. More than once, I've discovered mule deer living along creek bottoms adjacent to farms and, a number of times, I've flushed them from standing cornfields while I was hunting pheasants.

A muley must have food, water, and shelter to survive. If those three ingredients are present, a mule deer will call practically any place home.

There is a surprising exception to the three ingredients, however. Allan Whitaker, a wildlife officer with the Colorado Division of Wildlife, made an intensive study of mule deer watering habits in Mesa Verde National Park. He found that deer commonly drank no water at all, and obtained the necessary moisture from the food that they ate.

This information sheds interesting light on mule deer populations that dwell where water is scarce or absent. Many times, I've been puzzled at the presence of deer in areas where I couldn't find a trace of water for miles. I assumed that the deer were drinking from a water hole that I couldn't find. In light of Whitaker's study, though, I'm not so sure.

Several years ago, I hunted desert bighorn sheep in Utah and walked several miles each day in searing heat. I was amazed to see deer tracks in that inhospitable desert. Every now and then, I discovered a small seep issuing from springs, but I never saw deer tracks around them. I'm sure that I didn't find all the watering spots available, but the sheer steepness of the country seemed totally inconsistent with the typical mule deer territory with which I am familiar. Game trails often descended into deep canyons along sloping walls that defied anything with four legs to walk down them, but deer used them anyway.

While hunting mountain goats in Montana's Bitterroot Mountains recently, I commonly saw deer tracks in the cracks and crevices that goats walked on. Some of these prints were enormous, but I never saw the deer that made them. Maybe that was just as well, too. While I had a deer tag, I didn't want to complicate the goat hunt by killing a huge muley.

Photo by Conrad Rowe

If a muley has shelter, water, and food, the deer can call anywhere home.

It would have been tough, though, to pass up a record-class deer, even if I had to hunt him on those high, dangerous slopes.

What this means is that mule deer can adapt to almost any environment and weather extreme that nature can dish out. That's why you'll find muleys almost anywhere. They're tough and furtive enough to hide without being easily spotted.

Deer carcasses along highways are clues to the presence of muleys in places where you'd never think to look for them. Once I saw a doe that had been struck by a car in an area that I thought was barren of deer. Because there was snow on the ground, I parked my vehicle and looked for more tracks. Sure enough, I found where a small deer herd had been traveling from a series of bald hills to an alfalfa field adjacent to the highway.

I mentally filed the information and returned to the hills during deer season. It didn't take me long to find a buck for the freezer and tie my tag to his antlers.

One of the craziest places where I've found deer is next to busy highways during the peak of deer season. Mule deer, even wary bucks, may bed down close to a road as long as the topography is such that they can remain relatively hidden.

Several years ago, I was driving along a well-traveled highway when I noticed a colorful stand of quaking aspens. The trees were in superb fall foliage, showing brilliant shades of orange and yellow. I pulled off the highway to take pictures of the trees and walked about 50 yards across a small draw. As I walked, dozens of vehicles carrying deer hunters roared by. Like the hunters, I had no idea that deer might be present.

After crossing the draw, I walked another 100 yards along a low ridge. Finding a good vantage point for taking pictures, I was preparing my camera when a deer snorted from the brush just a few dozen yards away. I looked to see a small doe staring at me. I froze and watched her, surprised that deer would be so close to the highway—especially since it was either-sex season and the doe was legal game.

A moment later, I saw motion in the brush a few feet from the doe. Presently, a buck stepped out where I could see him. He was a handsome three-point with a wide, high rack.

I had a deer tag in my pocket, but my rifle was in the truck, which was almost 200 yards away. I was disgusted with myself for not carrying the rifle along, but it was too late to do anything other than watch. The doe had my number, and I knew that she'd soon spook and take the buck with her.

Sure enough, the doe spun around and ran for a brushy draw that led away from the highway. The buck instantly followed, and I was shocked to see another buck pop out of the cover—this one a small four-pointer.

As soon as they disappeared, I made a mad dash for my truck. I grabbed my rifle and made a big circle, trying to cut them off. It was no use. They dropped into a deep canyon and there wasn't enough shooting light to follow.

Another time, when I had pulled off the highway and was just 20 yards from the road, I heard a deer burst from the cover in front of me. I jumped up on a big rock and saw a nice buck bounding away. As in the other instance, deer season was open and heavy traffic whizzed by close to the deer's hideout.

Although it would seem that deer should shun busy highways, they apparently ignore traffic if they feel secure in their beds. Along many busy roads, the absence of vehicle pullouts precludes anyone from stopping and investigating roadside areas.

I've learned my lesson, and I frequently park my rig and check out areas near roads. Obviously, safety is a primary consideration when shooting near highways, and state laws generally prohibit shooting across a thoroughfare or from the side of a road. It's also necessary to be sure that the land adjacent to a highway is public. Otherwise, you'll need permission to hunt it. Quite frequently, hunters will spot a deer next to a road and, in the excitement, never consider who owns the land. Plenty of tickets are issued by game wardens for these types of trespass violations.

One of the most ignored environments for mule deer is the sprawling pinyon/juniper forests that occupy low elevations. Millions of acres of such forests grow in several Western states, notably Colorado, Utah, Nevada, New Mexico, and Arizona. The forests are hunted extensively in places where few other trees exist but, in areas where there is traditional mountain country, hunters drive past the forests to get to the higher elevations where aspens, pines, and firs grow.

The pinyon/juniper forests are difficult to hunt in, which is one reason why they're passed up by hunters. Noisy shale rock covers much of this habitat, and visibility is poor. Deer often hear or see hunters first, and then scoot out of the country without being seen.

Plenty of hunters are unaware of the number of deer that live in these lowland forests. A few years ago, I was dragging a nice buck out of an arid juniper forest, and a party of hunters saw me as I approached my truck. They were driving up into the mountains when they spotted me.

"Did you kill that buck down here in the scrub trees?" asked an incredulous hunter as the group gathered around to look.

"Sure did," I said. "There are always a few deer in these junipers."

I'll be darned," another hunter said. "We've been driving by here for years and never thought to give this area a try. You're the first person I've seen hunt this low country."

The men helped me load the buck in my pickup and we chatted a bit afterward. They asked me a few questions about hunting the junipers, and I encouraged them to try the area.

Two of the hunters returned the following weekend and called me afterwards. They had killed a pair of muleys—not trophies, but nice bucks nevertheless. The rest of their party hunted the higher country and never saw a buck.

Nighttime is when deer move about, unafraid of humans and the noises and sights of civilization. It's the best time to spot deer in out-of-the-way places, especially bucks that are hidden during the day. To find these deer, take a drive at sundown and look for deer in the waning light.

I like hunting deer in places where people give me funny looks. It's a great coup to take a buck in spots where they aren't supposed to be, and I grin all the way to my freezer.

Muleys In The Grass

By Ron Spomer

Last October, there was a mule deer lying out on a grassy flat, right in the open for the whole world to see. He wore heavy, chocolate-colored antlers that stretched out beyond his ears. The sun was beaming from a clear sky, it was 2 P.M., and the Rocky Mountains were 300 miles away. The deer wasn't lost. He was a grassland muley.

Grassland mule deer are nothing new. They were living where man and his cattle now prosper long before domestic ungulates set hoof on this continent. When the Herefords and Angus moved in, the muleys moved over, but they didn't move out. Today, they prance across broad wheat fields in the moonlight, slink down brushy coulees at dawn, and hide out in wrinkles and folds of a land that you'd swear couldn't conceal a snake. When muleys think that they can get away with it, they also bed in the middle of open flats, frustrating hunters who can't crawl within 600 yards before they're seen.

This doesn't mean that grassland muleys are unapproachable. Hardly. In fact, statistics indicate that they are the closest thing to a sure bet for filling a tag. Success rates for mule deer hunters in Plains States such as Kansas, South Dakota, and Nebraska ring in annually at 60 percent or better. In good years, when the weather is dry and mild on opening weekend and the deer have bred themselves into abundance, more than 85 percent of licensed hunters take home venison. Not much of it, though, wears big antlers.

Because they're relatively easy to find, open-country mule deer are killed at a tender age. Fork-horns are the rule, spindly four-points the exception, and heavy and wide four-points the bragging rights. Precious few live long enough to grow thick bases and tall tines that fork twice and reach well beyond their outstretched ears. Those that do are masters of escape in a land that appears to be escapeproof.

The first-time grasslands hunter, especially one skilled in the pursuit of woodland deer, gazes across the gently rolling wheat fields and pastures of eastern Montana and asks "Where?" Well, where are the deer? Obviously they can't hide in the trees, but they can slip into the earth.

A wise old muley buck can spot the slightest dimple in a plot of ground, then mold himself into it so that not even his mother could spot him. Last fall, I watched such a contortionist saunter across a quarter mile of table-flat grass, then disappear. I studied the creek 300 yards beyond the flat for an hour, but the buck never showed, so I went looking.

When I neared the spot where the four-point had vanished (identifiable by a lone yucca), I found a shallow dip—the beginning of a drainage. I followed it cautiously around a 45-degree bend until I could look down its length to where it emptied into the wide, barren creek bottom. No deer. I scratched my head and pondered this one. Here was the only possible place that the buck could have gone, unless he'd found somewhere to hide in the creek. I walked down the grassy swale and practically fell on the old boy. He bounced up out of nowhere—one second he wasn't, the next he was—and thundered back across the flat. He'd been holed up in a four-foot-

deep, three-foot-wide erosion cut shrouded by grass, and he left me holding the camera. I never seem to have a rifle when I could most effectively use it.

At least I found that buck. Most hunters walk or look right past them, disbelieving that anything bigger than a grasshopper could hide in grass. This attitude has contributed to many muley buck birthday parties. Way back in 1963, when mule deer were still noted for their stupidity in the face of fire, South Dakota wildlife biologists couldn't find a young four-point muley that was wearing Blaze Orange streamers and a radio transmitter that beeped researchers to within a few hundred yards.

The biologists had captured and radio-collared the animal shortly before the deer season opened. On the first day of the hunt, the men watched a group of hunters walk draws and thickets to within a quarter mile of the radio-collared buck before it sneaked away. When they moved still closer, it slipped around a height of land and returned to the cover that they'd already worked. After an hour, the group returned to their vehicle, fired a couple of practice rounds at a rock, then drove within 40 yards of the Blaze Orange decorated deer on their way to the road.

Two days later, several hunting parties passed within 200 or 300 yards of the buck. On the fourth day, it bedded in a barren draw within 200 yards of a highway. Several hunters stopped to glass but saw nothing of interest, so two researchers decided to try their luck at flushing the deer. They took a final check of the beeper and moved into the eroded draw, pushing out only does and fawns. They returned to the beepers and discovered that their target had moved 100 yards from its original position. They tried again and did much better. This time, they found its tracks.

That afternoon, three men repeatedly located the deer with the radio, walked the 150 yards to where it was supposed to be, and instead found empty hiding places.

This called for reinforcements. The next day, five men entered the battle and, by late afternoon, one of them finally stumbled onto the buck accidentally while returning from yet another unsuccessful search.

The lesson here is: be diligent and perseverant. Glassing is a wonderful technique for locating these grassland deer but, when that doesn't produce, it's time to cinch up the boots and kick those obscure dips and cuts and isolated snowberry patches. Don't take anything for granted. If an area looks like it couldn't hide a mouse under a ton of topsoil, it's probably sheltering a dozen muleys. Think of them as fourlegged, antlered pheasants, just as prone to sneaking off on their bellies, crawling into the most unlikely cover, and hiding their heads in the sand until you boot them in the tail. Trust neither shouting nor rock throwing nor gunfire to roust them from their sanctuaries.

Prairie muleys don't always stick to cover like cockleburs to setters. They're just as likely to light out and never look back. One year, a friend and I were dragging ourselves back to camp after a hard morning spent thrashing every leaf and twig, every cut and gopher hole, in an attempt to roust a muley, when here comes a deer parade. Moms, kids, and the family patriarch bringing up the rear. They trotted by out of range and disappeared up the canyon that we'd just worked—the farthest one from camp.

Dedicated to a fault, we hiked back, our eyes glued to the horizon lest they depart early. We never saw them leave, but they must have when we dropped—just for a minute, mind you—into one of those common erosion cuts because, when we finished our second thrashing of the big draw, it was again uninhabited.

Three long miles later, when we were within smelling distance of the camp stew pot, we looked left to see our band of deer lining out of the camp draw—again out of range. This time, they marched over a broad flat until distance alone hid them. We never saw them again.

With all this against him, the grassland muley hunter has to play smart and hard. He should begin with careful selection of his hunting grounds. States that offer grassland mule deer habitat include all those from North Dakota south to Texas and west to the Pacific Ocean—in other words, the traditional mule deer states plus the Plains. In the mountain states, you'll find grass muleys in the foothills and the broad agricultural valleys between mountain ranges. On the Plains, look for them west of the 101st meridian or, roughly, U.S. Highway 83. This is the eastern fringe of the Rocky Mountain rain shadow, where mule deer quickly give way to whitetails and wetter things.

Within this half continent, there is much mediocre country. It is easily avoided by keeping to the rivers, creeks, badlands, canyons, and other geography that puts relief in the landscape, creating pockets of brush and deep grass in which the deer can hide and winter. From here, they drift up to the flats to feed on the native forbs and man's crops.

If you haven't time to research these places, write or call fish and game departments and ask about the better grassland mule deer hunting units. Request harvest statistics and hunter success rates, remembering that the unit giving up the greatest number of deer doesn't necessarily have the largest bucks. So ask about big bucks, too. Often, they'll be in rugged areas where vehicles cannot penetrate. Many times, they're scarce on public lands—those under the Bureau of Land Management and National Grasslands—but they're more common on bordering private lands where the harvest is limited.

Earning permission to hunt good private land can be tough but not impossible. Begin by uncovering the names of landowners in the area of your interest. These can sometimes be obtained from state agencies and often from county agricultural businesses such as feed stores, implement dealers, and livestock associations. Request the names of ranchers who might talk with you about deer hunting, then write a few

Diligence and perserverance are the tactics you need to get a grassland mule deer.

letters of inquiry or make a few polite phone calls and see what happens.

Anytime you strike out with a prospect, ask him if he knows of any neighbors who might allow hunting. While some ranchers have a steady clientele of sportsmen, others often complain of too many deer and too few hunters, and the rural grapevine passes this information along.

If you can't, or don't want to drum up private land, turn to the public acres. Maps showing ownership, roads, and waterways are usually available from fish and game agencies. Once you've selected a hunting unit, plan to visit places on the map that are laced with broken terrain far from roads. These areas are less likely to have been hunted hard in the past, and may provide undisturbed resting places for deer during the season.

When you leave for your hunt, try to do so several days early, even if it means sacrificing an equal number of hunting days. This will allow you to scout many areas during critical dawn and dusk periods when deer are moving. By the time the season opens, you should be in position for the biggest buck in the county. In contrast, if you arrive bleary-eyed at 2 A.M. on opening day, half the decent bucks will be shot while you're scurrying for a place to hunt.

If you haven't found a proven muley travel route by your first morning's hunt, I recommend that you sit on a promontory between feeding areas and bedding grounds—the closer to the beds the better.

Here, you'll be in position to glass and stalk—the second most productive prairie hunting technique—and intercept deer fleeing from drive-and-poke, the most productive deer killing technique.

Drive-and-poke permit holders ride their pickups across the prairies, poking into canyons and coulees for a quick look before hurrying on. These are the types who drove up to the Blaze Orange, wired muley in that barren South Dakota draw without seeing it. They kill a lot of deer, but few trophies, and they spook a lot of deer, many of which will file past you if you're in the right place.

When you spot an animal worthy of a stalk, move quickly to intercept it if it appears to be heading out. If it beds down, give it time to relax while you study the terrain carefully and plan your approach. Then get to it before a poker drives up. Comb that cover if you don't immediately find your deer. Examine all side draws and drainages, even the shallowest. Any patch of cover that's more than two feet high could be hiding something.

If by noon you haven't seen what you were hoping to spot, stretch your legs with a ten-mile hike to all appropriate muley coverts. This is the time to hunt them as if they were pheasants. You may have to drive several miles to other areas with suitable cover—pockets of vegetation sprinkled sparsely over the pastures and grainfields.

If you're hunting a private ranch, find out the location of the winter pasture or bull pasture. These areas have the densest brush and grass cover because they've seen little or no domestic livestock all summer. If there is a cottonwood-lined river in your unit, walk it anytime after opening morning. This is usually whitetail habitat, with the muleys sticking to the drier and more open terrain but, under pressure, the long-eared deer will move into the river bottom.

Traditional Western rifle calibers with flat trajectories are ideal for grassland shooting. You can expect clear shots out to 600 yards or more and, although I insist that you not try such long shots, it's good to carry a rifle that will reach accurately to 400 yards. That potential may allow you to finish a wounded and escaping animal. Normal ranges will vary from point blank to 350 yards. There isn't much to lean against out there, but short grass and rolling terrain make prone shooting possible, and a practiced marksman can take standing game at 300 yards confidently—with no wind.

Because even a big grassland muley weighs just 200 pounds field-dressed, big calibers aren't as important as accurate ones. The .243 and 6 mm are good minimum cartridges, the .25/06 and .270 ideal, and the .30/06 more than enough. In some Plains states, .22 centerfires are legal. Many local hotshots use 50- to 60-grain bullets that don't have the mass to bull through bone and meat and reach a vital target. Miss the vertebrae or heart and lung area and you're trailing a wounded animal. When you finally get a 50-yard shot at a wily, heavy-beamed, long-forked grassland muley that's running straight away, you don't want to have to pass it up.

Aspen Pocket Muleys

By Kathy Etling

It was a glorious autumn day. Sunlight sparkled and bounced off the golden aspen leaves, scattering bright pockets of color over the landscape. We were hunting mule deer in south-central Wyoming, and the weather seemed to be custom-made for success.

The area we were hunting was ideal: Sagebrush, bitterbrush, and mountain mahogany dotted the foothills, each plant a staple of the mule deer's diet. Higher up, the dark green of a mature pine forest covered the mountain's steep sides.

I was off chasing an elusive forkhorn that we'd spotted earlier in the day. Bill Rooney, Editor of *American Forests* magazine, and *Outdoor Life* Editor-at-Large Jim Zumbo decided to sprint along the mountain's jagged crest with me in what turned out to be a wild-goose chase. My husband, Bob, was luckier.

While we were scrambling and sliding around on the ridgetop, Vin Sparano, Executive Editor of *Outdoor Life*, Hal Nesbitt, Director of the Boone and Crockett Club, and Bob plotted a one-man drive—with Vin as driver. They decided to concentrate on the tangled aspen pockets that were growing along the runoff rills.

Vin was elected to drive because he'd already collected a nice seven-point buck earlier in the day. He shot the muley as it was feeding toward an aspen pocket. That buck and previous encounters with mule deer put the handwriting on the wall for Bob. He knew that the one place they were bound to be during the midday doldrums was the aspen pockets.

Aspen thickets provide muleys with an abundance of preferred food. A one-man drive accounted for this plump buck. Shown with it are Jim Zumbo, left, and Bob Etling.

Photo by Bill Rooney

Hal and Bob each chose a vantage point from which to cover the aspen patch. When they were in position, Vin began to slowly walk into it. The wind was at his back, blowing his scent ahead of him. The wind does it all.

Vin had no sooner set foot in the aspens when a deer exploded from the cover on Bob's side. Bob only got a glimpse of the animal before it bolted quickly into a small depression and was hidden from view.

Bob guessed where the deer would top the ridge and concentrated on that spot. But he still didn't know whether or not it was a buck, and only bucks were legal in our area.

The aspens were full of deer. Vin barely took two more steps when he nearly stepped on a deer.

"Buck!" he yelled, as a heavy-bodied six-point

scrambled to his feet and then barreled out across the sagebrush.

Once again, the deer exited on Bob's side of the aspens. This deer was definitely a buck, so he quickly swung his .300 Weatherby back around and picked up the fleeing buck in his scope. As the animal raced past, Bob swung ahead and fired three times. The deer stumbled several times but kept right on going. Bob chambered another shell but, before he could squeeze off another shot, the buck disappeared.

"You got him," Vin shouted, then hurried over to help in the search.

Bob and Vin headed in the general direction of where the buck was last seen. Because of the waist-high sagebrush and similar-looking terrain, they feared a difficult tracking task, but Bob found the deer fairly quickly. The buck had been hit twice and both shots were good ones. That muley turned out to be one of the heaviest we've ever seen. It had put on layers of fat in preparation for the rut and winter. The antlers, while nice, weren't as good as they could have been. The winter had been particularly brutal in this section of the state and the muleys, therefore, had smaller racks than normal. This symmetrical six-point rack had an 18-inch outside spread.

Our hunt took place on land owned by Elk Mountain Safari near Saratoga, Wyoming. Ed Beattie, Elk Mountain's general manager, offers a variety of hunts on 1,300,000 acres either owned outright or leased. The area that we hunted lies squarely in the middle of a major mule deer migration route.

Throughout the Rockies, most mule deer are migratory. They spend their short summers high in the mountains and, in autumn, snow drives them down to lower elevations. By the time Region D opens for deer hunting in October, the migration is usually well underway. Finding an area where deer area on the move increases the chances for success. Fortunately, there are many such areas.

Bob and I discovered the benefits of hunting aspen pockets a couple of years before when we concentrated our efforts 20 miles southwest of Rawlins. We were hunting north of the Atlantic Rim in rugged sagebrush hills. As we glassed from the tops of ridges, the land around us seemed devoid of life. But then Dennis Smith, the game warden in Rawlins, visited us and clued us in on why deer like aspen pockets.

Aspen thickets provide an abundance of preferred food. Snowberry, bitterbrush, serviceberry, mountain mahogany and, of course, aspen are all muley favorites and grow in and around these pockets.

In terrain where sagebrush is dominant, aspen groves also provide needed cover. While mule deer don't crave heavy cover as much as whitetails do, they still feel more secure when they can hole up in some sheltered nook. Aspen pockets are made to order. Within one pocket, there is usually a diversity of cover ranging from impenetrable thickets, where moving is nearly impossible, to openings littered with leaves that make desirable bedding areas. Deer feel safe in this kind of cover.

Once located, aspen pockets can be hunted in a variety of ways.

If the aspen pocket is fairly small or narrow, one-man drives can pay off. Always take advantage of the wind. Make it work for you, not against you. Shooters should position themselves where they can cover the greatest amount of territory without being in the line of fire. And, if conditions are right, noise isn't necessary.

Drives using several men are also effective. I got my first aspen pocket muley as a result of a three-man drive. I was sitting on a point overlooking an aspen draw that necked down and finally gave out altogether. It was a frightful day with slashing sleet and a buffeting north wind.

This aspen pocket was much larger than usual, and the drivers were taking their time covering it. Hunting like this is extra thrilling because of all the deer that bound out of the drivers' way.

On this particular day, I was seeing a lot of does. The drivers got closer and closer, and I'd just about given up when I noticed movement directly below. My eyelashes were almost frozen together, but I finally recognized the form of a deer—its coat completely covered with sleet—picking its way across the valley floor. The deer wasn't in a big hurry and, as it walked along, I could see a nice six-point rack.

I took the time to get set up in the sling, bracing my elbows on the insides of my knees, and found the buck's shoulder in the crosshairs of my scope. One shot from my .30/06 dropped the muley immediately. And I became an aspen pocket believer.

As strange as it may sound, a hunter can be successful conducting lone-man drives. Find a thicket that looks promising but that is small enough so that a deer, if jumped, will try to escape out the other side while still being in range. Use the wind as an ally, travel slowly, and stay alert, Bob discovered the rewards of hunting like this a couple of years ago.

He'd been watching an aspen grove from before dawn until about 10 A.M. No bucks had been spotted, so he decided to climb over the ridge behind him and explore a likely looking patch of aspens that he'd noticed while scouting the day before.

Right away, he realized an important fact: The new aspen patch was located so that the sun shone directly on it. This can make all the difference in country noted for its harsh weather. Deer take advantage of small luxuries like this. The aspens that he'd been hunting were still shaded by the high ridge behind.

He tested the wind and found it blowing from behind him, pushing his scent right into the quakies ahead. Moving slowly, a third of the way down the eastern slope, he carefully watched for any movement below.

In just a few minutes, he spotted his first deer. It was a good ten-point that had been browsing along the edge of the aspens. Buck and man stared at each other for long seconds. As Bob raised his .300 Weatherby, the deer bolted into the quakies and promptly dropped out of sight in a deep wash. Long moments passed before it bounded straight out of

Photo by Tom Huggler

This forkhorn muley exited aspens to feed on sagebrush and was shot by hunter.

the gully and charged up the opposite hillside. One shot from the .300 Weatherby, and the buck fell near the top of the ridge. Bob's hunt was over.

One other method of hunting the aspens is to find a place to sit, watch, and wait. This kind of hunting is very similar to whitetail-deer hunting, only on a much larger scale. It's a good idea to have a friend pace off a variety of distances upon reaching muley country. Distances can be deceiving, especially when the only object around to compare a deer to is a clump of sagebrush. Sometimes, an easy 100-yard shot turns out to be well over 200 yards . . . and no sure thing.

Be on your stand well before dawn. Mule deer like to travel during low light. Thoroughly scout any area you plan to cover. Learn where game trails are, where they merge, and where they top ridges. Be sure to stay alert, because I've seen muleys stand so still that only the flicker of an ear or a tail gave away their position.

It's important to stay on stand until legal shooting

hours are over. I prefer to stay on stand all day when a front is moving through. Avoid walking on game trails whenever possible. Mule deer can be as wary as whitetails if they get a whiff of human scent where it shouldn't be.

One final tip: When checking likely looking aspen pockets, avoid being skylined. Remember, if you can see deer moving below, they most certainly can see you—especially if you're silhouetted against the sky. By walking a few yards under the rim, you can avoid this problem.

Aspens thrive throughout most of the West, primarily in elevations between 7,000 and 9,000 feet. They can be found within a pine/fir forest or hidden along drainages in rolling sagebrush. They nearly always hold deer.

Hunting aspen pockets is both productive and fun. It's a good way to see the best that the West has to offer while collecting a fine mule deer in the bargain. And it's addictive. Once you've tried it, you may never hunt mule deer any other way!

Methods For Mature Muleys

By Doyle Markham

Most hunters will admit that one of the easiest ways to take a big mule deer buck is through hiring a competent guide. Guided hunts, though, are not for everyone. Because of the cost and the desire to go by themselves or with buddies, most hunters prefer not to use a guide's service.

But many hunters who don't employ guides are also consistently successful in shooting big muley bucks. These hunters typically use several methods or factors in their hunting—and guides commonly use the same techniques. No matter where you hunt mule deer, you can increase your chances of harvesting a mature buck with these methods.

One of the important factors in consistently collecting mature bucks involves the time of the season you hunt. Hunting the late season, when the bucks are in rut and snows have forced the deer to concentrate at lower elevations, is unquestionably one of the most productive times for seeing the big bucks, and it is one of my favorite times to hunt. Recently, in a fenced test area in Montana, mule deer were hunted throughout the general season. Data was gathered from hunters about the number of deer seen, their sex, and the number of hours hunted. The area was open to either-sex hunting and received hunting pressure throughout the season. The results of the study indicated that does were easiest to harvest at the beginning of the season but became increasingly difficult to see and shoot as the season progressed. Conversely, the bucks were much more difficult to collect during the opening week but became more visible as the season progressed.

Mule deer typically begin the rut by November 1. After this date, the bucks are generally more active and less cautious. To increase your opportunities to shoot mature bucks, plan your hunt, if possible, as late into November as the season will allow. Additionally, during later seasons, hunting competition is greatly reduced. In Montana, the deer season generally runs from mid to late October through the end of November. While hunting in Montana during the last 2½ weeks of November, I've encountered but a handful of deer hunters.

Preseason scouting and becoming familiar with your hunting area is another important factor. If you don't already have a favorite spot, contact a guide or talk to your hunting buddies. Some of the best contacts are the fish and game department employees who work in the area where you wish to hunt. I've enjoyed many hunts that were planned over the telephone with a topographical map in front of me. You may bag a big buck during the first day in a new hunting area, but it often takes several days to locate a big one.

Invariably, my wife and I hear comments on how lucky one of us is for having shot a nice buck. There's no doubt that luck is one of the factors. Being in the right place at the right time when a big buck suddenly appears is lucky, especially if it's a real trophy.

During the 1981 deer season, a friend, Jack Connelly, and I were hunting on the opener. It was one of those days when you wondered if you made the right decision in taking a day off from work. Two of the weather conditions were great for deer hunt-

Photo by Tim Christie

ing—cold and a few snow flurries—but the third, fog, wasn't. Deer may have been standing everywhere, but we couldn't see anything because the fog was so thick that it limited visibility to a maximum of 200 yards and, at most times, a lot less.

We were working a patch of aspen on the northeast slope of a small drainage. Jack was walking up the draw on the treeless slope opposite the trees, and I was walking on top of the ridge above the trees about 500 yards up from Jack. As we approached the upper end of the draw, the fog thickened and I no longer could see the area where Jack was supposed to be. Not far from the top of the draw. I hurried into a 600-yard-wide basin covered with sagebrush, bitterbrush, and juniper trees.

The fog receded a little as I reached the middle of the basin. Several does and fawns darted out of the junipers, and I watched each of them with my binoculars to make sure that one wasn't a buck. As I watched the last two slowly disappear into the fog, the quietness was interrupted by a sound similar to that of someone running a stick along a picket fence. I strained my eyes toward the sound and waited. Suddenly, a huge buck appeared, ghostlike, out of the fog, running full speed in my direction. I dropped down and landed in the sitting position

with my elbows resting on my knees. I missed the first shot but the second .243 bullet put the buck down. His antlers had a spread of 33 inches.

Although luck is certainly involved in harvesting mature bucks, other important factors are a prerequisite for luck. People who appear to have more than their share of luck are usually the ones who consistently work the other factors.

You should be a fanatic about keeping your gun sighted in, and you should know exactly where your bullet will hit at various distances. Most of us don't shoot as much as we should anyway, particularly offhand. Certainly shooting offhand at reasonably close distances ought to be a routine part of our rifle practice, but everyone shoots better with a rest than offhand. When shooting at a deer, use a rest if at all possible. It takes only a second to find a bush or tree to rest a gun on, or to shoot from the sitting, kneeling, or lying position. Hunters I know who practice shooting faithfully and who have trained themselves to use a rest whenever possible seldom miss deer. You may only get one shot all season, so you must be able to shoot accurately.

All of these factors are crucial for shooting deer—whether you consider yourself a meat hunter, a trophy hunter, or both. But if you're after a big buck, there are several additional factors that you'll need to consider. One of the simplest yet toughest rules is: Don't shoot small ones.

There's also the danger of passing up a nice four-point, in the hope that you'll see a bigger one, and then later wishing that you had taken the four-point. That happened to me in 1982 while I was hunting near Miles City, Montana. I purposely waited until mid-November to hunt because the bucks would be in full rut by then. At 10:30 A.M. on my first day of hunting, I was using my binoculars to search the small side draws that dipped into a large canyon. After about 20 minutes of searching, I finally spotted a buck and a doe across the canyon in the bottom of one of the draws near some scattered ponderosa pines. I slowly made my way around the steep head of the canyon and along the opposite side.

It took me about 15 minutes to reach the small draw where I had last seen the deer. As I started to peek into the draw, the doe spooked and the buck followed her, but both stopped in the open sage-brush on the opposite ridge. The doe stared at me as I lay in the snow, but the buck acted unconcerned. I studied both with my binoculars for several minutes. The buck had four long tines on each side, and each side of his rack was perfectly matched. I realized that it would be my third largest rack if I took advantage of my opportunity. But then again, I had three more days to hunt, and I found him so easily— surely I'd get a chance to shoot a bigger one. So I got up and slowly walked away. As I took my fourth step, the deer bolted over the hill.

During the next three days of hunting, I passed up 12 additional bucks—and not one of them was a mature four-point. On the morning of the fourth day, I decided to shoot the first buck I saw because I had 560 miles to travel to get home. I found one just as legal shooting time started—and it was the smallest buck that I'd seen on the entire hunt. I still think about that lovely four-point buck standing there 100 yards away in the sagebrush and snow.

The single most important physical item in any hunt for mule deer bucks is a pair of good binoculars. My favorite pair is an 8X40 that I've carried for 19 years. But whatever power you're comfortable with, this is one piece of equipment that the serious mule deer hunter shouldn't scrimp on—quality optics are essential and cannot be an option.

Almost ever year, I see hunters using their binoculars only to check out a movement in the distance or to be certain that the brown figure they've seen is a deer.

Those hunters are missing many deer that could be readily spotted if they used the binoculars routinely. Although it's difficult and tiring to use your binoculars consistently throughout the day, doing so is one of the most productive deer hunting habits that you can develop, especially during the first few hours of the morning and the last few hours of the day.

Once, while hunting with my wife, Cherrie, in Colorado, we hiked two-thirds of the way up a

Photo by Erwin and Peggy Bauer

mountain and were sitting down catching our breath and enjoying a mid-morning snack. We had seen several does but no bucks. As usual, we were scanning the surrounding hillsides with binoculars, looking for deer. I soon spotted a buck about three-quarters of a mile away, the early-morning sunlight reflecting from his polished rack as he walked into a group of four trees. Surprisingly, these trees were the only ones on the southern-facing slope and were only 100 yards from the main trail near the bottom on the mountain.

We watched the trees for several minutes to make sure that the buck was going to bed down. A couple of hunters, unaware of the buck, hurried up the trail below the deer without spooking him. Right then, we knew that we had a reasonable chance of taking him. Hiking back down the mountain to the trail and following it to the trees would put us below the deer, offering him an easy escape route upward. There-fore, we decided to go alongside the adjacent can-yon, just out of sight, and come out above and op-posite the deer.

After a brisk 30-minute hike, we climbed the few feet up the top of the ridge and started down through the trees on a north slope, which we hoped would bring us out on a treeless area directly across from the buck. As we broke through the trees, a quick look with the binoculars barely distinguished the head and shoulders of the deer lying under the trees, but the white face of the buck stood out like a billboard—a sure sign of a mature buck.

We approached within 250 yards. My wife rested her rifle and squeezed the trigger. The buck never moved but kept staring in our direction. Cherrie's next shot killed him instantly. We found that the first shot had hit the ground right by the old boy's shoulder, spraying some dirt on his side—but he never moved. He had escaped several hunters that morning just by lying still. We certainly wouldn't have seen him, either, had it not been for our trusty binoculars.

When deer think that they're well hidden, they are usually reluctant to move. During the middle of the season a few years ago, I was hunting near Challis, Idaho. I had worked my way up a steep mountain to a large rock slide near the top and decided to take a breather. I was using my binoculars to search the trees all around the head of the rock slide. On my third sweep of the trees on the side of the rock slide, a white face materialized within the trees some 275 yards away. I could only see a face and a portion of a neck. Although the top of the head wasn't visible, that white face had to belong to a mature buck. Even if I was wrong, the area was open to either-sex hunting, anyway.

The deer didn't move a muscle as I began to build a shooting platform of rocks so that I could shoot over the brush. Finally, I slipped out of my pack and placed it on the platform to form a cushion for the rifle. But I could still see the top of the brush through the bottom of the scope, so twice I added more rocks and replaced the pack. The deer continued to watch

without moving. Finally, my scope cleared the brush and the crosshairs were solid as a rock on the bottom of his neck.

At the shot, the buck whirled and disappeared into the thick trees. After ten to 15 minutes of searching and going back to the shooting platform to get my bearings, I finally found the buck ten feet from where he had disappeared at the shot. He had the best rack that I had collected up to that date. Without the binoculars, I never would have seen him.

Early in the morning, bucks will often stand motionless at the edge of a group of trees. If a hunter moves into the opening, the bucks drift undetected into the trees, and the hunter never sees them. The four-pointer that I shot in Idaho during the 1982 season was one of those "before dawn" bucks. My wife and I were on the top of a ridge, looking down over a sagebrush-covered slope into a small basin. Trees covered its northern slope. Even with the binoculars, the deer looked like a ghost standing on a small open ridge within the trees. But there was no mistaking that unusually high rack. I called to Cherrie, who was farther up the ridge, and pointed out where I had last seen the buck. She guided me with hand signals to the area. When I arrived on the ridge where the buck had been standing, the light was still so poor that I couldn't see Cherrie without using the binoculars.

Deer blend in well with their surroundings, particularly when they are on a hillside that's covered with several types of brush. Hunters can easily miss seeing them, even in the middle of the day. In Colorado, on one clear sunny day, I was sitting down opposite a largehillside covered with browse. I'd been there looking around for a few minutes when I saw a movement out of the corner of my eye. I

To remain hidden while maintaining a good vantage point, older bucks will often bed in or near a copse of trees. This and all other types of potential deer-holding habitat should be closely inspected with binoculars.

Author thoroughly scouted an area in southeastern Idaho to collect this trophy buck.

hurriedly brought the binoculars up to my eyes. To my surprise, not one but 12 deer were out there. Through the binoculars they were all obvious—standing out in the open.

Although working tree-covered draws and north slopes in otherwise open country with one or two buddies is a productive method of hunting, most of the mature bucks are difficult to "brush out." The old boys have likely played this game before and the only way that they'll move is if a hunter almost steps on them. If they are scared out of their bed, they often will quietly slip out of the trees.

Cherrie and I never have been very successful in brushing out the bigger bucks unless we happen to know their specific location in the trees. Once, while hunting near the Utah/Idaho border, we were glassing several open slopes just after legal shooting time began. We saw two mature bucks walk into a long, thin strip of aspens in the bottom of a small draw. Without binoculars, we couldn't see them, even when we knew where to look. After a half-mile hike, we approched the trees where the bucks had disappeared. I began throwing large rocks into the narrow stand of trees, which was no wider than ten feet across. On the fifth rock, one of the bucks jumped right from where the rock had landed and made the mistake of running out on the other side of the trees. If we hadn't thrown the rocks directly at the place

where the buck was bedded, it's likely that he would never have moved. And, without binoculars, we would never have seen the deer.

Our binoculars delivered another four-point that evening. After hunting all day without seeing another deer, my wife and I wearily approached our parked car just at dark. The car was in a broad saddle where sagebrush and bitterbrush-covered hills met. Just over the hill was a small cattle water pond. As we arrived at the car, I took a last look at the facing slope with my binoculars. Standing perfectly still in the middle of it was a nice four-point buck. He had probably seen us coming down the slope where he had been headed for water only moments before and had realized that his best defense was to remain motionless. It was so late in the day that the buck was only visible with binoculars and, luckily, in the riflescope as well.

Was this entirely luck—or just an isolated incident? No, the binoculars were responsible and, more than once, we've scored on a couple of four-points in the same day by continuously glassing them through our binoculars.

Although the effort necessary to collect a big buck isn't for everyone, the potential to shoot mature mule deer bucks is certainly available to most hunters. The only things necessary are hard work, persistence—and a little luck.

How To Hunt For Success

By Bill McRae

H ow can one guy be so lucky?" The comment
came from a man standing beside me. We
were part of a crowd of bowhunters gathered
around a converted horse trailer used by Calvin
Coziah to display some of the heads and horns of
the more than 100 trophies that he has taken with
bow and arrow.

"I don't think luck is much of a factor," I said.

"Oh yeah? Well how do you explain this kind of
hunting success?"

I don't recall where the conversation went after
that—probably nowhere—but I've thought a lot
about the incident and have come to realize that,
while most of us admire and even envy successful
hunters, we don't really understand the reasons behind their success.

Setting out to tell the whole story about any subject
is an awesome undertaking, especially if your ideas
are contrary to popular misconceptions and illusions.
It might be presumptuous on my part, but I am going
to try to tell the truth about hunting success.

I don't have a master's degree in any field even
remotely related to hunting success, but I have
hunted for at least 40 years and have taken a few
respectable trophies. I've also been privileged to
know many of the most successful hunters of modern times, people whose names appear frequently
in Boone and Crockett, Pope and Young, and Row-
land Ward. But the only hunter I'll mention by name
is Calvin Coziah—for several reasons.

First, I have great admiration for what Calvin accomplished. He has taken more than 50 trophies that

Photo by Mary McRae

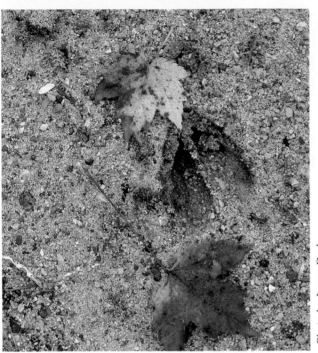

Photo by Larry Dech

One major reason why most hunters never bring in trophy-class animals is because they spend their time hunting in areas where such animals simply don't exist.

qualify for the Pope and Young record book, including 13 antelope, 28 mule deer, 14 elk, and two mountain goats. For a gun hunter, that would be an outstanding record but, for a bowhunter, it borders on the incredible. Second, what he has done could conceivably be duplicated by anyone with sufficient dedication and determination. He is a man of common means who hunts on public land and does his own thing in his own way. Third, while most of the successful hunters I know are honest, conscientious, well-balanced individuals, some of the things that I have to say about some of them may be taken as less than complimentary.

Here, then, are the keys to the kingdom of hunting success.

AN EXCEPTIONAL PLACE TO HUNT

One major reason why most hunters never bag trophy-class animals is because they spend their time hunting in areas where such animals simply don't exist. There may be plenty of game about, but the animals don't live long enough to grow outstanding heads. As Coziah says, "If he's not there, you're not going to get him."

So, to be an exceptional hunter, you need exceptional places to hunt. Such places fall into two categories. The first consists of private holdings with very limited access. These exist in infinite variety, ranging from private game preserves, where animals are selectively bred and fed mineral-rich diets to produce trophy racks, to huge Western ranches that are off-limits to hunters in general and, in some cas-

es, block their access to adjacent public land. Except for the matter of blocking access to public land, there's nothing wrong with these, but to take an outstanding animal under such conditions takes no great talent.

Most hunters, however, are not blessed with such opportunities. And the alternative to owning your own hunting preserve, or paying a large sum to hunt on someone else's, is to find your own exceptional hunting spots either on public or private land. It can be done. Perhaps the most outstanding facet of Coziah's success is that all of his trophies were taken on Bureau of Land Management and Forest Service holdings—land that's accessible to anyone willing to expend the effort, ambition, and intelligence required to hunt it.

As Coziah told me, "In Idaho, where I live, most of the best hunting is on public land."

Unfortunately, this is not true in many other parts of the country. In Texas, for example, most of the good hunting land is privately owned. But it's amazing what can be done in gaining access to posted land, if the hunter is willing to give as much as he takes. Try offering to help a farmer or rancher with some of his chores. You'll gain a new appreciation for this hard-working segment of our society, and you'll make friends. Respect the owner's wishes, treat his property better than if it were your own, always say thanks, and send a small remembrance during the holidays.

It is important to understand that public areas with easy road access are apt to be overhunted, while out-of-the-way, hard-to-get-to spots are rarely, if ever, hunted. The animals know where these places are; you have to find them. It also helps to be close-mouthed—a good hunting place shared by a lot of hunters seldom remains one.

SUCCESS TAKES TIME

"The most important factor in hunting success is time," according to Coziah, who spends from 25 to 30 days in the field every fall with bow in hand. "My main objective is trophy mule deer bucks. The elk are taken incidentally."

Coziah also spends a lot of time outdoors fishing and trapping and, while he may not be actively hunting, he is observing and learning.

One super-successful elk hunter I know spends 30 to 40 days per fall hunting trophy bulls in a couple of Western states. Most of us can't spend that much time hunting, but it does prove that the investment of time afield will pay off.

THE HUNTING FANATIC

A common characteristic of many successful hunters is that they tend, at least to some degree, to be fanatics. Their tunnel vision often extends only to one species: sheep, whitetails, elk, and so on.

There's nothing wrong with pursuing one cause, but I do know several people who have sacrificed everything that most of us hold dear—home, family, friends, security, and their own futures—to the god of the hunt.

I asked Coziah if he was a fanatic.

"Not really," he said. "I hunt because I enjoy myself and I try not to lose sight of that fact. I'm out there to have fun."

THE LUCK FACTOR

Someone (probably a hunter) once said, "Without believing in luck, it would be hard to explain other peoples' successes or our own failures."

When asked what part luck played in hunting success, Calvin Coziah replied, "There are times when luck plays a part, but I feel that 90 percent of the time, you make your own luck."

It is obvious that outstanding trophies are occasionally taken fortuitously, but this is the exception, not the rule. You may be sure that those who take good trophies, season after season, are "making their own luck."

USE YOUR HEAD

Probably the most significant thing that Coziah told me was, "I never spend a day hunting that I don't learn something. I believe that a lot of people just don't open their eyes or they don't comprehend what they see. You have to understand what you see, learn from it, and apply what you learn."

To put it plainly, all consistently successful hunters are smart! They may not have a lot of formal education—some do, many don't—but in all cases, they are perceptive people who comprehend the things that go on around them. When it comes to wildlife, they know what is happening and why it is happening. If something doesn't work, they're not afraid to try something new. They make mistakes, but seldom the same ones twice.

It isn't coincidental that the best elk hunter I've ever met has an encyclopedic knowledge of the species. He knows where they are apt to be at any given time, and how they are apt to respond to any situation. He literally talks their language and can bugle like a bull, bark like a cow, and squeal like a calf. As might be expected, he reads everything that he can find on elk and elk hunting. But more important is the fact that he never misses an opportunity to spend time in elk country. He will follow an elk for hours—not because he expects to get a shot at it, but to see where it goes and to find out what it will do when it's spooked. He is just as apt to backtrack it to see where it had bedded or fed when it was not disturbed. He is just plain interested in elk!

LEARN TO SHOOT

Another hunter friend says, "If you can't hit 'em, you can't get 'em." The final test of the hunter, after he has done everything else right, is his ability to shoot. And there is no excuse for not becoming a reasonably good shot. Furthermore, there is no justification for shooting at an animal unless you are reasonably certain that you can kill it. I may be labeled a heretic for saying this, but I believe that proving your ability to shoot should be a prerequisite to getting a hunting license.

In any event, successful hunters tend to be good shots with the weapons of their choice. They may not be Camp Perry champions, but they know their firearms, have confidence in their ability to use them, and know how to pick their shots.

Coziah also said, "Attitude is all-important. There was a time when I used to be astounded if I hit something, but now I'm astounded if I miss."

He explained that his change to positive thinking and, consequently, better shooting, came about "sort of instantaneously" early in his hunting career. Coziah shoots a bow, which is somewhat harder to master than a rifle. However, with either a bow or a gun, good marksmanship is largely a matter of practice. Practice brings skill, which in turn leads to success, and success begets the kind of self-confident attitude that Coziah has—when he shoots at something, he expects to hit it.

HARD WORK HELPS

Arthur Brisbane said. "The dictionary is the only place where success comes before work." Successful hunters work hard at their sport. As a rule, they are up early, they go far, and they are out late. On this point, Coziah is something of an enigma. He told me that his normal hunting day begins "when I feel like getting up—usually well after daylight." That has never worked for me, and I think that the reason it works for Coziah is that his specialty is stalking to within spitting distance of animals that have bedded down for the day, and animals don't bed down until well after daylight. However, I also learned that he isn't averse to hard hunting and hard work.

THE NEED FOR PATIENCE

Hard work alone is not enough. Many hunters work their fool heads off and never get game. Effort must be tempered with a liberal dose of patience. Time, again, becomes an important factor. It takes patience to locate game in the first place, to allow hunting situations to develop, to make a good stalk, and to wait for the right shot. If you're in a hurry and act rashly, nine times out of ten, you'll blow your chance for a trophy.

Hunting success, then, depends on our reasons for hunting in the first place. One person may consider himself successful because he bags an exceptional trophy, while another may measure success by the tenderness of a good piece of meat. And who is to say that a hunter isn't successful if he goes home empty-handed, as long as he has a good feeling about the hunt and about himself?

Tracking A Trophy Area

By Maury Jones

Photo by Erwin and Peggy Bauer

The thundering crash of the huge boulder echoed through the canyons. Dust billowed in the still air as the rock dislodged numerous small stones and crunched through hillsides of scrub oak. The violence of the moment had barely subsided when two deer burst from the cover some 300 yards below us. They scrambled up a small ridge and stopped, breathless and confused, wondering what all the uproar was about. It was difficult to determine with the naked eye anything other than that they were Arizona Coues deer with antlers. A quick check through binoculars showed that one of them was an exceptional trophy. The Husqvarna .243 cracked, the buck's knees buckled, and he slowly toppled over and rolled down the hill. My partner, Steve, pounded me on the back and exclaimed, "That one will go in the book for sure!"

Many minutes later, when we finally arrived at the buck—following a harrowing slide down the 60° slope—we had a chance to examine my trophy more closely. The mouse-gray buck had a beautifully perfect rack, one that eventually ranked No. 28 in the Safari Club Record Book. The antlers had four perfectly matched tines on a side. That buck was 91 of the heaviest pounds I've ever had to wrestle out of a nearly inaccessible canyon.

A trophy in the record book. A magnificent animal on the wall. All of us have dreams of someday getting a bragging-size trophy. Each year, this dream is realized by a few lucky hunters. But how about the other guys who go home skunked? Some of them have tales of the one that got away, but most go home having seen just small bucks and does or nothing at all. Could it be that the majority of these hunters are hunting in the wrong places?

Since October 1974, when I shot that Coues buck, I have killed or guided others to killing a number of trophy and record book animals. Luck? Part of it is. There is an element of luck in all hunting. But the one element common to all of these trophy kills is

that we were hunting in an area that qualified as a trophy area.

The one thing all hunters must do when after trophy-class animals is to hunt where they are. "You'll find 'em where you find 'em," as someone not so rich and not so famous (and slightly balding) once told me. So where do you find 'em? To kill a real trophy, you must first qualify your hunting area. Take the following checklist and go shopping for an area with wall-hangers.

1. A trophy area must have a *short hunting season*. It is a biological fact that for a buck or a bull elk to develop full antler growth, he must be at least 5 years old. He is really in his prime at age 6 or 7. (Beyond that, he tends to go downhill, much like an older man tends to lose some of his muscle tone.) If a hunting season is long, sooner or later a buck or bull is going to run out of luck and bump into a hunter. An area with a long season doesn't give many animals a chance to age.

How do you define a long season? Well, that is up to you, but I would think it depends somewhat on hunting pressure, ruggedness of terrain to be hunted, and so on. Generally, I would say that you can take the state in which you are going to hunt and immediately eliminate 90 percent of the areas, using as a criterion the length of the hunting season. Be careful in doing this, however, because some areas may have had their season length shortened recently because of previous overhunting. Take a five-year average just to be safe.

2. Your trophy area should have some restriction on the *size* animal that can be harvested. Look for an area that has a "four-point-or-larger" hunting restriction, or in the case of elk, "no shooting of spikes." It is well known that spike deer are inferior genetically, but such is not the case with elk. Once again, this helps the animals get older, and in the process they get smarter. Smarter animals live longer and get bigger.

3. Soil with *good mineral content*, particularly calcium and phosphorus, makes for big racks. Antler growth in elk, deer, and moose depends to a great extent on the amount of calcium their bodies assimilate. Phosphorus acts as a catalyst to react with calcium and make it available in a usuable form to the animal, much as enzymes help in the digestion of food. The U. S. Geological Survey can help you determine which areas are high in calcium and phosphorus.

4. Along with nutrition, a *good gene pool* is very important. Just ask a breeder of fine racehorses. If you want speed, get a fast mare and a fast sire. If you want antler growth, get a big buck to breed your does. How do you find out about the gene pool? Go on to No. 5.

5. Your area must be a *consistent producer of trophies*. This is proof of the genetic makeup of your herd. Any area can produce an occasional trophy. Also, some areas have produced many big racks in the past but are only so-so at this time. A prime example of the latter is the Kaibab Plateau in northern Arizona.

Once *the* place to go for a trophy buck, it is now only mediocre. True, an occasional monster still comes out of there, but not very many as a percentage of the deer herd or compared with what it used to produce. An area must have *recent* trophies.

One good way to find out is to call local taxidermists and ask them about the racks coming out of their herds. They will tell you whether the hunting has been excellent as far as trophies go. If the trophy quality has been poor, they will be glad to tell you, as they want less hunting pressure to enable the number of trophies to build back up. If the hunting is great, they want dedicated trophy hunters, not local meat seekers. Trophy hunters become a taxidermist's customers; meat hunters don't. A taxidermist will generally level with you. He gains nothing if you come and don't kill a big buck.

You can also check the record books for recent scores, but there often is a delay of a year or two in getting scores into the books, and some hunters don't bother to score their trophies. This method is not infallible but can be helpful.

6. Your area must have *limited hunting pressure*, which is usually the result of some kind of "drawing for permit" system. Hunter numbers must be limited or the area gets overhunted. A prime and current example of this is the San Juan National Forest in Colorado. Because of much publicity and unlimited numbers of permits being issued, the numbers of big racks being taken there is declining. I guided there for six years, in the very area where the world-record mule deer was killed. During those six years, I saw hunting pressure increase to the point at which the quality of the hunting severely declined. About 90 percent of the elk killed in my area were spikes. The game department openly admits it is managing for numbers and not for racks. I cannot speak for all areas of the San Juan, but the mountains northwest of Durango have been overhunted. So both hunters and outfitters must move on to areas that are harder to get permits for but offer better hunting.

7. A trophy area must have lots of *rough, rugged terrain*. This eliminates 90 percent of would-be trophy hunters. Deer, elk, and moose must be able to hide. The area must be *difficult* to hunt: rough, steep, thick, tangled, abrupt, precipitous—all those adjectives. Find a place that looks like hell stood on its end, and you will find trophy country. The simple reason for this is less hunting pressure.

For example, this past December I made my annual pilgrimage into the Coues deer habitat of southeastern Arizona. I'm hooked on hunting these little deer, and their season is this Wyoming outfitter's off-season, so it satisfies my trophy hunting appetite. I took a couple of friends with me. They claimed they were trophy hunters, but after three hard hours of horse-backing over a genuine mountain, they took one look from the top and decided to look for trophy bucks down in the flatter country. I persuaded them to stay and try the back side of the mountain for a while, but after a couple of hours they'd had enough, even though we saw several nice scrapes and some promising tracks. Just too tough to hunt for 95 percent of hunters.

Even those hunters who get a good outfitter and have a good horse under them are bucking the odds. *But that's where the big ones are.* You've got to hunt where they live regardless of the inconvenience to yourself.

8. The area should have a *few local meat hunters.* This goes right along with item No. 7. If the area is so rugged that it is inconvenient for meat hunters to hunt there, they won't accidentally blunder into one of your animals. If the area is easy to hunt, you can bet the meat hunters will overhunt it. I've heard local guys say, "You hunt up there? You're crazy! That place can kill you! Besides, those big old bucks are tough eating. Give me a fat forkhorn off the hay fields. Now that's fine eating!" Leave the local meat hunters down below. Come on up where the hunting is tough but great.

9. A trophy area should have *no rifle hunt during the rut.* Big bucks and big bulls get stupid during the breeding season. They also get thinned out.

If you can bugle bulls in and shoot them with a rifle, you are going to kill off a lot of the population. If bucks are looking for mates instead of for an orange-clad hunter, they are going to end up as venison. The result? Fewer bucks and bulls around next year to grow big racks. Incidentally, the animals that are hunted prior to the rut are super smart. They don't come easy, but there are a lot more record book animals in an area like that than there are in a hunt-during-the-rut area.

The rut in most of the Rocky Mountain region takes place in November for mule deer, and September and early October for elk. Check with local game departments for any possible exceptions.

10. The area you choose to hunt should have *no late hunting season* when there is the likelihood of deep snow. It is easier to spot animals and hunt them in deep snow, and the migration to winter feeding grounds bunches them up, so the result is fewer record book heads in an area like that.

11. Last but certainly not least, you need to hunt *with an outfitter who specializes in trophy hunting.* The do-it-yourself hunter can be successful, but more often he comes home skunked. And it usually takes him three trips to the same area just to adequately learn it so he has a chance at these super-smart old animals. If he doesn't have a horse that is used to the altitude and to climbing mountains, forget it. Trying to get a bull elk out of one of these rugged areas with a good stout horse is next to impossible.

All reputable outfitters (those duly licensed by the state and with a Forest Service permit) have good horses, the right equipment, and a knowledge of the country, and are familiar with game movements. But an outfitter who specializes in trophies will do his utmost to see that you get that wall-hanger. His reputation is at stake if you kill a minnow. His reputation is enhanced if you kill a mossyhorn. Many outfitters will try to fill their hunter's tag with the first legal animal they see. After all, they have already been paid for the hunt, and if the hunter fills out early and goes home, the outfitter gets some much needed rest. Also, it looks good on the brochure or reference sheet if he can say, "80 percent of our hunters were successful last year." How do *you* measure hunting success? Will your guide try and talk you into shooting a "good" buck when what you really want is a *great* one? Does your guide really know the difference between a good buck and a record book head? Is he a trophy hunter himself, or does he just "take out" trophy hunters? (When you grill him about this last point, be fair. He may be a dedicated trophy hunter and still not have heads in the book that he personally killed. After all, he is usually working all through the hunting season. Rather, ask what percentage of his clients have killed wall-hangers.) Does he bow-hunt? An outfitter who loves to trophy hunt often takes up bowhunting to get in more hunting time. During rifle season, he is working full time. Is he dedicated to the fact that you are his client, you have paid for the hunt, and your wishes are the reason he is in business? Ask references about this.

Will your outfitter/guide give you an honest appraisal of the buck you are glassing? The following is the basic idea of what an outfitter should say in such an instance: "That one is better than 90 percent of the bucks in this area. It will spread about 28 inches and should score high, but it is not a record book head. If you decide to kill it, you will have a nice trophy to hang on the wall. If you pass it up, you may not get another chance at a buck that nice, but there are some bigger bucks out here. It is your decision." That's what a trophy hunting guide is for.

Make an actual checklist of the above items. Do as much background work as you can before you call the outfitter. When you call the outfitter or one of his references, have a written list of well-thought-out questions to ask him. Realize that not all outfitters in a qualified trophy area are dedicated trophy outfitters. If they don't have the right answers, don't make them feel uncomfortable, but don't string them along and let them think you are going to hunt with them. Level with them, but be tactful about it: "Thank you for your time, but I believe I am looking for a different type of hunt."

Finally, realize that the trophy outfitter is not Father Nature. He cannot produce a trophy animal at the drop of a hat. He will do his best, work hard, and try to put you in the right place at the right time, but it does take some luck as well as preparation and skill to put a rack in the books. If it rains for ten days straight during deer season (as happened in 1983), or it is dry as a bone and hot during elk season (as also happened in 1983), or someone puts a tent smack in the middle of the best deer area and you discover it on opening morning after a hard three-hour horseback ride in the dark (as also happened that same year), remember that this is why they call it hunting instead of shooting.

PART 4

GUNS AND SHOOTING

How To Buy A Used Gun

By Russ Carpenter

The second-hand gun is close kin to the second-hand car. By exercising care and using some basic knowledge, you can buy a second-hand cream puff that's a joy to behold or you can get a very bad deal. This story will be of no help when buying a used car but, if you take it seriously, it can help you to become the proud possessor of a second-hand gun that will provide you with pleasure afield at a budget price.

What to buy and where to look for it are certainly problems for the novice. A good buy can, at times, be found listed in your local newspaper. However, unless you have a reasonable amount of gun smarts, this is risky ground for a beginner. There are also times when a trusted friend or hunting acquaintance may want to sell a gun suitable for your type of hunting, and that may work out well. Generally speaking, however, a reliable gun shop is the best place to look for a used gun, and most prospective nimrods live close to one. When you buy a used gun, factory warranties are usually void but, with most reliable dealers, there is a semblance of guarantee. Check with the dealer about his policy. Will he foot the cost of repair if needed? Can you return your purchase in a limited time for full credit on a different gun? Don't expect a cash refund; it seldom happens.

To the experienced hunter, the basic choice is usually easy. He knows the suitable calibers for big game, the gauges and chokes for scatter-gun hunting, and the calibers and type of handguns suited for the outdoorsman. He also has knowledge concerning the type of action that will best serve his special needs. On the other hand, there is the average Joe who wants to go hunting for the first time. The first shocker for our friend Joe, for instance, is often the price tag on a new deer rifle. However,

Joe's new deer hunting buddy comes to the rescue and suggests that Joe look over the used-gun rack at a local gun shop. I'll add a piece of advice and tell Joe to take along his new hunting buddy as an advisor, provided he really knows something about firearms. The local dealer may be honest enough to qualify for saintdom, but he wants to sell what's in his gun rack and without advice, our budding nimrod could end up with a rifle that's unsuited for the area where he will be hunting deer. The caliber could be inappropriate, the bore could be marginal, and many other things could be wrong. Another piece of good advice is not to wait until the week before opening day to look for a used gun. Selections are very limited then, and Joe needs at least a month, and preferably longer, to check sights and learn how and what to expect from his new smokepole.

Guns wear with use, but how much wear is too much? Contrary to some thinking, a gun can wear until it is unsafe as well as unreliable. Before someone is injured or killed, any gun in this category should be junked. During the many years that I gunsmithed for a living, many proud owners came into my shop with a piece of pure scrap made originally for the budget trade around the turn of the century. They left my shop all bent out of shape when I told them that their treasures were neither safe nor worth the cost of repair.

Dealers, gunsmiths, and manufacturers are all very safety conscious these days. This is because of the proliferation of product-liability lawsuits during the last decade. This has become a serious problem because many of these lawsuits are frivolous in nature. Court and insurance costs have driven up the price of both new and used guns. Because of this, however, dealers and gunsmiths are now more inclined to check the firearms that they sell. Most new guns come from the factory with instructions for safe use, and the manufacturers urge those who purchase one of their guns on the used market to write to the factory for a copy of the instructions. By all means, you should do so.

I don't consider it necessary for the dealer to test-fire every second-hand gun. However, any big-game or varmint rifle that has been fired a great deal should have the headspace checked. (Headspace is the length of the chamber.) If the locking lugs wear or are hammered back into the receiver in firing, the chamber lengthens. The tolerance is small and, with excess headspace, the brass cartridge case must stretch on firing. Too much stretch and the brass may rupture, damaging the rifle and possibly injuring the shooter. A no-go headspace gauge is a precision-made piece of steel that duplicates the maximum safe length of the cartridge case. The no-go gauge is placed in the chamber and, if the action will not close and lock, the headspace is proper and will retain the cartridge case within safe length limits. If the dealer you are buying from does not have a proper no-go head-space gauge, I suggest taking the rifle to a local gunsmith who does. You can also ask about the general condition and the appearance of the bore.

Photo by Tom Yates

There will be a modest fee for this service, but it's worth it for the peace of mind. If there is doubt about the chambering, have the gunsmith make a chamber cast and identify the cartridge.

After World War II, surplus and liberated military rifles were converted to sporters by the thousands, and these reworked rifles keep showing up in used-gun racks. Thousands of these rifles were rechambered and others were rebarreled, some to standard cartridges and others to nonstandard wildcats. Most of these conversions are safe and suitable for hunting. In fact, many of the converted Model 98 Mausers and 1903 Springfields are truly excellent hunting rifles. However, some conversions were by "shade tree" gunsmiths who lacked both knowledge and the proper tools. Many do not have correct caliber markings, and the risk of using improper ammunition is present. I'll tell you about one of the more common conversions that is dangerous if it is not done properly.

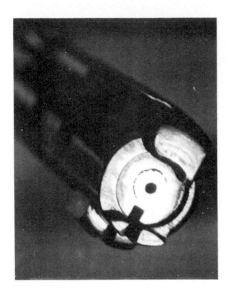

Gauge in rifle's chamber indicates excess headspace if bolt will close on it. Too much headspace can cause cartridge case to separate on firing. Gas leaking around primers cuts circular groove in bolt face. A deep groove indicates the rifle was fired a great deal.

USED-GUN PRICE GUIDE

Prices listed are for guns in "excellent" condition. Some models in "perfect" condition will be worth more. Those with appreciable wear, requiring parts replacement and refinishing, are only worth approximately 50 percent of the price listed here. Costs may vary with demand and geographic location.

Lever Actions

* Browning BLR and BLR-81: chambered for eight varmint and big-game cartridges from .222 Remington through .358 Winchester—$275.
* Marlin Model 336 and several similar models: .30/30, .35 Remington, .444, .45/70—$150.
* Mossberg Model 472 and Model 479: .30/30 and .35 Remington—$110.
* Savage Model 99E and Model 99C: chambered for five cartridges from .250 Savage through .358 Winchester; made from 1960 to date—$200.
* Winchester Model 94: .30/30 and .32 Special; postwar to 1964 and current model—$200; carbines made from 1964 to 1972—$100.
* Winchester Model 88: obsolete but in demand by hunters—$350.

Pumps

* Remington Model 760: chambered for ten cartridges from .223 Remington to .30/06 Springfield—$250.

Autoloaders

* Browning BAR Grade I: chambered for six popular cartridges from .243 Winchester through .300 Winchester Magnum—$400.

* Remington Model 742: this is the most popular autoloader: chambered for five cartridges from 6-mm Remington through .30/06 Springfield—$300.
* Ruger Model 44: chambered for .44 Remington Magnum only—$200.
* Winchester Model 100: obsolete, but in demand by hunters—$400.

Bolt Actions

* Browning BBR: chambered for cartridges from .22/250 through .300 Winchester Magnum—$350.
* Harrington & Richardson Model 340: chambered for cartridges from .243 Winchester through .30/06 Springfield, including 7-mm Remington Magnum—$250.
* Interarms Mark X Standard Model: Mauser-type action chambered for cartridges from .22/250 Remington through .300 Winchester Magnum—$225.
* Mossberg Model 800 and Model 810: chambered for cartridges from .222 Remington through .338 Winchester Magnum—$200.
* Remington Model 722 (short action) and Model 721 (long action): the current Model 700 is a refined version of this model; chambered for cartridges from .222 Remington through .300 H&H—$200.
* Remington Model 600 and Model 660: carbine chambered for cartridges from .222 Remington through .350 Remington Magnum—$250.
* Remington Model 788: chambered for cartridges from .222 Remington through .308 Winchester—$190.
* Remington Model 700 long- and short-action ADL grade: chambered for cartridges from .222 Remington through 7-mm Remington Magnum; there are numerous grades and a left-hand model at higher prices—$250.

It was several years after the war before 6.5 hunting ammunition for the Japanese Arisaka rifle was imported from Norma in Sweden. In the interim, many of these rifles were rechambered for the .257 Roberts cartridge. Properly done and checked with a headspace gauge, this was a safe conversion, but accuracy was terrible. The .257 Roberts bullets were .007 too small for the 6.5-mm barrel. Of course, the answer was to load 6.5-mm bullets in the .257 Roberts brass but, unless the gunsmith who cut the chamber had a special reamer to enlarge the neck area, the bullet could bind in the cartridge neck. When forced into the chamber and fired, this com-

To test-fire, prop rifle in an old tire and pull the trigger with a lanyard from a safe position behind a tree or down in a ditch.

bination could send pressure skyrocketing. This is a buyer-beware condition and is a good example of why you should have *any* converted military rifle checked by an expert gunsmith.

If there is any doubt about the reliability of a rifle, it should be test-fired. This does not mean using a deliberately overloaded proof cartridge. A heavy standard factory load is adequate. Mount the rifle with the butt stuck inside an old automobile tire with the forend resting on the other side of the tire. Aim the barrel at a safe backstop. With a stout cord rigged as a lanyard, fire the rifle from a remote position behind a wall or stout tree. The old tire absorbs the recoil, and the shooter is protected if something is wrong. If no problems arise after firing two or three rounds, you can be fairly sure that the gun is safe to hand hold.

There are obvious telltale signs that warn a prospective buyer about second-hand guns. One of the most important is the internal appearance of the barrel. Many unknowing buyers look down a blackened barrel that resembles the inside of a stove pipe and, if they can faintly discern the twist of rifling, they boldly declare the barrel to be very good. To be accurate, a barrel must be smooth and bright. Before inspecting it, ask the dealer to run a dry patch

- Ruger Model 77R: chambered for cartridges from .22/250 Remington through .338 Winchester Magnum—$250.
- Savage Model 110: various models chambered for cartridges from .22/250 to .338 Winchester Magnum—$200.
- Savage Model 340: chambered for cartridges from .22 Hornet through .30/30—$125.
- Smith & Wesson Model 1500: chambered for cartridges from .243 Winchester through 7-mm Remington Magnum—$225.
- Winchester Model 70 Pre-1964 Model: chambered for cartridges from .22 Hornet through .375 H&H—$600; 1964 through 1972: chambered for cartridges from .22/250 Remington through .338 Winchester Magnum—$200; 1972 to date: chambered for cartridges from .222 Remington through .300 Winchester Magnum—$250.

Autoloading Shotguns

- Browning B80: 12 and 20 gauge—$300.
- Ithaca Model 51: 12 and 20 gauge—$275.
- Remington Model 11–48: 12, 16, 20, 28, and .410 gauge—$225.
- Remington Model 1100: 12, 16, 20, 28, and .410 gauge—$300.
- Savage 755: 12 and 16 gauge—$150.
- Winchester Model 1400: 12, 16, and 20 gauge—$200.

Pump Shotguns

- Browning BPS: 12 and 20 gauge—$225.
- High Standard Flite-King: 12, 20, 28, and .410 gauge—$150.
- Ithaca Model 37: 12, 16, and 20 gauge—$250.

- Marlin 120: 12 gauge—$200.
- Mossberg Model 500: 12, 16, and 20 gauge; many variations and features—$200.
- Remington Model 870: 12, 16, 20, 28, and .410 gauge—$250.
- Savage Model 30: 12, 16, 20, and .410 gauge—$150.
- Winchester Model 1200: 12, 16, and 20 gauge—$175.

Side-by-Side Doubles

- Browning BSS: 12 and 20 gauge—$375.
- Ithaca SKB Model 100: 12 and 20 gauge—$300.
- Savage Model 311: 12, 16, 20, and .410 gauge—$175.

Over/Under Doubles

- Browning Citori: 12 and 20 gauge—$500.
- Harrington & Richardson Model 1212: 12 gauge—$350.
- Ithaca SKB Model 500: 12 and 20 gauge—$500.
- Ruger Red Label: 12 and 20 gauge—$550.

Handguns

- Colt Python: .357 Magnum—$350.
- Ruger Blackhawk: .357 Magnum, .41 Magnum, and .45 Long Colt—$150.
- Ruger Super Blackhawk: .44 Remington Magnum only—$275.
- Ruger Redhawk: .44 Remington Magnum—$300.
- Dan Wesson Model 44V: .44 Remington Magnum—$275.
- Thompson/Center Contender: chambered for numerous varmint and big-game cartridges, including .44 Remington Magnum, .30/30 and .35 Remington—$200.

Very few dealers will try to sting you with a useless gun but, unintentionally, even the best dealers may have defective firearms in the rack.

down the bore. Don't let him use an oil-saturated patch because any barrel looks better with a fresh coating of oil. This trick can mislead a novice gun buyer. To inspect the bore of a rifle with a breech-block or bolt that cannot be removed, open the action and arrange a piece of white paper in the rear of the breech opening so that it will reflect light into the bore. With a bolt action, remove the bolt and view the bore from both muzzle and breech. A less than perfect barrel may still be accurate enough for close-range brush shooting but, if you want to hit the vital area of a whitetail at 50 yards or more, the bore had better be perfect. Rusing or pitting near the muzzle has a greater adverse effect than the same imperfections near the breech end. It is difficult for anyone but an expert to discern normal wear in what may be a well-cared-for barrel. Such wear shows as rounding of the sharp edges of the rifling and graying of the surface of the bore ahead of the chamber.

Rifle barrels sometimes suffer wear from improper cleaning. A dirty or gritty cleaning rod can wear the rifling near the muzzle. It may not be visible to the eye, but even a small amount of wear at this point can cause accuracy to suffer. Only range testing will tell the story, but a gunsmith can remove an inch or two at the muzzle to eliminate the worn area and restore accuracy.

The face of the breechblock or bolt will tell you if a gun has undergone an excessive amount of shooting. Erosion in the form of a circle indicates a lot of shooting and, of course, this could mean excessive barrel wear.

Excess sloppiness in an action or binding when the action is obviously well lubricated may indicate wear that can lead to grief. However, some seemingly sloppy conditions are the normal nature of the beast. For instance, most pump guns rattle and the forend may seem overloose, but this is normal with these guns. Most Mauser-type bolt-action rifles ap-

pear to have sloppily fitted bolts when the bolt is fully open. Again, play is normal in these arms.

Any second-hand gun that has been carried a lot will show surface wear but, because many such guns have been fired only a minimal amount, they can provide the new owner with many years of good field service. On the other hand, an abused rifle may show similar outside wear and be in even worse shape inside. Touch-up blue may have been used to improve the appearance of the metals, and stock finish or wax may have been applied to the wood. This is not exactly cheating on the part of the dealer, but an unknowing buyer could be fooled into believing that the rifle or shotgun has seen only a little use.

Another pitfall for the novice gun buyer is the caliber of that second-hand beauty. Is it a converted military rifle that digests hard-to-find sporting ammo or, perhaps, an American classic chambered for an obsolete cartridge? The Model 99 Savage and Model 94 Winchester are still manufactured but, at one time, they were chambered for cartridges that are now obsolete. Obsolete rifles such as the Model 141 Remington and the Model 81 Remington were chambered for the obsolete .25 Remington and .32 Remington cartridges. These same rifles, in good condition and chambered for .300 Savage of .35 Remington, are good for deer-size game. In obsolete chambering, you end up with a white elephant. On the other hand, foreign ammo manufacturers are now making cartridges that were formerly hard to find, and they are also making some old American cartridges—for instance, the .22 Savage Hi-Power. Swedish-made Norma ammo, thanks to a new distribution system in the United States, is breathing new life into these rifles. All this boils down to the fact that a used-gun buyer should be sure to check the availability of suitable ammunition before he opens his wallet.

The usual "buyer beware" warnings apply to the

purchase of a .22 Rimfire rifle, and a few special tips may prove helpful. Most of the rimfire rifles made during the last 35 years are dependable and accurate. Unless badly worn or abused, most of the used rimfire rifles have a lot of life left in them. Some of the earlier models that were made since the turn of the century are still mechanically sound and, if they were properly cared for, may be great buys. Prior to 1930, however, rimfire ammunition was very corrosive, and this ammo was still around and being fired for several years after the advent of the noncorrosive variety. This means that there are many mechanically sound used .22 Rimfire rifles that have poor or marginal bores.

Rimfire rifles, with the exception of most autoloaders, usually fire .22 Shorts, Longs, and Long Rifle cartridges interchangeably. The extensive use of Shorts, especially the old corrosive variety, caused problems. The chamber would foul or errode ahead of the short cartridge and, when a Long Rifle was fired and expanded in the chamber, the fired case would stick and cause a malfunction. This defect is hard to detect without firing, but it is quite common among older .22 rimfire rifles.

Like centerfire rifles, the rimfires should be checked for ammunition availability. Many older rifles are chambered for oddball cartridges that are no longer manufactured. To the novice, a rifle marked .22 WRF may appear to be just another .22 Long Rifle, but the .22 WRF is a larger cartridge and is no longer made. A rifle chambered for it is worthless as a shooter.

The Model 591 and Model 592 Remingtons are rimfire rifles of modern manufacture, but they are chambered for the 5-mm Remington Rimfire Magnum, and this cartridge is also no longer made. It was introduced in 1970 and only lasted about 10 years. Without ammo, these rifles are of no practical use. Even if you handload, no one can reload fired rimfire cases.

Choosing the right shotgun is a chancy affair, but I'll offer a few tips. Most shotgunners shoot better with a single sighting plane than with a side-by-side double, which means that a pump, autoloader, or over/under is the better choice. Budget-priced pumps and autoloaders shoot loose faster than the better-grade models, and they should be carefully checked for dependable operations.

A double, either a side-by-side or an over/under, should be checked for excessive side-to-side wobble when the action is open. An insecure lockup when the action is closed means excessive wear or abuse. The gun should lock tight before the top lever returns to dead center. If there is erosion around the firing-pin holes in the standing breech, the gun has done a lot of shooting.

Check the barrels carefully for dents, bulges, and pitting. Dents can be ironed out, within reason, but bulges are usually unrepairable. A lightly pitted bore may be useable, but overall value is lessened.

Chokes are commonly altered and, if you are looking for a shotgun for turkey or pass-shooting ducks, you could find that a barrel marked Full actually throws a wide Improved Cylinder pattern. Full-choked guns used in steel-shot areas often have their chokes hammered open by the hard shot. It takes a lot of shooting, but it does happen. On the opposite side of the coin, you may find a shotgun with a Full Choke barrel that's a better-than-average buy, but you want to hunt upland birds and need an open choke. You can have the barrel shortened or the choke opened up. Interchangeable barrels are available for many modern shotguns, which means that a new barrel could make an unattractive gun a good buy.

Check the chamber for erosion. In the age of paper shotshells, this rarely occurred because the chambers were coated with the wax that impregnated the paper tubes. When a modern plastic shell is fired in a pump or autoloader, it heats the chamber. When it is ejected and quickly replaced by a cool, unfired shell, condensation forms when the humidity is high and this can be the beginning of rusting. This erosion can cause problems with extraction but, in most instances, this erosion can be polished out.

Buying a used hunting handgun can be easy if you know a few mechancal points and the calibers best suited for your needs. The autoloader is seldom used for hunting deer-size game but, for a camp gun and for putting small game in the pot, the .22 Long Rifle autoloader is a good choice. These guns seldom wear out, which means that outside appearance is the main concern.

Revolvers in all calibers are popular with hunters. The small kit-gun types are popular as camp guns, and the big .44 Magnum is the top choice for deer-size game. The buyer of any double-action revolver should check the cylinder lockup and cylinder timing. Cylinder timing is equally important if the revolver is a single-action. The locked-up cylinder that feels sloppy was probably owned by a pistoleer who snapped the cylinder closed with a flick of his wrist. This strains the parts and soon produces a sloppy lockup. A properly timed revolver locks up with a chamber in line with the bore as the hammer reaches full cock. A worn hand or other internal parts can allow the hammer to reach full cock with the cylinder short of the in-line lockup.

Single-shot pistols are popular among hunters, and there is seldom a mechanical problem with this type. Finding the right caliber and outside appearance is the primary concern.

The greatest change in sporting arms and ammunition this century came about when production resumed after World War II. Many of the popular models of the prewar years were never made again. Most of the popular rifles and shotguns and at least half of the popular cartridges are the products of the postwar years. Many of the prewar models are now collectors' items and are priced out of reach for the buyer who is looking for a field gun. However, there are plenty of late models in used-gun racks and, I hope, the tips that I've covered will help you select the gun that's suited for your special needs. 🦌

Zero In On The Perfect Scope

By Bob Bell

Photo by Stanley W. Trzoniec

Nobody doubts that a scope is superior to iron sights for precision shooting. It presents a magnified target; it can be easily and exactly zeroed in; it has a comparatively clear and bright field with a conspicuous aiming point, even in near darkness; and it does not conceal the lower half of the field of view, as V-notch iron sights do. Yet many hunters still do not feel comfortable with scope sights, and some just don't trust them.

Most of their reasons stem from unfamiliarity. Almost all air rifles, plinking .22s, and even centerfire rifles come with iron sights. Hard as it is for gun-cranks to realize, most shooters begin with such outfits—and a lot stay with them. Simple observation tells them that scopes are practical—everywhere they look, they see others using them—but lack of experience makes them stick to irons. It's still hard for some shooters to believe that anything having lots of glass in it is durable enough to hang together in a heavy-recoiling rifle. Others reject scopes because of bad personal experiences, which almost invariably are the result of using the wrong kind of scope for their particular needs. All iron sights used in the field are essentially short-range units because you can't see well enough with them to aim at small, indistinct targets at long range. However, different classes of scopes are designed for optimum utility at different distances. For complete satisfaction, a user must understand some basic optics.

Magnification, or power, is the scope characteristic of most interest to prospective users. Beginners tend to opt for high powers—they think that the larger the target appears, the easier it will be to hit. That belief has some validity if the target is motionless and if a support for the rifle is available. These conditions often occur in certain kinds of varmint shooting, so a scope of 10X or even higher power is a fine choice. But if that scope is mounted on a .35 Remington and taken into typical whitetail cover, any deer seen will be at short range and it will be in view for only seconds. That superprecise 10X will be useless. Its field of view is too high and its exit pupil is too small for quick alignment. Further, it won't transmit enough light for the gloomy cover. If the hunter does happen to see something through the scope, its high magnification presents such an unusual view of branches, shadows, glitters of light, and patches of snow that everything will appear in utter confusion.

An experience such as that can make anyone swear off scopes forever. But such results must be blamed on the shooter, not on the scope. He used a fine tool for the wrong job. When the target is large and the range is short, as in most big-game hunting, the ideal scope is one of low power. High magnification simply isn't needed (even a small deer is a big target compared to a prairie dog), and the low power means that you get a comparatively big field of view. That's a law of optics: As power goes up, field goes down—and vice versa.

Another law is that the amount of light passed through a scope depends primarily on the ratio between the scope's magnification and the diameter of the objective lens (the one farthest from the viewer).

Author's favorite deer rifles are, from left: .284 Winchester on 98 Mauser action with 2½× Lyman Alaskan; Model 700 Remington 7mm/08 with 2½× Lyman AA; and Model 788 Remington 7mm/08 with 1½×-to-4½× Redfield.

Dividing the diameter of the scope's objective lens by its magnification—2½X, 4X, 10X, or whatever—gives the diameter of the scope's exit pupil in millimeters. (The exit pupil is the circular bundle of light rays that enters the eye.) However, when an exit pupil is larger than the eye's entrance pupil, the excess light is wasted because it simply cannot be used. This means that an exit pupil larger than 5 mm is optically unnecessary because the human pupil does not exceed 5 mm in diameter, except in total darkness, when it might reach 7 mm. Because sport hunting is normally illegal after dark, there is no real need for the 8-mm or 10-mm exit pupil commonly available today. One minor advantage does accrue to the larger exit pupil: It makes it a bit faster to aim when the rifle is shouldered rapidly for a shot. However, if the rifle fits the shooter well, he or she will have no trouble getting aligned with a 5-mm exit pupil.

These basics are pointed out because they can affect scope design and size. If you keep in mind that the optimum size for the exit pupil is 5 mm, it's ob-

vious that a 4X scope needs only a 20-mm objective lens to deliver all the light that the eye can absorb (20 ÷ 4 = 5). And, because a 20-mm objective lens is a lens with a diameter of less than one inch, a big-game scope can be built much smaller and lighter than a high-power varmint or target model. A magnification of 10X would require a 50-mm objective lens (slightly more than two inches in diameter) to supply a 5-mm exit pupil. Try to imagine what that would look like and how it would handle on a .30/30 carbine.

Fortunately for big-game hunters, the optical laws that make high-power scopes ideal for small, motionless, distant targets also make low-power scopes ideal for fast-moving big game at short range. The lightly magnified image that they provide blends naturally into the view seen with the off eye, everything looks essentially normal, and the field is big enough to easily find and retain even a whitetail in high gear in the brush. For example, the 45-foot field at 100 yards—typical of a 2½X scope—still provides 15 feet at 30 yards or so where many thick-country deer are taken. By comparison, a 10X scope would have a four-foot field at that distance—not even enough to enclose a deer standing broadside.

The hunter who wants even more adaptability than a straight low-power scope can choose a small variable-power model. Many are available in the 1½-to-4½X range. Most of these are built on unenlarged-objective one-inch tubes, so they are in the size and weight class of the small straight powers. They have the advantage of an extremely wide field at bottom power—about 65 feet—and enough magnification at the top end to permit precise shot placement on deer to 400 or so yards. Few hunters should try shots at longer distances with any scope or rifle. In my opinion, a top-quality 1½-to-4½X is the optimum big-game scope.

Besides the optical efficiency and reasonable weight and bulk of the low-power scopes, they have another important thing going for them: They can be mounted low on the gun, which is important when fast shooting is required. The large objective of a high-power scope requires high-mount rings to clear the barrel. The ocular (rear) end of the scope, of course, is as high as the front end, which means that it is considerably above the comb of the stock where it supports the cheek. Ideally, when the cheekbone is pushed down hard onto the comb, the eye should align perfectly with the exit pupil of the scope. This means that the vertical distance from the top of the comb to the centerline of the scope should equal that from the bottom of the cheekbone to the pupil of the eye. However, on the bolt-action rifles so popular nowadays, the comb must be low enough to allow functioning of the bolt. This requirement plus the mechanical design of most mounts today and the large eyepieces of modern scopes mean that it's impossible to get perfect eye alignment with bolt-action rifles. It would be easy to get the comb higher on autoloading rifles, say, or pumps or single shots, but it isn't done, probably because of esthetics or

Because scope is mounted high to clear large objective unit, shooter's jaw, rather than cheekbone, must rest on stock comb.

habit. In the end, things work reasonably well with the smaller scopes, but fast-aiming efficiency quickly deteriorates as scope size goes up.

It isn't enough to have the scope mounted low. It also has to be mounted in the correct front-to-rear position. A scope's full field of view can be seen only at a certain distance behind the scope. This distance is called eye relief. There is a little fore-and-aft leeway, depending upon the included angle of the peripheral light rays and the diameter of the eye's pupil at the moment, but it isn't very much.

Fast gun alignment is necessary for much big-game shooting. This means that the scope's full field must be visible the moment the rifle hits the shoulder—which requires exact positioning for eye relief. This isn't as simple as it seems. Fore-and-aft scope movement is limited by the tube length, the adjustment turret, the power-selector ring (if the scope is a variable), and enlargement of either end of the tube.

Mount design is also a limiting factor. If one or both mount bases sits on the action, mount-ring separation will vary according to action length (although extension rings offer adaptability in some cases). Some sidemounts offer more flexibility, but are rarely seen nowadays. Furthermore, eye relief is affected by the thickness of the clothing on the shooter's shoulder. If the scope is perfectly fitted while wearing a T-shirt during summer, a heavy winter jacket may move the scope too far forward,

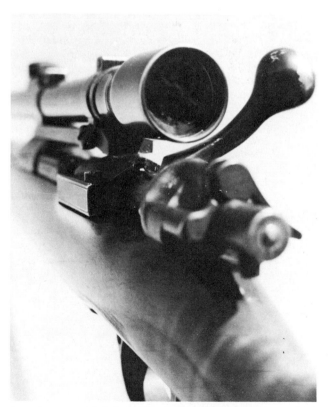

Less than one-eighth-inch clearance between ocular lens and bolt handle means scope can't be mounted any lower on this rifle.

thus requiring further adjustment. On some occasions, it is necessary to alter the length of the stock to get perfect eye relief.

When the rifle is shouldered, the scope's reticle or aiming point should be immediately and conspicuously visible. Its design is important. For generations, the flat-top post was recommended for woods use because it was big enough to be easily seen—even in poor light. It also provided a familiar image to shooters accustomed to the blade-type iron front sight. Crosshairs (actually wires) were first choice for pinpoint aiming at long range because they concealed much less of the target. However, they could vanish in dark woods. For some years now, the so-called Duplex reticle has been the choice of most hunters. It combines the best features of both post and crosshairs, having fine wires in the center and four posts projecting inward from the perimeter, overlying the wires for much of their length. The thin crosswires permit precision aiming whenever the light is reasonable, while the posts are visible for any conditions under which it's legal to hunt.

The Lee Dot also is excellent. It is perhaps the fastest of all to use because it's perfectly natural to plaster that round black dot onto the target, wherever it is, whatever it's doing. It is important to get a fairly big dot. Most new users want them too small. Forty years of Lee Dot use makes me suggest three or four minutes (three or four inches at 100 yards) in a 4X scope, or inversely proportionate to this in other powers (six or eight inches in a 2X for example, and so on).

Zeroing in is absolutely necessary, but there's nothing difficult about it if you have a solid rest and a safe place to shoot. Just put up a big target at 25 yards, hold center, and adjust the reticle until your bullets are hitting a whisper under the crosshair intersection. This should put you somewhere close to center at 100 yards. Try it there, and adjust to center your group three inches high. With most of today's high-velocity cartridges, this should put you a little high at 200 yards, maybe seven inches low at 300. Often, though, if you check this out, you will find a surprising variation. Recently, my groups out of a 24-inch-barrel .30/06 with factory-loaded 150-grain ammunition were +3, −4, and −13 inches, respectively, at these ranges. Accuracy was excellent, but the groups were nowhere near where published tables indicated that they should be. They could have caused vertical misses even at 200. It's impossible to know such things unless you check them.

Basic zeroing and trajectory determination should be done long before the hunting season and should be verified occasionally. Stock warpage, changes in humidity, bouncing around in a pickup's rack, maybe even what you had for breakfast before shooting can change a rifle's zero. So it should be checked, especially just before the hunt.

It's during the months before the season that a shooter can learn to trust his scope. The trick is to gain confidence in it, which is only accomplished by

use. It isn't necessary to shoot the rifle, but it is necessary to handle it—preferably daily. Dry firing an empty rifle is the answer. I don't mean just the aim-and-squeeze technique so beloved of old-time military men and target competitors, but rapid-handling dry firing.

You can do it in your den, bedroom, or backyard, but make triple-certain that the rifle's chamber and magazine are empty first. Then pick out a small object at the other end of the room or across the yard—a light switch, a tiny shadow in the bark of a tree, or a distinctive leaf. For a few minutes, that object is going to be the biggest whitetail you've ever dreamed of, or the most magnificent elk.

The rifle should be in standard carrying position: at the ready in both hands, across one elbow, down at the side in one hand, or even slung on the shoulder, though it's just as well to reserve the last for later. Stand facing the target. At some signal to yourself, move your feet into shooting position and bring the rifle to the shoulder, shoving the safety off as you do so. With both eyes open, find the target in the scope, slide the aiming point onto it, smoothly but quickly squeeze the trigger, flip the bolt open and slam it shut (open and close the bolt *hard*; it won't break). Make a habit of repeat shots: Aim—squeeze—flip—slam—aim—squeeze— flip—slam.

A few minutes a day of much rapid-handling dry firing will bring almost full familiarity with your rifle and scope. It cannot substitute completely for actual shooting because there is no recoil effect, but it's the next best thing. Most important, it will prove that you can see your target in the scope the moment the rifle butt hits your shoulder—even at close range where the field is small. That's the main bugaboo of most hunters who are leery of scopes. They're convinced that they won't be able to find the target quickly enough. But this kind of familiarization with a low-power, low-mounted scope shows how easy the whole thing is. In a short time, it will be easy to hit that leaf and even to hold on birds flying across the backyard.

As preparation for typical deer, elk, or bear hunting, such close-range training with a scope is vital. For most long-range shots, there is time to study the situation, get into a solid position with some kind of rest, get your breath under control, mentally review everything that you should do, and squeeze. There's a surgical precision about it all. But at short range, even though the target may be big, it's probably moving fast—and you have to hit it *now*. Despite the shifting shadows and lousy light, or driving rain or snow, or the fact that you're out of breath or excited or maybe scared, chances are you'll have but a few seconds to do whatever is necessary. It usually takes a lot of hard hunting and a lot of money to get an opportunity for a shot, and what you do in the space of a few heartbeats can mean the difference between success and failure. You'll find that practice of the kind suggested will turn such opportunities into successes.

Good Shooting In Bad Light

By Bill McRae

It was 5:31 P.M. and there were exactly ten precious minutes of legal shooting time left. The sun had disappeared behind an escarpment to the west an hour and a half earlier—it had officially been down for only 20 minutes—and heavy, snow-promising clouds had moved in from the north, cutting out the little sky light that remained. It would be a dark night in the mountains and, with camp two miles away through choice grizzly country, I had an uneasy feeling that I should be going. It was already so dark that objects in the bottom of the draw at timber's edge were indistinguishable but, being a die-hard, I'd have one last look around.

The meadow (a park to Westerners) was located on a steep mountainside. Tracks and droppings indicated that bull elk were feeding there nightly and, by staying until dark, I had hoped to see them. A battered old Bausch & Lomb 7X50 binocular gave a picture, amazingly bright and clear, as it opened the shadows of the park's perimeter. There, halfway up the other side and about 100 yards away, two bulls were feeding.

Shouldering the Model 70 Winchester .30/06, I full-well intended to send a 180-grain-Nosler greeting to the larger of the bulls but, when I looked through the 2.5X scope mounted on the rifle, my heart sank. Instead of the bright picture that I had gotten through the binoculars, I could see only faint light blobs that I assumed were the bulls. Worse still, the scope's thin crosshairs were not visible at all. A shot still might have been possible, but I deemed it too risky. Following wounded game with a flashlight doesn't appeal to me and, with snow in the offing,

my blood trail would be obliterated by morning. Besides, elk, if left unattended, spoil quickly.

Failing to get the elk was a great disappointment for a young hunter, but there were valuable lessons in that long-ago experience. I already knew that the edge of night, either morning or evening, was the best time to hunt. But I learned the importance of good, low-light binoculars. The real revelation, however, was that a riflescope should be equal in light-gathering ability to your binocular.

While good light-gathering optics are most useful at dawn and dusk, under certain conditions they can be helpful any time of day. For example, thick tamarack or cedar swamps can be mighty dark on heavily overcast days. Even on sunny days, because your eyes become accustomed to the bright light, it's hard to see into deeply shaded spots, which are the places where game is most apt to bed. A bright scope or binocular will open up the shadows and let you see what's there.

What makes binoculars or riflescopes suitable for low-light use? There are three major factors: exit-pupil diameter, which translates directly to relative brightness; magnification, a term interchangeable with power; and light transmission. (As you read on, you may want to occasionally refer to the Glossary of Optical Terms in this chapter.

EXIT-PUPIL SIZE

The exit pupil is a bundle of light rays that emerges from the eyepiece of an optical instrument and enters the viewer's eye when it is positioned correctly at

117

Although quality light-gathering optics will do yeoman service at dawn and dusk, you may find them most useful when peering into deeply shaded sopts, which are the places where game are most apt to bed down. A bright scope will help open up the shadows and let you see what's there.

the proper eye relief. It can be seen as a round spot of light in the eyepiece when the viewing instrument is held at arm's length and pointed toward the sky or toward a brightly lit background. The amount of light that the exit pupil can transmit is determined by its diameter. To find the metric diameter of the exit pupil, divide the diameter of the objective lens by the rated magnification. Thus, the diameter of the exit pupil on a 7X35 binocular is 5 mm (35 ÷ 7

= 5); on a 4X28 riflescope, the diameter is 7 mm (28 ÷ 4 = 7). Relative brightness is the square of the diameter of the exit pupil and, using the preceding examples, it is 25 and 49, respectively.

Why bother to square the exit pupil's diameter? Because by doing so, we get its area (since the exit pupil is round, to find its true area multiply the relative brightness by .7854) as opposed to its diameter, and area better indicates the exit pupil's ability to transmit light. Note that when the diameter of the exit pupil is doubled, its area is quadrupled and four times as much light is transmitted. For example, if you compare a 7X50 binocular (exit pupil diameter is 7.14 and relative brightness is 51) with a 7X5 binocular (exit pupil diameter is 3.57 and relative brightness is 12.75), the 7X50 transmits four times as much light as the 7X25. Other things being equal, the 7X50 weighs roughly four times as much, while the diameter of its objective lens doubles. Compared to a 7X35 (exit pupil diameter is five and relative brightness is 25), a 7X50 transmits twice as much light, weighs roughly twice as much, and is about 30 percent larger.

The diameter of the objective lens (the lens nearest a viewed object) controls brightness in a very simple way. The larger the opening, the greater the amount of light that goes into the optical system—it's like comparing large windows to small ones.

From this, you might conclude that, to make scopes or binoculars brighter, all a manufacturer need do is increase the objective-lens diameter. This is true, but only to a point. The first problem, as we've already seen, is that the size and the weight of an instrument increase with the increases in objective-lens diameter. However, the immutable, limiting factor is the entrance pupil of the human eye, which plays a role in the optical system of any visual instrument. The eye has an iris diaphragm that determines the size of the eye's entrance pupil according to the prevailing light conditions. The pupil gets larger in low light, smaller in bright. The catch is that even under the lowest light conditions, the pupil of the human eye can open up only to 7 mm and is seldom larger than 5 mm in most low-light hunting situations. If an optical system provides an exit pupil with a diameter larger than that of the pupil of the human eye, the added light is wasted.

It should be noted, however, that an instrument with a slightly oversized exit pupil is more comfortable to use because it allows more latitude in the position of the user's eye. The hunter does not have to place his eyeball exactly in line with the exit pupil.

MAGNIFICATION

Magnification significantly improves low-light performance, and the twilight-factor formula takes this into account. The way this formula works is simple. Magnification makes objects appear larger, and the larger something appears—especially in low light—the easier it is to see.

Let's suppose that, on a wilderness hunting trip,

you left your horse tied to a tree and, as a result of hunting too long, you must find the horse in the dark or walk several miles back to camp. In the daylight, it had been possible to see the horse a mile away but, in the darkness, you must get within ten yards before you can see it. Now, for the sake of simplicity, let's say that you are using a 7X binocular that delivers an image equal in brightness to the naked eye (most 7X glasses do much better). You will now be able to see the horse at 70 yards because, through the binocular, it will appear as large as if it were only ten yards away. You could see the horse at 80 yards with an 8X binocular, at 100 yards with a 10X, and so on.

It is important to note here that, while increased magnification does make objects appear larger and thus easier to see in poor light, it does not make them brighter. This is where the twilight factor, if carried to the extreme, breaks down. High magnification is helpful *only* if it is combined with a generous-sized exit pupil. A case in point is a 30 X 60 spotting scope: It has a very high twilight factor of 42 (see the Glossary of Optical Terms to learn how this was computed), but has an exit-pupil diameter of only 2 mm and a relative brightness of four. This makes it nearly useless in low light.

LIGHT TRANSMISSION

The third major factor in low-light performance is light transmission. It is the very important but little-talked-about stepchild in the world of optics. Relative brightness and the twilight factor are mathematical formulas that only tell how instruments *should* perform in low light. Theoretically, binoculars or scopes of equal magnification power and with lenses of the same objective diameter should be equally bright. In the real world, however, optical instruments that have the same identification numbers do not necessarily perform equally well under low-light conditions—and the reason for this is the light-transmission factor.

Unfortunately, there is no industry-wide standard for evaluating and reporting light transmission—in spite of the fact that light transmission can range from as low as 40 percent in systems with uncoated optics to more than 90 percent (70 percent is good).

Among the things that can affect light transmission, antireflection coating is the most important. It reduces the amount of light reflected away from the highly polished glass surfaces on the lenses of a binocular or a spotting scope. The coating material most often used is magnesium fluoride. An optimum

thickness of this, deposited on an optical surface, will reduce the amount of light lost from that surface from about 5 percent to about 1 percent. When you realize that a binocular or riflescope may have ten or more air-to-glass surfaces, it is easy to see why antireflection coatings are important. The new multicoatings are even more effective.

Other factors affecting light transmission are the clarity of the optical glass and the detail-robbing glare that is most noticeable when you're looking into the sun at dawn or dusk.

Without uniform standards, how can you be sure that the optics that you select yield good light transmission? The best assurance is to buy from a manufacturer that has a reputation for quality and dependability. Unfortunately, this rule of thumb makes short shrift of some small manufacturers who produce top-quality instruments.

Another option is to visually compare different models: Look into deep shadows to see how bright they are and then toward a light source to check for glare. You'll be surprised at the differences that you find. As Ken Woytek, riflescope engineering manager for Bausch & Lomb, points out, "The human eye is not of itself a good instrument for judging optical quality, but it is great for making comparisons."

BINOCULARS

What does it take to have a good low-light binocular? At the risk of being disagreed with or even denounced, I am going to arbitrarily set minimum standards for both relative brightness and the twilight factor. Here they are: Relative brightness should be at least 25, with a twilight factor of at least 17—and not one or the other, *both*! This leaves out all of the compacts and many fine full-sized binoculars. By this standard, the venerable 7X35 doesn't make it—its twilight factor of 15.6 is too low. The much-proclaimed 10X40 doesn't cut the mustard, either—while it has a high twilight factor of 20, its 4-mm diameter exit pupil yields a relative brightness of only 16. I said that I was being arbitrary!

Realizing that I am ignoring other binoculars that are equally deserving, I am going to talk about some of my favorites. The 7X50 Bausch & Lomb is one and, because it has been around for a long time, it has fought in several wars and has sailed the seven seas. Its almost-identical twin, the 10X50, is also a fine low-light glass.

A Bausch & Lomb binocular that really excites me is the new 8X42 Roof Prism Elite. This glass is the nurtured child of optical engineer Al Akin. In fact, Al was so fussy about having his personal quality standards met on this binocular that production was delayed for more than a year. His goal was to make "the world's best binocular." Whether he succeeded or not, I'm not qualified to say but, when looking through the Elite, it isn't hard to believe. It has wonderfully long eye-relief, is very bright, very sharp, easy on the eyes, and priced accordingly.

Zeiss binoculars have impressed me to the point that my wife describes our family's financial status as "Zeiss poor." Every Zeiss binocular is good—you can count on it—but some are better than others, particularly in low light. With a relative brightness of 49 and a twilight factor of 21.16, the Zeiss 8X56 is probably the king of the night glasses. A lighter

GLOSSARY OF OPTICAL TERMS

- **Magnification or Power:** Let's use the 7×50 binocular as an example. The first figure, $7 \times$, denotes the magnification. This means that distant objects will appear seven times larger than when viewed with the naked eye or, conversely, you will view them as though they were one-seventh of their actual distance away.
- **Objective Lens:** The objective (front) lens is the lens nearest a viewed object when the binocular is in use. The number immediately following the $\times$ in the identification number (such as 50 in 7×50) is the objective-lens diameter expressed in millimeters.
- **Ocular Lens or Eyepiece:** The ocular lens is the lens that is held nearest the eye when binocular is in use.
- **Exit Pupil:** Hold the binocular at arm's length and point it at a broad source of light. The small circle of light that you see in the eyepiece is the exit pupil. Exit-pupil diameter is stated in millimeters and is computed by dividing the diameter of the objective lens by the magnification. A 7×35 binocular, for example, has a 5-mm exit pupil ($35 \div 7 = 5$).
- **Relative Brightness:** This factor serves as a traditional guide for comparing image brightness between binoculars of different magnification and objective-lens sizes. To determine relative brightness, divide the diameter of the objective lens by the magnification and square the result (which is the diameter of the exit pupil). For example, an 8×40 binocular has a 5-mm exit pupil and, thus, a relative brightness of 25. Even under the lowest light conditions, the human eye cannot utilize a relative brightness greater than 50.
- **Twilight Factor:** A newer and perhaps more reliable guide for comparing low-light performance of binoculars is the twilight factor. It differs from relative brightness in that it takes magnification into account. To determine the twilight factor, multiply the magnification of the binocular by the diameter of its objective lens, then find the square root of the result. For a 10×40 binocular, the formula looks like this: $10 \times 40 = 400$, and the square root of 400 is 20. Thus, the twilight factor for the 10×40 binocular is 20. The higher the twilight factor, the more detail will be visible in dim light.
- **Eye Relief:** This is a term that refers to the distance that the ocular lens (eyepiece) of the binocular must be held from the user's eye in order for the binocular's full field of view to be visible. Long eye relief is an important feature for those individuals who must wear eyeglasses.

The Bausch & Lomb 8×42 Roof Prism Elite binocular.

and small Zeiss, almost its equal, is the 7X42. It has a generous 450-foot field of view and, at 28 ounces, it is a great all-around hunting glass.

Remember, these are simply examples of fine optics. There are others, indeed.

TELESCOPIC SIGHTS

What should you look for in a riflescope? Beginning with the exit pupil, a scope that is going to be used in low-light conditions should have an exit pupil no smaller than 7 mm in diameter—8 mm is even better. Why 7 mm instead of 5 mm, as was the case with binoculars? Because scopes have exceptionally long eye relief, which makes perfect eye alignment harder to achieve, and the larger-diameter exit pupil leaves more room for lateral eye movement. Incidentally, the 2.5X scope that let me down on that elk hunt wasn't lacking in exit-pupil size. With its 20-mm objective lens, it had an 8-mm exit pupil, but it lacked magnification, good light transmission, and a decent reticle.

High magnification helps but, on a fixed-power scope, it presents a problem. It enhances low-light performance, but it is a detriment when shooting in thick cover or at running game. The solution is a variable-power scope, preferably with a 3X-to-9X range. Such scopes usually have the large objectives needed to gather light, and the twilight factor improves as the power is turned up.

In low light, especially in the evening when there

is little time for tracking wounded game, pinpoint shot placement is a must. It is vital that the reticle be seen clearly. Among the conventional reticles available to American sportsmen, the Duplex, which was invented by Leupold and copied by everyone else, is the best.

Bushnell's Lite-Site riflescope is another option. Under normal light conditions, the reticle of the Lite-Site looks like any other dual-thickness crosshair but, in low light, a switch is turned on that causes a red dot to be projected in the center of the reticle. The 3X-to-9X model that I tested gave a bright image, and the dot was very apparent even in situations where any other reticle would have been lost. However, be sure to check the hunting regulations for the area where you'll be shooting before using this scope. As of last season, it was illegal to use the Lite-Site in Pennsylvania. Other states may have similar regulations in force.

Good low-light performers that grace rifles in my gun cabinet are Leupold's Vari-X III 2.5X-to-8X, a Bausch & Lomb 3X-to-9X, and a Zeiss 4X. They have never let me down.

As far as recent developments go, Bruce Cavey, sports optics division manager for Zeiss, assures me that by the time you read this a Zeiss 8X56 riflescope will be available in this country. The 8X56 has long been a favorite in Europe where hunting is often done in low light. I have ordered one, mainly because I'm so fond of my 8X56 Zeiss binoculars. It will go on a flat-shooting Remington Model 700 .225/06 and do double duty on varmints. The price will be a little over $500.

Another point of interest is that Nikon, a company that is world renowned for fine cameras, is making a strong entry into U. S. sporting optics. Along with a very fine line of binoculars, they are offering two multicoated riflescopes, a 4X and a 3X-to-9X variable. Both have 40-mm objective lenses, and the optics are what you'd expect from Nikon—bright and sharp!

Now some loose ends: What about spotting scopes? For reasons already noted (small exit pupils), they are not very useful in low light.

Do yellow shooting glasses help in low light? Definitely not. Yellow glasses filter out scattered blue light, thus increasing contrast and sharpening detail on foggy or hazy days. They are, however, optical filters, and all filters reduce—in one way or another—the total amount of light that passes through them. We want to increase light, not reduce it.

All optical instruments perform best if they are kept clean. I've seen hunters' scopes and binoculars that were so dirty I could hardly see through them in *good* light. I could only imagine how useless they would be in poor light.

And, finally, three very important points: Know the legal shooting hours and follow the law to the letter. Play it safe—if you don't know where the bullet is going, don't shoot. And don't shoot if you're not sure of making a clean kill. You owe this to yourself, to the sport, and to the game.

Big Game At Long Range

By Jim Carmichel

Whenever someone brings up the subject of long-range shooting, my first remark is that the shoot is always more important than the rifle. Sadly, no hunting rifle yet devised will compensate for poor marksmanship. A hyper-velocity hotshot magnum in the hands of an inexperienced nimrod will not extend his effective range—and it may even be a handicap.

Many years ago, I read an article about long-range shooting that was a remarkable manipulation of logic. The author, whose name I hastened to forget, allowed that a lousy marksman has a better chance of hitting a deer at long range than does an accomplished rifleman. According to the writer's reasoning, it takes more than one shot to connect at extreme range and that the better marksman, with his steadier aim, will keep missing the same way, shot after shot. The poor shot, however, will scatter bullets all over the countryside and one of them might accidentally hit the target.

The failings of this logic are several, with the first error being the shooting-gallery approach to long-range marksmanship. A knowledgeable hunter plans to get his first shot on target and makes a precisely calculated effort to do so. If the first shot misses the mark and there is a *reasonable* opportunity for follow-up shots (long-range shooting at running game is not reasonable), the experienced rifleman will make adjustments in his aim, especially if he or a companion can see where the previous bullet hit.

It is equally true that only an experienced rifleman can take advantage of today's long-range rifles, cartridges, and scopes. Less experienced hunters often make the mistake of assuming that by using one of today's high-performance rifles, they compensate for their lack of skill. This is a pitiful situation because, not only are they usually doomed to disappointment, but the awful truth of the matter is that inexperienced or unskilled shooters are frequently intimidated by magnum-class, long-range rifles and may not shoot one as well as they do more ordinary equipment.

Quite often, I am asked to recommend a rifle and caliber for a first-time-ever hunt for elk or other Western big game. Invariably, the hunter anticipates that he will be shooting halfway across the state and needs an ultra-long-range rig. Sometimes, I recommend a rather ordinary caliber such as the .30/06 or .270 Winchester. Other times, I might suggest a 7-mm Remington Magnum, .300 Winchester Magnum, or even one of the hot Weatherbys. Why do I recommend a particular caliber one day, then change my mind the next? I'm simply trying to match the caliber to the shooter. A relatively inexperienced rifleman will have a better chance of making a long

bered for a magnum caliber, either a 7-mm Remington Magnum, one of the .300 magnums, or a related wildcat. Magnum calibers have extra velocity, which transmits into less wind drift. These fascinating and wonderfully accurate rifles usually weigh from 12 to 14 pounds, which of course, is too heavy a weight for a hunting rifle.

Even heavier rifles are used by a group of long-range fanatics in Pennsylvania. These good folk shoot for group at 1,000 yards from a benchrest using rifles that may weigh 20 pounds or more. Needless to say, such rifles are too heavy to tote when hunting, but they are used for a special sort of benchrest deer hunting at unbelievable ranges. According to what I'm told, these fellows consider a 1,000 yard shot at deer nothing out of the ordinary, and make hits at even greater ranges. Naturally, their rifles are specially built affairs, and the cartridges are impressive wildcats. I understand that one of their favorite cartridges is the .378 Weatherby Magnum case necked down to .30 caliber.

The only reason I mention this type of shooting is to give you an idea of what the outer limits of long-range sport shooting are, and the types of equipment needed for it. When we try to build long-range capability into a hunting rifle, a number of compromises are called for. Obviously, a hunting rifle has to be carried a lot, so that alone rules out the excessive weight that characterizes high-performance, long-range, target-type rifles. We also have to fire a hunting rifle with relative comfort, so an oversize magnum is out of the question. The recoil of a .300 Weatherby Magnum from a nine-pound rifle is about all the self-inflicted abuse that any of us want to tolerate. After all, the essence of long-range shooting is not to stop a charging elephant but, rather, to precisely place a bullet on target.

We hear all sorts of wild tales about game being hit at outrageous distances. Nine out of ten of these stories can be discounted because distance is hard to judge and hunters, for some reason, tend to tremendously overestimate distances. If your hunting pal tells you that he smacked a pronghorn at 500 yards with his .270 Winchester, you might casually ask how high he held over the critter's shoulder. Even with a 130-grain pointed bullet sighted in dead on at 300 yards, he would have to hold about *two feet* over the animal's backbone to get the bullet where he wanted it. In case you're curious, he would have had to hold 4½ feet high if the antelope had been 600 yards off. At 1,000 yards, the necessary "Kentucky elevation" would be more than 23 feet! After taking into account ballistic tidbits such as this, it is easy to see why most tales of long-range hits on big game need to be taken with several pounds of salt.

With this in mind, let's establish a reasonable definition of long-range shooting, and then consider what rifles and calibers offer us the best chance of killing game out in telescope country where the yards are long. To my notion, 500 yards is the far outside edge of reasonable game shooting distances. In fact,

shot with a milder cartridge, especially if it's one that he's accustomed to using. If I figure that a hunter can perform well with a hotshot magnum, though, that's what I recommend he buy.

If this sounds like a bit of philosophical moralizing, please be assured that it is intended as such. I'm convinced that any discussion of long-range rifles should begin with a sermon and end with a prayer because of the ease with which the topic can be misinterpreted. The parable of the long-range rifle is that by the time a hunter gains the experience and skill to use one effectively, what he will have learned best—if he has learned at all—is that the long shot is only a last resort and should be avoided by the hunter if at all possible.

By way of reference, the most common long-range shooting done with sporting rifles is 1,000-yard NRA-type competition. Shooting is from the prone position, using both telescopic and iron (peep) sights. The center X-ring is ten inches in diameter. To be competitive, a rifle has to be capable of ten-inch or smaller groups, even if the shooter isn't. Most of the specialty rifles used in this competition are cham-

anything beyond 300 yards is beginning to let our reach exceed our grasp. The problem, by the way, is not a matter of horsepower. Most of today's high-intensity cartridges have more than enough remaining energy to kill even the biggest North American game at ranges well beyond 500 yards. If you check your ballistic charts, you'll discover that there are several loads that deliver more than 1,000 pounds of energy at 500 yards.

The problem, therefore, is simply *hitting* the target at long range. This problem is made up of four major factors. The first two are the accuracy of the shooter and the accuracy of the rifle. (Because we're talking mostly about rifles, let's leave off the human factor and assume that we're all dead shots.) The third and fourth factors are range determination and bullet trajectory—the real nuts and bolts of long-range shooting.

Most hunters can judge distance pretty well out to about 250 yards. After all, we watch enough football to know what 100 yards looks like. Out at 300 yards, however, it is not uncommon to make errors of as much as 100 yards one way or the other. At 500 yards, estimates may vary by as much as 200 yards. Sadly, it is out past 300 yards where we need a precise knowledge of the distance. Here's why: Let's say that you're using a .270 Winchester with 130-grain bullets, a popular caliber for its flat trajectory and long-range potential. By sighting in the rifle so that it is dead on target at 200 yards, you don't have to worry about range out to 250 yards because the trajectory is so flat that the bullet will hit within three inches of where you aim, meaning that you will be in the vital area of any big game. But at 300 yards, the bullet has lost nearly one-third of its original velocity and is beginning to curve downward more sharply. At 300 yards, the bullet hits only about seven inches below where you aim but, at 400 yards, it is 20 inches low. Out at 500 yards, it is more than 40 inches low. If the animal is actually 400 yards away and you make an error of range estimation of 100 yards either way, the bullet will wind up either over or under where you want to hit by an excessive mar-

gin. At longer ranges, as the bullet pitches down ever more sharply, the allowable error in range estimating becomes less and less. Out around 600 yards, for example, a plus or minus error of only 50 yards will mean the difference between the bullet passing harmlessly either over or under a deer-size target. So even if we memorize the trajectory curve of a given cartridge and know how much to hold over the target at all ranges, we're still operating under a tremendous handicap because of the difficulty of accurately estimating distance. I've never met anyone who can consistently estimate true range within 50 yards at distances beyond 400 yards.

To some extent, we can make up for poor range-estimating skills by using telescopic sights that feature range finders. Small, hand-held, optical range finders are also available but, unfortunately, both of these devices become less precise out where we need the most precision. (Some hunters who specialize in ultra-long-range shooting use large tripod-mounted range finders, but these aren't practical for normal hunting situations.)

Once we accept the fact that we can't reliably judge distances well enough to know exactly how much Kentucky elevation to allow for a long-range shot, we begin looking elsewhere for a workable solution. This is where we pay closer attention to cartridges having the flattest long-range trajectories.

Before getting out the ballistic tables, let's establish a maximum allowable hit area. In other words, if you are shooting at a distant deer, how far can the bullet deviate from your point-of-aim and still hit the vital area? Moose and elk have quite large vital areas, but the heart/lung area of a pronghorn antelope or deer is relatively small. So let's establish a maximum allowable kill-zone diameter of ten inches. The bullet cannot hit more than five inches above or below the point-of-aim. Now let's check the ballistic tables and see which cartridges best meet our criteria. Needless to say, the calibers that do it best are those that have the higher velocities.

One of the fastest of the hotshots is the .257 Weatherby Magnum, which spits a 100-grain spitzer

The .300 Weatherby Magnum V Bicentennial (upper left) is accurate beyond 400 yards. Popular Winchester Model 70 (above) is available in a variety of long-range calibers.

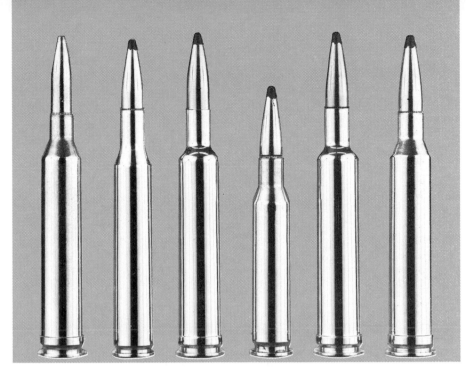

Some of the better medium-caliber cartridges for long-range shooting include, from left: .264 Winchester Magnum; .270 Winchester; .270 Weatherby Magnum; 7mm/08 Remington; 7mm Remington Magnum; and 7mm Weatherby Magnum.

MAXIMUM FOOLPROOF RANGES OF POPULAR CARTRIDGES

Caliber	Bullet Weight	Muzzle Velocity	Maximum Foolproof Range
.243 Win.	100	2,960	345
6-mm Rem.	100	3,130	365
.240 Weatherby Mag.	100	3,395	400
.25/06 Rem.	100	3,230	375
.25/06 Rem.	117	3,060	355
.264 Win. Mag.	140	3,030	365
.270 Win.	130	3,110	360
.270 Weatherby Mag.	130	3,375	400
7-mm/08 Rem.	140	2,860	345
7-mm Rem. Mag.	175	2,860	350
7-mm Weatherby Mag.	175	3,070	380
.308 Win.	150	2,820	335
.308 Win.	180	2,620	315
.30/06 Springfield	150	2,910	340
.30/06 Springfield	165	2,800	340
.30/06 Springfield	180	2,100	330
.300 Win. Mag.	150	3,290	380
.300 Win. Mag.	180	2,960	355
.300 Weatherby Mag.	150	3,545	420
.300 Weatherby Mag.	180	3,250	385
.338 Win. Mag.	250	2,660	335
.340 Weatherby Mag.	250	2,850	355

(Ranges at which the bullet is no more than five inches below point-of-aim and never more than five inches high)

out at more than 3,500 fps. A bit of arithmetic tells us that the .257 Weatherby offers us a foolproof trajectory out to 400 yards—a good load. Is anything better? (To see how a few stack up, see the table.)

Accurate bolt-action rifles, or good single shots, are the only really viable choices for long-range shooting. In fact, nearly all of the better long-range calibers come in bolt configuration anyway. If I were buying a rifle or having one built just for long shots at game, I'd strive for a compromise between portability and weight. Rifles with heavier barrels hold steadier, an important factor when aiming at a distant target. A rifle that need never be carried far from the vehicle or saddle can weigh upwards of ten pounds. One that has to be carried up mountains, however, gets mighty tiresome if it weighs much more than seven pounds.

I'd also want plenty of barrel length, probably 26 inches for a magnum caliber because of the better velocity yield. With a high-intensity cartridge, a 26-inch barrel will offer about 100 fps more velocity than one that's two inches shorter. I'd also have the rig accuracy-tuned, so that I could depend on the first shot out of a cold barrel being perfectly on target.

My selection in aiming equipment would almost certainly be one of the new variable-power scopes that has 12X magnification on the high end. Or, I might just settle for a fixed-power glass in the 10X or 12X range. You can't hit it if you can't see it.

Even if you own the finest long-range rig in the country, don't plan on using it for a long shot unless you must. Remember, a long-range rifle works wonderfully well at short range, too. Though rifles and ammo are better now than ever, hunting is still the same and you're doing it best when you're up close.

How Far Is Too Far?

By Jim Carmichel

My wife and I had been shooting prairie dogs all afternoon and had only a couple of .220 Swift cartridges left when we headed back to town.

"There's another one," she said, pointing at a spec on the horizon.

It was a long way, too far for sensible shooting, but I wanted to burn the two remaining rounds. So I set up the sandbag, laid out my rifle, and took a look at the distant target through my 12× varmint scope.

There was absolutely no wind and only a faint wiggle of mirage rose from the crusty, dry high-plains landscape. Even so, aiming was difficult—the crosshairs almost completely covered the target at that extreme range. There wasn't much of a chance of hitting that dog because, even with a rifle capable of better than minute-of-angle accuracy, group sizes at 500 yards, for example, will be about six inches with perfect conditions. Thus, even a perfectly aimed shot could miss a target as small as a prairie dog at long range. But prairie dog shooters can't resist attempting an occasional long shot and know that, every once in a while, a bullet will find its way to the target.

Unless the wind is really whistling across the dog town, which it usually does, a 100-yard shot is dead easy, even with a rifle of just so-so accuracy. Two hundred yards is considered a normal prairie dog distance and, if a shooter has good equipment, he should expect to make a solid hit. At 300 yards, the shooting gets a bit tricky and even the better marks-man won't get every shot on target, especially if there are changeable crosswinds. Beyond 300 yards, the variables, such as range estimating, wind, mirage, rifle accuracy, and marksmanship become major forces, and the ratio of shots missed to shots attempted climbs. At 400 yards and beyond, it takes a big dose of luck to hit a prairie dog.

I held the crosshairs a foot or so over the prairie dog's head and gently ticked the Canjar set trigger on my varmint-barreled Ruger Model 77 bolt rifle. After a measurable moment, there was a puff of dust in front of the target, indicating that the bullet had hit short. The dog seemed untroubled, so I fed my last round into the chamber and aimed again, adding the inches that the bullet had hit low to the inches I held over the target. Now I was aiming about 20 inches over where I wanted to hit.

"Bet I hit close enough to make him move this time," I said to my wife, and then touched the trigger again.

"Did you hit him?" she asked.

"Can't tell for sure. But at least he's not standing anymore."

Overwhelmed by curiosity, I had to pace off the distance. Exactly at my 500th long step lay an extraordinarily unlucky prairie dog.

After connecting on such a small target, totaling no more than a dozen or so square inches to aim at, at so many yards, I could easily be rushed to the conclusion that I can hit a much bigger target at the same distance. A deer or sheep should be a pushover by comparison, and a game animal as big as an elk

How far away is that 12-pointer in your binoculars? Probably too far for an offhand shot. You're better off placing elbows on knees and using the rifle's sling to steady hold, as shown above.

or a moose should prove ridiculously easy. But we know that big game can be extremely hard to hit at much closer range. Why? How can we hit a prairie dog at 500 yards and miss deer at half that distance?

On the day I made that 500-yard hit, I'd also nailed a lot of prairie dogs at about 300 yards. I'd set up a portable bench and, with my rifle solidly rested on sandbags, I was connecting on about four out of every five shots. During a break for lunch, while I was cooling in the shade, a coyote came trotting through the dog town, picking at the scattered remains. Sprinting to the bench, I loaded a round and tried to settle the crosshairs on the coyote's shoulder. But every time I was about to fire, he would move and I'd have to wait until he stopped to examine a prairie dog. Finally, when he looked as if he would stand still for a moment, I rushed off a shot—and missed. My wife was as amazed as I was.

"How can you hit tiny prairie dogs," she asked, "and then miss a big coyote at the same distance?"

The reason I missed, strange as it seems, was because the coyote was *too far* for the conditions under which I was forced to shoot. Let's take a look at the factors that can make a shot "too far" simply be comparing the situations.

When I was making hit after hit on prairie dogs at around 300 yards, I had maximized the probability of making a hit by eliminating as much of the human factor as possible. For example, I was shooting from a solid benchrest with the rifle supported by sandbags so that the crosshairs didn't jiggle when I touched off a shot. When I fired at the coyote, however, I had to rush the shot because he had stopped for only a moment. Further, even though I fired from a rest, the rifle was at an awkward, poorly controlled angle with no solid support under the butt. Perhaps the main reason I missed was because I was excited and in a hurry to nail the coyote.

A couple of years back, when a few of my pals and I were hunting in British Columbia, we set up a target near camp and fine-tuned our rifle sights so that we could easily swat a billy goat at 300 yards. The next day, we ran across a pretty nice moose, and my companion wasted three shots before he finaly got a bullet on target. Would you believe that the range was only 60 yards? If the distance had been another 40 yards, that old bull would probably still be loafing in the wilderness. So how could my hunting buddy, an experienced hunter and rifleman, hit a one-inch bull's-eye at 100 yards when we were sighted in at camp, and then miss a six-by-six-foot target at 60 yards? The same way I missed the coyote: it was too far for the conditions that prevailed when he began shooting. He was firing offhand and he's terrible at it. This factor, added to his excitement, caused his string of misses.

The point of these rather extreme examples is to illustrate that maximum shooting range is not just a matter of distance, but of prevailing conditions when you pull the trigger. Crazy as it sounds, I'd bet a dollar or two that more deer are missed at 200 yards than at 300 yards. The reason is that 200 yards is a

pretty long shot for what is normally a short-range hunting sport. When a brush hunter who has his equipment and shooting technique geared for ranges of less than 100 yards is suddenly presented with a 200-yard shot, he is usually forced to apply his equipment—and his technique—to a very difficult set of circumstances. If the range is 300 yards, he simply doesn't try. But there are deer hunting conditions where a 300-yard shot is routine. In some Southeast states, for example, deer are commonly hunted around vast soybean fields, where the hunters shoot from platforms using highly accurate long-range rifles. These guys put markers in the field so that they will know the distance to within a few yards and, with a solid rest, can hit a beer can a long way off. Very seldom do they miss at 300 yards—and they kill a lot of deer. These specialists would tell you that pulling off a 300-yard shot is simple. But if they had to stand on their hind legs and shoot without a rest, they would do a lot of missing at 200 yards and less.

To get an idea of how far is too far for offhand shooting, let's take a look at the game of silhouette shooting. At 220 yards, the target is a steel profile of a chicken, which is roughly equivalent to the heart and lung area of a whitetail deer in terms of total target area. The silhouette shooter uses a medium-weight rifle and fires five shots in 2½ minutes from an unsupported standing position. His rifle is generally highly accurate and precisely zeroed but, even so, it is so difficult to hit five chickens in a row that if he does get all five he gets a special award. And keep in mind that these are top marksmen accustomed to shooting under pressure. The lesson here is that few of us are good enough with a rifle to hit

MAXIMUM DISTANCES

Position	Range
Standing without sling	70 yards
Standing with sling	75 yards
Standing with side rest	120 yards
Kneeling without sling	85 yards
Kneeling with sling	95 yards
Sitting without sling	120 yards
Sitting with sling	190 yards
Sitting with side rest	220 yards
Prone without sling	160 yards
Prone with sling	220 yards
Prone without sling over rest	280 yards
Prone with bipod rest	280 yards
Benchrest with sandbags	300 yards

How can we hit a tiny prairie dog at 500 yards and miss a big buck at half that distance? The reason is that the deer was probably too far for the conditions under which we were forced to shoot.

a deer at 200 yards without some sort of support to steady the rifle and comfort our aim. Even with the rifle rested alongside a tree, 200 yards is still a tough shot in many cases, unless the hunter can sit down as well.

If an experienced rifleman can fire from the prone position with the rifle rested over a log or rock, he can expect to hit a deer-size target at 250 yards—*provided* he has the right rifle for the job and it is correctly sighted for the distance. If he is really good, he can stretch the range another 100 yards or so but, beyond that, other factors take their toll.

Riflemen who compete in long-range tournaments regularly fire at 600 and 1,000 yards, with the best of them keeping most of their shots in the six-inch X-ring at 600 yards and the ten-inch X-ring at 1,000 yards. It would seem that riflemen of such skill could easily hit a deer or elk at long range, until you consider that one of the reasons they hit targets at such distances is because they know the distance *precisely.* If one of these riflemen were suddenly confronted with the task of putting his first bullet on target at some unknown distance between 300 and 500 yards, he would be hard pressed to do so.

That's why Carmichel's first law of long-range shooting is: "It is too far when you don't know how far it is." Within certain limits, errors in range estimating are automatically corrected by modern high-

velocity cartridges. For example, let's say that you sight in your .270 to hit dead on at 200 yards. If you get a shot at a deer or any other big-game animal out to nearly 300 yards, you can hold in the center of the vital area and expect to hit within six inches of point-of-aim. But what if the deer is at 400 yards and you estimate it to be 500 yards? You hold over the target by the correct amount for a 500-yard shot but, because of the error in range estimation, you miss by nearly two feet. It is extremely difficult to estimate ranges beyond 300 yards and, at 500 yards, errors of 200 yards either way are not uncommon, especially in typical big-game country.

A few years ago, I assembled a number of more or less knowledgeable and experienced big-game hunters at a rifle range to conduct a series of performance tests. We used paper plates for targets and fired from a variety of positions, and what we learned was a bit surprising. The table on the facing page summarizes what we found out about how far is too far when shooting modern scoped hunting rifles and flat-shooting centerfire ammo.

The acceptable level of performance was established as being 80 percent, meaning that four out of five shots had to hit the plate. The range was shortened if the average fell below 80 percent, and the range was increased if the average was significantly more than 80 percent.

Perfect Blackpowder Load For Deer

By Rick Hacker

It seems to be a yearly ritual and it usually occurs in late August or early September. About that time, I can always be found hunkered down at the shooting bench at the Angeles Shooting Range in Southern California, firing a .50- or .54-caliber muzzleloading rifle at 50- and 100-yard targets in preparation for the upcoming deer season. I'm shooting, filing the front sight down, drifting the rear sight with a brass hammer, swabbing out the bore, loading, and shooting.

It is a leisurely, relaxing procedure for me, and the entire exercise of working up a perfect blackpowder load for a new rifle normally takes about half a day. However, it never takes more than 30 minutes after the first thick white cloud of blackpowder smoke drifts across the firing line for some yahoo from the smokeless-powder section to come shuffling up behind me. After about five minutes of watching my antics, he will wait until the precise moment when I have the black bull delicately centered around the silver blade front sight and am just about ready to touch off the three-pound pull of the set trigger. At that crucial instant, the self-contained-metallic-cartridge shooter will lean over my shoulder and say: "Nice looking smokepole, but can it kill a deer?"

I usually blow the shot, but my typical reply is, "Well, I know of quite a number of bucks that would answer in the affirmative, if only they were still around to nod their heads."

The number of deer rises almost every year. Sometimes it has remained frozen for two years at

a stretch but, normally, when antlered game is within range and in my sights, I consider it tagged at the moment the hammer falls. Whether flint strikes steel or the hammer pops a percussion cap, I have never lost a big-game animal when hunting with blackpowder. There are reasons for this that transcend luck and skill.

First of all, I hunt with a muzzleloader that is of sufficient caliber to drop any buck. My choices, for this reason, are .50 and .54. Second, I never fire at a deer unless I am well within range, which is rarely more than 100 yards and sometimes closer than 30. I have passed up record-book animals that I felt were too far away, even though the distance may have been less than 150 yards. It is not sporting to wound a magnificent animal just because you're anxious to get a shot at a big buck. And, finally, my muzzleloading rifle is always stoked up with the best blackpowder load that I can devise for the game that I am hunting.

For deer, I want a muzzle velocity of well over 1,000 fps and a minimum striking energy at 100 yards of approximately 500 foot-pounds. That's with round balls. With conical bullets, which I prefer, I want substantially greater velocity and energy, and my basic rule is to develop blackpowder loads that generate at least 1,000 foot-pounds at 100 yards. With a heart/lung hit, that will put your deer on the ground for good.

Just what constitutes a perfect deer load has always been a matter of debate among blackpowder hunters, and the discussion had its origin long before the era

of Crockett and Bridger. In the early days of American hunting, conserving hard-to-get powder and lead was a necessity on the frontier, and impractical light loads were often used on nondangerous game. Fortunately for today's buckskinners, we no longer have a supply problem with blackpowder or Pyrodex. For big-game hunting, my thinking is that there is no such thing as being overgunned—within reason, of course. I, therefore, select rifles that throw a ball of at least a half inch in diameter (.50 caliber) and work up loads that represent the best compromise between accuracy and power. Unfortunately, those two qualities are not always compatible. A superaccurate load may lack sufficient killing power; a magnum charge of blackpowder may scatter your bullets all over the target. Consequently, a lot depends upon the rifle you choose, the kind of projectile you load, and how much powder you pack behind it.

Although the .50-caliber rifle is by far the most popular for deer hunting, my favorite is the .54 because it is the best all-around muzzleloading caliber—not only for deer but for black bear and elk, as well. I have also found that it provides the best compromise between power and accuracy. This is not to say that a .50 will not drop a buck; it most assuredly will. I have taken coastal blacktail deer using a Dixie Tennessee Mountain Rifle in .50 caliber, powered by 100 grains of FFg blackpowder. However, a .54 hits

with approximately 25 percent more power than the .50, and this increase can mean the difference between a buck on the ground and a buck on the bound. The .58 caliber has even more striking power, but it loses out in the accuracy department with heavy loads—although I definitely prefer it for dangerous game. I took a Kodiak .58 double rifle with me to Africa and did not regret it for one instant.

When discussing any form of blackpowder big-game hunting, the choice between using a round ball and a conical always raises much heated debate, but the facts speak for themselves. Conicals carry about twice the weight of a round ball in the same caliber. Because the muzzleloading hunter is primarily concerned with striking energy, the more weight you have in a bullet, the harder it will hit. Consequently, the conical is more effective by far on any big-game animal. For example, 100 grains of FFFg blackpowder behind a 220-grain .54 round ball produces about 522 foot-pounds of energy at 100 yards. The same 100 grains behind a 410-grain .54 Minie ball slams home with 1,034 foot-pounds of energy at the same distance—almost twice the amount of energy using the same powder charge. In the round ball's defense, however, I must say that it will shoot flatter, and a round-ball rifle zeroed in for 50 yards will still strike in approximately the same target area at 100 yards. Because a conical is heavier, it travels at a slower rate of speed, and the drop will be greater at 100 yards—usually somewhere between two and four inches for a rifle zeroed in to hit dead on at 50 yards. This means that those shooting conicals have to use a bit of Kentucky elevation at longer ranges, but I feel that the benefit of greater killing power is worth it. My personal goal is to always have a big-game hunting load that will produce at least 1,000 foot-pounds of energy at 100 yards. It is humane, effective, and sportsmanlike to load that way.

Although round balls are slightly more accurate than conicals, as a rule, they cannot be loaded as fast in the field. They require a greased patch that must be centered over the bore. The ball is then placed over this patch, which acts as a gas seal and takes a grip on the rifling when the rifle is fired. Minie balls and other conicals, on the other hand, are greased before they are loaded in the bore and require no patch. The soft lead of the bullet is engraved by the rifling during loading or when the bullet expands on firing.

There are three types of conicals from which the hunter can choose. Maxi-Balls, which are made primarily for Thompson/Center muzzleloaders, have a thick lead bearing that must be pressed into the rifling when the bullet is forced into the muzzle. This makes for slow and sometimes awkward loading in the field, especially in a situation where a fast second shot may be needed. Minie balls, on the other hand, are loaded with ease because they are cast slightly smaller than the bore. The hollow base of the Minie expands and fills the rifling when the rifle is fired. Minies work best in rifles with fast twists (for instance, one in 48 inches), but too heavy a powder charge can cause these bullets to strip completely out of the rifling, resulting in a keyholing effect.

Buffalo Bullets, representing the third type, are the newest entry in the conical category and they are my favorites for hunting. They have a tapered base, which allows for easy, thumb-pressure loading just like a Minié bullet, and they also have a thick knurled center section that enters the rifling on firing. Hollow-based Buffalo Bullets come in three grain weights in .54 caliber. The 460-grain bullet is most effective in fast-twist barrels, while the two lighter bullets—425-grain hollow point and 435-grain round nose—work best in slow-twist barrels, which are normally reserved for round balls. The company also makes .45- and .50-caliber bullets, in hollow-based or solid.

Once we have selected the bullet, we next have to determine how much powder should be poured down the tube in order to achieve an optimum deer hunting load. Of course, only blackpowder or Pyrodex RS should be used. Smokeless powder will take you and your rifle out of deer season forever. Although many hunters use FFFg powder, I prefer FFg for .50-caliber and larger rifles. It burns slower and produces less pressure while providing more velocity, grain for grain. FFFFg powder should only be used to prime the pans of flintlocks and Fg should be left to people who like to shoot cannons. Stick with FFg in big-bore muzzleloaders.

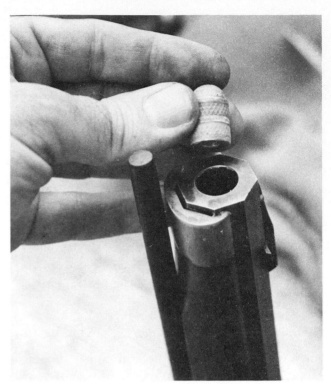

This Buffalo bullet has a tapered base and enters the bore easily. A patch is not needed.

In working up a hunting load, the usual rule is to start with one grain per caliber (for instance, a .54 rifle would first be loaded with 54 grains of powder). Frankly, I have found that this is fine for the target shooter who is only concerned with putting his projectile inside the X ring. The deer hunter has a minimum striking energy requirement to meet. Therefore, I can save you a lot of time and powder by stating that for .50- and .54-caliber shooters, the best hunting loads using round balls are somewhere between 80 and 120 grains. With conicals, it is normally best to stay between 60 and 90 grains in these calibers. Even in these days of mass-produced charcoal-burners, each muzzleloading hunting rifle has its own requirements. It is up to you to find out what they are. Because of this, the author and *Outdoor Life* cannot be responsible for mishaps. We have no control over how you measure your charge or load your gun, and we have no control over the quality of the piece that you are firing, so we accept no responsibility for the results. Hunting with a muzzleloader isn't dangerous, but you do have to be careful, especially when loading.

Before going to the range, be sure your thunderstick is in top shootable condition. Have a gunsmith check it out if you're in doubt, perhaps because you bought it used. New guns are usually covered by a warranty but, unfortunately, most manufacturers only recommend very mild, ultrasafe loads. Be sure that you are shooting a quality blackpowder arm made by one of the leaders in the field—Dixie, Lyman, Navy Arms, Allen Fire Arms, CVA, and

Loading a patched round ball in a rifle requires short starter to enter it into the muzzle.

Thompson/Center, just to name a few.

For the blackpowder hunter, it is important to define just what you are seeking in accuracy. For example, my .54-caliber Mountain Hawken rifle with 100 grains of FFg behind a 435-grain Buffalo Bullet prints two-inch groups consistently at 50 yards. At 100 yards, this group opens up to four inches, and the group center is two inches low. Any more powder and the group spreads out. With less powder, I don't feel I have the energy that I need to kill a big-game animal cleanly. This, then, is my standard hunting load in that rifle, and I stick with it season after season. There is no reason to vary because I know what it can do. It is nice to be able to punch cloverleafs in paper targets, and many round-ball guns can do just that—but often at the cost of sacrificing striking energy. When trying to place a heavy lead bullet in a buck's vitals, we are aiming at a pie-plate-size target. For practical hunting, any shooter who can keep his offhand shots in an area as wide as his hand is going to score if he, his muzzleloader, and the deer all come together at the right moment.

Blackpowder hunters who use smooth bore muskets, which are required by law in some states, should be equally concerned about working up a good deer load. The lack of any rifling normally limits the effectiveness of these guns to 40 or 50 yards. A 60-grain charge of FFg in a .75-caliber Brown Bess, for instance, will produce about 530 foot-pounds of energy at 100 yards. That's rather substantial, considering you are shooting a 545-grain round ball. It is interesting to compare this energy figure with the 875 foot-pounds of energy that a one-ounce 12-gauge shotgun slug produces at 100 yards. The shotgun slug, of course, is conical. Unfortunately, conicals will not stabilize in a smooth bore front-loader, so the musket hunter is relegated to using patched round balls. However, even with a smoothbore musket, groups can be surprisingly tight at fairly short range. For example, using a greased linen patch and .590 ball in Dixie's .60 Northwest Trade Gun, I have consistently fired four-inch groups at 50 yards, which I consider more than adequate for deer hunting. However, I was able to achieve these results only by spending time with that flinter to work up the perfect powder/patch/ball combination.

Normally, I take about three hours at the range to work up a perfect deer hunting load for a new muzzleloader. That is because I do not hurry through the process, lest I forget to pour in the powder before I ram down the ball or make any of many similar goofs. In addition, to obtain optimum accuracy, the bore must be wiped out with blackpowder solvent and dried after every shot. If you neglect to do this, you will never really know where your ball will hit on the first shot when hunting. Blackpowder fouling can drift the strike of the ball noticeably from shot to shot. Additionally, the amount of fouling increases with heavier hunting loads, although the deeper rifling of some of the Hawken-style hunting guns can lessen this effect somewhat.

Consistency in loading is the key in obtaining the tightest group with any load. The amount of powder, the thickness of your patch, and even the force with which you ram your ball home can all affect the impact point. I usually shoot three shots with a given load, firing each shot as if it were my first of the day. I increase my powder charge in five-grain increments and stop when the spread of the group becomes too great or when my powder charge is approaching what I consider to be the maximum limit for my rifle and myself. After determining my optimum deer hunting load at the bench, I take a break and then fire three shots from the offhand position at a 50-yard target; then three more offhand shots at a 100-yard target. Fifty to 100 yards probably represents most shooting situations that you will find yourself in during deer season. Once you have your hunting load worked up, it pays to become intimately familiar with it before opening day. Always wear shatterproof shooting glasses and protective ear muffs (or plugs) at the range.

Once you have your three-shot group printing right and delivering sufficient knockdown power, you still have to adjust your sights so that your rifle will be shooting to the point-of-aim. This differs from sighting in a cartridge rifle, for which everything is premeasured for you right out of the box. With a blackpowder rifle, each variation in powder charge, bullet weight, and other things will place your shot in a different spot on the target. First, determine your hunting load, then get it in the black. Chances are you will never have to touch the sights or change the adjustment of your powder measure again.

PART 5

BOWS AND HUNTING

World's Best Bowhunter?

By Jeff Murray

For most deer hunters, especially bowhunters, luck plays a mighty big role in determining the outcome of each season. You know—being in the right place at the right time and all that jazz.

Not for Myles Keller, a 39-year-old highway maintenance man for Dodge County, Minnesota.

Come on, a guy who's arrowed 18 Pope and Young whitetail bucks—more than anyone else in the world—must have had a few lucky days behind him. And what about those five record-book black bears? You mean to say that there isn't a close-shave story, either?

Nope. Dull hunts. Boring shots. All of them.

But this guy, Myles Keller, now he's quite a story. Nothing mundane about his whitetail knowledge and the strategies that he has refined over the years from successful hunts. He's got his tactics down pat—to the point that, when he sets up for a particular buck and finally makes his move, it'll be history for another trophy deer.

How does he do it? You can't put it into a 25-words-or-less capsule but, by taking a close look at each component of his technique, you'll get a good feel for what true trophy deer hunting is all about. Myles Keller is not interested in anything unless it has a direct bearing on mature, large-racked bucks. Of course, that really narrows the field down, yet he somehow manages to pull it off every year.

And he does it just about every place he hunts. He does it elk hunting out West (his Pope and Young bull was the best taken in the entire state of Colorado in 1974, during both the gun and the bow season); he does it whitetail hunting in Wisconsin (his big eight-pointer scored a whopping 175⅝ inches and remains that state's No. 1 bow kill); and he does it black bear hunting in Minnesota (until 1984, his 510-pound, 21⁴⁄₁₆-inch Pope and Young bear outranked

Most bowhunters would be proud to have just one of these trophies hanging on the wall. Surrounding this bull elk are a few of Myles Keller's record-book bucks.

Photo by Tom Huggler

"Bucks—really big bucks—don't normally travel along the same trails as does and immature bucks," says Keller.

the state's No. 1 Boone and Crockett entry). He has also placed whitetails in the books from Michigan and Missouri.

But like I said, his actual hunts are pretty boring. He doesn't go near selected ambush sites until he's confident that everything is just right. It may take a week, a month, or a season to get to that point, but he seems to get there like clockwork.

It's hard to believe that a man who has amassed such an unprecedented record almost quit bowhunting altogether before he fulfilled his destiny as one of the world's greatest deer hunters. As a young teenager, he walked to the headquarters of Herters, the once-famous sporting-goods mail-order house, to buy his first bow. On the way home on that same day, he shot his first deer, a doe feeding at the edge of a field.

An eight-pointer was his next target, but a misplaced shot—high and toward the stomach area—taught Keller the necessity of clean kills in the sport of bowhunting. When he couldn't find the deer after hours of searching, he went back to the farm to tell his father that he wasn't going to ever hunt deer with a bow again. The thought of losing such a beautiful animal was more than he could bear. But the next morning, he had a change of heart. Aided by his father's sharp eye, they found the deer—less than 100 yards from where the shot was made. The arrow somehow made its way into the artery just below the backbone, and the deer bled to death within minutes. Later, the young Keller learned that

one of the bow's limbs was badly twisted; it was a wonder that he hit the deer at all.

Despite all his travels, Myles Keller does 80 percent of his bowhunting (he doesn't even own a rifle) within a ten-mile radius of his home in Claremont, Minnesota. It is, indeed, a worthwhile area for a serious bowhunter who intends to consistently score on trophy-class bucks; rich farm soils laced with lush river bottoms are the perfect complement to a decent gene pool of high-racked bucks. But Keller by no means considers this territory holy ground for record-bound deer.

"There are a lot more big bucks out there than the average hunter thinks," he said. "The trouble is, they don't give the mature bucks credit; if a guy shoots a 1½- or 2½-year-old deer, he starts thinking that all the rest of the bucks act or react the same way. Bucks old enough to grow a large set of antlers are wise to the day-in and day-out ploys of most hunters."

Keller feels that modern deer hunting is often approached much like a man punching in at work—you just put in your time and sooner or later, the bonuses will come. Keller does just the opposite. He never goes near a selected stand site unless he's absolutely sure that the buck he's after will be "working his route" in an *unalarmed* manner.

"I don't like to hunt escape-route bucks," he told me. "It's hard enough to fool a buck on even terms, let alone one that's on edge, working his senses overtime."

What's wrong with a little Russian roulette on a deer stand? Plenty, according to Keller. On rare occasions you may by chance intercept a nice buck but, almost always, the buck will wind you and you'll probably never know that it exists. This becomes part of the vicious cycle that reinforces the notion that there aren't any big bucks in your area.

To get around this, Keller is able to scout his deer out so well that he knows every stretch of their home territory to a T.

"I never stop scouting," he explained. "Whether it's a trip to the grocery store or out on the grader plowing a county road, I'm looking for tracks and racks."

And he looks for something that most bowhunters never consider, something he calls the big picture. Instead of keying in on a particular runway that a buck is most likely to use, he first tries to establish a buck's routine. Without doing this, finding the weak point in a buck's travels could not be accomplished. Typically, a mature animal travels the safest routes, where it can rely on its keen senses to keep it out of danger. Putting yourself on equal footing with those senses is useless, Keller insists, but find the one part of a buck's pattern where he isn't using his senses to full advantage, and you'll quickly gain the upper hand. That's basically how Keller outwits trophy bucks.

"There aren't any shortcuts to a trophy deer," Keller maintains. "But they all make mistakes eventually. It's up to the hunter to predict them before they happen and to be ready when the opportunity presents itself."

The story of how he recently took a Pope and Young buck illustrates this point perfectly. By putting together the deer's overall routine, he was able to determine that, each morning, the buck would head out of a breeding area and follow a ditch bank toward a ten-acre woodlot, which he would circle a full 360 degrees before entering it to bed down for the day. Just before the big buck got to the woodlot, however, he would feel relatively confident and would cut the corner from where the ditch ran by the woods. At this point, the deer would also be quartering against the wind. Keller reasoned that if he approached this spot from the opposite side of the tree line and positioned himself in exactly the right place, the buck would not be able to wind him while he was cutting the corner. It worked out for a 15-yard shot, and this particular pattern has repeated itself on other occasions in different areas.

One of Keller's favorite ways to figure out the big picture is by posting on a fenceline. These are obvious travel routes leading to and from bedding and feeding areas, and they afford the added benefit of openness—you can see for miles, in many instances. Keller spends countless hours waiting—observing deer from fencelines.

"To me, a fenceline is like a window to a buck's living room," he said. "I can look in without being detected and get a good feel for where the kitchen and bedroom are. And I can do all this without going in and disturbing a thing."

But don't get the idea that all Keller does is chew Copenhagen while glassing deer from a distance. He cuts no corners to set up over a buck's apparent Achilles' heel. On a normal year's hunt, he's usually got at least a dozen or more stands carefully erected at locations that he knows could produce a trophy buck. The real trick is choosing the right one. And should he make a mistake so that a buck picks him up, he'll yank that stand out and completely relocate it, provided he finds another weak link for another setup. And after the move, he won't touch the new stand for at least a few more days, even if he moves it only 20 yards.

Over the years, a number of reliable setup areas have emerged from Keller's copious field notes and observations. One such pet place is what he calls perimeter trails.

"Bucks—really big bucks—don't normally travel along the same trails as does and immature bucks," he said. "I've found that they use their own travel lines off the well-beaten paths, instead. Of course, a lot depends on the terrain but, in farm country that's broken up by woodlots and creek bottoms, bucks will often utilize perimeter trails that skirt the edge of the heavier cover."

Keller has shot a number of dandy bucks off perimeter trails for the simple reason that these routes often lead deer along a route—even if it's for a short distance—where they can't use their nose. The irony here is that the reason why perimeter trails exist is because a buck has walked the woodlot, scent-checking for danger before deciding that the area's safe for spending the day. Again, by utilizing the wind at the precise place for his stand, Keller can intercept unsuspecting bucks.

This setup can be worked two ways. First, deer coming out to feed in fields at the end of the day can be seen before last light, whereas the hunter who watches over the actual field edge will be lucky to see fawns and yearlings. And second, the tactic works on deer coming out of the fields in the morning, looking for a safe place to hide out for the day. Earlier in the year, prior to heavy rutting activity, Keller feels that perimeter trails, when properly understood, can be very productive.

But given a choice, Keller, like most bowhunters, would much rather hunt during the rut. It's a time when he goes all out, squeezing as much energy as he can out of his body. But unlike many other hunters, he does not hunt over primary scrapes. Instead, he uses them to find shortcut-type travel routes where a buck is likely to take a chance for a short distance, rely on his eyes and not on his nose, and travel crosswind. Bucks that have been chasing does all night are often in a hurry to bed down, and a wise hunter can often pull this one off.

"This is the best and only reliable way to get at a big buck," he explained. "Besides being preoccupied with the sex urge, bucks are on the move a lot more than at any other time, so it really increases your chances."

The way Keller uses scrapes to his advantage is a trick that works equally well for farm-country bucks and deep-woods deer. Most hunters would like to believe that bucks check their scrapes during daylight hours, freshening them often. Keller doesn't buy that for trophy animals. Invariably, a wise older buck will scent-check his scrapes from downwind; in the process, most hunters are detected and easily avoided. So, what to do? Simple. Figure out how the buck approaches his scenting route and set up downwind—or preferrably crosswind—from that.

"I find that bucks usually check their scrapes at a distance of about 70 yards or so," he said. "I start there and work my way back and around from the primary breeding areas."

By primary breeding areas, Keller means only those scrapes that are really torn up, with numerous trails coming in and going out of them. They're a far cry from the isolated scrape made here or there on impulse by a lesser buck.

All of the scouting and all of the whitetail wisdom in the world is useless if a deer is able to get his nose on you. Nothing is more important to Keller than beating a buck's sniffer.

"That's the name of the game," he often says. "Bucks in more open edge country rely totally on their sense of smell; it never lets them down. But if you use your head the way a whitetail uses its nose, you're off to a good start."

The rituals that Keller routinely goes through to counteract his own body odor sound almost kinky. First, he washes *all* his hunting clothes (most hunters forget the underwear) in baking soda, using a box or so for one wash. Then he air dries them. And he never wears them around the house or camp where they could pick up undesirable odors; the minute he's done hunting, off they go. He also stores them in large plastic garbage bags, often with a tree branch of what's native to the area that he's hunting.

He also cakes his own body with baking soda and, whenever he's near water (a lake, river, or whatever), he plunges in no matter what the temperature. A clean body is essential, he insists; most hunters would agree. But Keller also has one ritual that tops them all.

"I don't know if you should print this—some people might think I'm weird," he told me. "But when I'm really serious, I put a plastic bag over my head [snugged over the top of his head down to his eyebrows]—you know, the lunch-bag size. Then I put on a fresh stocking cap—one that's heavily laden with baking soda."

Indeed, it sounds weird but, when he explains his line of reasoning, it seems to make sense: If most of the body's heat escapes through the head, then a lot of scent must also rise from that area, as well. By keeping a lid on it, so to speak, you can cut down on the amount of scent released, as well.

Keller takes other precautions that he considers mandatory. For one thing, he frequently hunts while wearing rubber waders because he knows from trapping that leather boots leave a scent trail behind in the woods. Whenever he climbs one of his tree stands, he dons a pair of surgical gloves. On stand, he does not sit atop a platform with an old piece of carpeting—that's like putting a big scent vent of human odors up in a tree, he explained. Instead, he'll make sure that the scrap piece of rug has been thoroughly washed—again, in baking soda—and hung in the breeze to dry. What's more, he never affixes it to the platform with any smelly glues. By keeping a plastic garbage bag snugged over it when the stand is not in use, he avoids noise problems when it freezes up. He simply removes the garbage bag with any built up snow and ice and is then able to sit or stand as quietly and odorlessly as possible.

Most commercially made scents are ineffective, according to Keller, especially the so-called doe-in-heat lures.

Keller does use fox urine and a couple of homemade concoctions that help to confuse deer about his ground scent, but he doesn't think anything can actually mask human odor. The only line of defense is to avoid sweating, keep immaculately clean, have plenty of changes of hunting clothing, and stay out of a buck's area until it's time for the kill.

Although most of Keller's trophies have been arrowed from a stand, as hunter pressure grows, stalking has become an increasingly important tool in his repertoire. A deadly method is to stalk bedding bucks lying in small depressions among farm crops. Cornfields especially lend themselves to this approach. Keller believes that stalking takes a little nerve but, more importantly, time.

One fall afternoon, he spotted a huge buck feeding on the periphery of a field of standing corn. It was already getting late, but the wind was right. Unfortunately, the ground was frozen and very crunchy, so he had to remove his boots and walk barefoot in order to avoid spooking the buck. He came to within 50 yards before he ran out of time—shooting light had finally vanished. His feet were frozen, but he almost bagged a trophy in the process.

If you carefully examined Keller's outer hunting garb, you'd notice that it is quite a bit different from the camo clothing that's sold over the counter today. He feels that the broken patches are too small and, beyond 40 yards, that they all tend to blend together. So he dyes his own to get the proper effect and plans on marketing a similar line for friends who agree with his ideas.

Other standard equipment includes a 75-pound Black Widow recurve that he shoots bare-handed—*without* a shooting glove or pinch tab. He likes Wilderness wooden shaft arrows, and his favorite broadhead must have a needle-sharp point with enough energy to drive through bone, if necessary. For that reason, Keller shoots nothing but Zwickey broadheads.

I've shot [this broadhead] through both shoulder blades of big bucks and have even broken the rear leg bone of a black bear," he said. "I don't like to hit bones, but sometimes it happens. What I do strive for is perfect placement so that the arrow is driven completely through the animal. Two holes are always better than one.

"And with that sharp point, I'm able to break the skin right away for good penetration. Other broadheads with the rounded-off points to go around bones and cartilage don't provide as much penetration, in my opinion."

With all those records to his credit and a system that appears unbeatable, what's the next hurdle for Myles Keller?

When I asked him, he just smiled and said, "Probably more rewarding hunts." But then he gave me a funny look. "You know," he added, "I feel like a bum for even saying this—lots of guys are always saying this—but there's a buck just a few miles from my house that could be the next typical world record. His last upward point is six or seven inches, and he's got six perfect tines to each side, plus mass and a tall wide rack. I've seen him several times and he'll go at least 190. That is what I'll be up to this year."

Keller told me that, last year, he hunted hard most of the season for that animal without catching a glimpse. When it was evident that the buck had been pushed out of its normal patterns, Keller helped a coworker, Mike Ness, bag his first Pope and Younger trophy by setting Ness up on a hotspot that he calls the firing line.

Why should Myles Keller be the next man to bag a world-record whitetail—hasn't he got enough trophies? Well, if pro hockey can have a Wayne Gretzky, is there any reason why the bowhunting world can't have a Myles Keller?

Rig Your Bow For Big Game

By Rich LaRocco

A bowhunter can do many things to improve his hunting success. One of the simplest, however, is to equip himself with the proper archery gear. The best bowhunters I know would no sooner carry some of the archery tackle that I've seen in the hands of novices than Roland Martin would rely on a $4 kiddy's rod-and-reel outfit. It's not that Roland couldn't catch bass on a cheap rod and reel, but he certainly wouldn't boat fish in the numbers and sizes that he'd like to.

While after mule deer last fall, some friends and I met a teenage bowhunter as he hiked out of a rugged canyon. His old recurve had twisted limbs, and his arrows were a mismatched collection of wood and aluminum shafts held dangerously in a foam-rubber bow quiver with no broadhead cover.

"That guy doesn't have a chance," one of my friends said later, "I'd be willing to bet that each one of his arrows flies differently."

"I'm sure you're right," another friend said, "but before we make too much fun of him, remember that we all started with pretty much the same kind of equipment."

Indeed we had. But it hadn't taken us long to learn that we needed to upgrade our gear. In those days, virtually all bowhunters used the cheap foam bow quivers that left the broadheads exposed. One day, my bow jumped upward while I was unstringing it, and one of the naked broadheads cut my right arm. Fortunately, the wound was minor. After that, I never went afield without a broadhead cover on my quiver. Nowadays, of course, the broadhead cover is an integral part of most bow quivers.

My friends and I also used a mishmash of arrows. An after-school job doesn't often provide enough income to allow the purchase of such luxuries as a dozen matched shafts, so we did with what we could. Now I wonder how we ever managed to kill any game at all. We certainly could have done much better if we'd owned better equipment.

Bowhunting gear should be durable, effective, and silent. For instance, a bow that shoots an arrow at record speeds is nice, but if it is noisy or likely to break down in the field, I want no part of it.

Space does not permit a complete comparison of various bows, so suffice to say that your best choice is probably a compound bow with an adjustable draw weight from 55 to 70 pounds. If you can't shoot a 55-pound bow, get the heaviest bow you can handle under hunting conditions. Don't overbow yourself. One very good hunter I know can shoot a 78-pound bow well, but it was too much for him to draw once when he had to twist to aim at a bull elk that came from an unexpected direction.

A compound's chief advantage is its letoff. My bow, for example, exerts a tension of 65 pounds at half draw and only about 35 pounds at full draw. Therefore, I can hold my bow at full draw far longer than I could hold my old 48-pound recurve bow. That ability has helped me to take several animals, such as my most recent elk. I had been waiting several seconds at full draw when the bull finally presented a clear shot. If I'd had a heavy recurve, I wouldn't have drawn my bow until the last moment. I'm positive that the elk would have seen the movement and fled before I could have shot.

I recommend getting a two-wheel compound instead of a model with four or six pulleys. The fewer moving parts, the more durable and silent the bow. Lately so-called programmed cams have become popular because they increase arrow speed substantially. Programmed cams exert a great deal of stress, however, so the limbs, cables, and bowstring are more likely to break. The last thing I want on a backcountry hunt is a broken bow, so I'm perfectly willing to put up with a little less arrow speed to get that extra reliability.

Another popular item is an overdraw attachment, which allows a hunter to shoot a shorter-than-normal arrow. An overdraw leads to much faster-flying shafts, but it also increases noise and reduces durability. Another disadvantage is that wide broadheads cannot be used.

Your arrows should be neither too stiff nor too flexible for your particular bow and broadhead. Mine are Easton XX75 aluminum shafts, which have a very high tensile strength, meaning that they resist taking a permanent bend when striking a tree or rock. the arrows are also anodized bright orange, so they're easier to find after missing or passing through an animal. I favor aluminum over wood, graphite, or fiberglass shafts because I've found them more durable in the long run.

Some bowhunters still cling to using feather fletching because it is said to be more forgiving of shooting errors. Feather fletching is not very durable and is useless when wet, however. I've tried silicone-based dry-fly dressing to waterproof the feathers, but the coating washed off after half a day in damp brush. Feathers also are noisy when rubbed against brush or other feather fletching. One day, I was hunting in Utah with a man who insisted on using feather fletching. We had stopped to rest, so my companion decided to lay his bow on a sagebrush. As we were sitting, three nice muley bucks fed their way within bow range before we noticed them. My pal grabbed for his bow, but his fletches scraped against the brush and against each other. The deer, naturally, heard the racket and wasted no time in looking elsewhere for the groceries.

Feathers are also noisy in flight. The last time I used turkey quills, I watched two bucks hear my arrows whistle through the air and bolt away from the noise as though my shafts were dive-bombing hawks. Plastic vanes are waterproof, extremely durable, and relatively silent, and I've seen some target shooters rack up some near-perfect scores with them, so I can't see using anything else for hunting.

Arrows can be fletched with three or four vanes. I prefer an arrow with four vanes because the fletching is properly aligned no matter how I nock the arrow. The fletching should be attached in a spiral so that the arrow twists during flight. Such fletching performs the same task as the lands and grooves in a rifle barrel, causing the projectile to act as a gyroscope, reducing the effect of any imperfections and leading to extreme accuracy. This is vital when shooting broadheads, which tend to plane if they don't spin.

The broadhead that you choose should penetrate well, which is largely a function of its design, and it should cut a wide enough section of tissue to kill an animal quickly. I favor a head that is at least one inch wide, and I believe that a four-edged blade is better than a two-edged model. The tip should be knifelike, with a flattened point that slices the instant it begins peneftrating hide. The broadhead also must be precisely made so that it is symmetrical and flies well without planing or whistling. I also like a head that is durable and rust-resistant. The model that I use can be shot into a tree or even a rock and will usually come out undamaged. All I have to do is rehone it.

An arrow rest is a necessity when shooting a compound bow. Some rests are well suited to target shooting but are too fragile for hunting. Three years ago, my friend Jim Craig sent me a fine Wing bow for field testing. It came ready to shoot, with a beautiful spring-steel arrow rest that helped me to obtain some wonderfully small groups. On the first morning I hunted with that bow, however, the rest caught on a branch and bent. I couldn't bend the rest back to its original position, so out came my field repair kit and off went the rest. In its place went my favorite arrow rest, an indestructible Hoyt Hunter. This is a simple soft-plastic affair with a flexible curved finger that keeps an arrow in place. A plastic bar is designed to provide cushioning between the arrow and the bow's sight window but, because I use a cushion plunger, I cut off the bar.

A cushion plunger, also called a Berger button, is a good accessory that can improve your bow's accuracy. It is a spring-loaded plunger that is screwed through the bow's riser and that touches the arrow as it sits on the arrow rest. By adjusting the button in and out or by inserting a stronger or weaker spring, you can use the plunger to eliminate such arrow-flight problems as fishtailing.

Arrow holders are nice little gadgets—when they work properly—but some hold the shaft too tightly or make too much noise when they release the arrow. A friend once had a holder that he liked a great deal until a cold morning stiffened the plastic. When he was drawing on a nice whitetail buck, the holder gripped the arrow and pulled it off the bowstring. The arrow fell to the ground, and the buck was gone.

Anything that you attach to your bow should be thoroughly tested before a hunt. Take, for example, a bow quiver. I bought one quiver that made noises like a pot full of nuts and bolts whenever I shot my bow. I couldn't quiet it down no matter what I tried because the quiver was poorly designed.

Often you can improve a quiver with a few minutes' work. One quiver that I bought had a simple quick-detach feature, but it was loose because there was too much space between the quiver and the bow

Photo by Dan Brockman

plate. I made a plastic spacer from a milk jug, hooked it to the plate, and my problem was solved. The quiver's broadhead cover didn't hold the blades firmly so they rattled against the cover. A chunk of soft foam rubber glued inside the cover corrected that, however.

Unless you're an experienced, instinctive shooter, I'd strongly recommend that you buy a bowsight. The sight should be durable and easy to adjust, but the pins should lock tightly into place. The sight should also have a pin guard—a bar that keeps the pins from being knocked off zero. Incidentally, a pin guard also protects *you*. A friend of mine, hunting with bare pins, fell on his sight, and a pin ripped a horrendous slash in his arm, ending his season.

If you need a set of Allen wrenches to adjust your bowsight, replace the Allen bolts with standard slot-head brass bolts to make field adjustments easier.

141

The jury is out on bow stabilizers: Some hunters think they aid shooting accuracy, while others think they make the bow more difficult to handle and carry.

To prevent arrows from rattling inside your bow quiver, insert a piece of hard or soft foam inside the broadhead cover to cushion them and still any noises.

Add lock washers to each pin and bolt to ensure that the sight stays adjusted, too.

Some fellows use lighted sight pins or tiny battery-powered sight lights for low-light shooting. I believe that if you can't see your pins, it's too dark for shooting, so I don't have such an attachment. Last year, I hunted bears in a state that allows hunting until one full hour after sunset. Believe me, it's much too dark then to consider shooting any sort of game animal with a bow and arrow, let alone a potentially dangerous bear.

One of the most common reasons that bowhunters miss their targets is poor range estimation. Consequently, so-called range-finding sights are popular. All those that I'm familiar with are based on perspective—the principle that an animal looks smaller the farther away it is. One popular model features bowsight pins tipped with metal or plastic rings of varying sizes. The idea is to use the pin that frames the animal's chest most closely.

This sounds nice but, in my experience, range-finder sights don't work very well. One problem is that individuals of any game species vary in size. Another is that it takes good vision and judgment to use such a perspective sight. Figuring that a bale of hay is approximately as narrow as a deer's chest, I tested a perspective range finder a couple of years ago. At a range of 40 yards, I couldn't tell whether the sight read 30, 40, or 50 yards. I can eyeball distance better than that.

If you often misjudge range, either practice a great deal or get a good-quality optical range finder. I've tried several of these instruments and found them suitably accurate at normal bowhunting distances, if the device is calibrated for measuring distances to 400 yards. The short-range models that I've tested aren't precise enough for me.

A peep sight can lead to better accuracy, but I don't use one myself because seeing through a peep in low light can be hard, and the aperture can fill with water, snow, or mud. One of my friends missed a big mule deer because he couldn't see through the peep sight when he drew his bow. He moved his shooting eye a little to one side, tried to adjust for the change, and ended up missing. Afterward, he saw that rain water had filled the sight.

If you use a peep sight, drill the hole bigger to improve low-light visibility. Get a self-aligning model because peep sights are inserted among the strands of the bowstrings and they tend to twist. Self-aligning sights feature a length of surgical tubing attached to the peep at one end and the bow at the other. When you draw your bow, the tubing stretches and aligns the peep.

Be sure to tie your peep sight securely into place with thread or dental floss. Having a peep sight that moves is like having a loose rear sight on a rifle. This is true also of your nocking point indicator. I like the small, rubber-lined brass type because it's easy to install and holds tight. Mount your nocking point indicator above the arrow. That way, you can nock an arrow without looking. In addition, if you hang your bow with an arrow already nocked, the indicator prevents the arrow from sliding upward off the string.

Background photo by Leonard Lee Rue III

Background photo by Leonard Lee Rue III

A cable guard is a necessary accessory of most compound bows because, without it, the arrow's fletching strikes the cables and the arrow will fly poorly. My first compound came without a cable guard. Three-fletched arrows flew well from it, but four-fletched shafts, because of the more acute angle of the vanes, struck the cables and fishtailed badly. I took that bow to California for a wild boar hunt with Chuck Adams, who took one look at my gear and suggested adding one of the newfangled cable guards. After that, my shafts flew much better, and we were able to tune up the bow until it was shooting perfectly.

Another popular accessory is a short stabilizer, which is a weighted rod that reduces twisting and tipping of the bow during a shot. I've used one for the past two years, but I'm not convinced that it helps. It makes the bow heavier and more ungainly and jabs me in the ribs when I carry my bow with a sling, so I doubt I'll use a stabilizer this year.

A bow sling is one accessory that you should seriously consider, particularly if you plan to carry your bow while riding horses or motorcycles. Mine is attached to small, inconspicuous sling swivels threaded into the riser. If you can't find bow slings at your archery dealer, I suggest you contact Wayne Carlton's Hunting Accessories, Box 1746, Montrose, CO 81402.

Some hunters use a string tracking device to help them recover arrow-hit animals. The device consists of a roll of filament mounted in a holder. The free end of the filament is tied to the arrow. When an animal is hit, the string pays out and is supposed to lead the hunter to his game. I don't seem to have problems finding animals I've killed, so I don't use a tracker, but, in some situations, I'd consider using one. While hunting whitetails in New Jersey swamps, I could see how blood trailing there could be extremely difficult. Though friends tell me that trackers work well at ranges of less than 30 yards, I'm reluctant to use one because I've heard of other hunters who have had bad experiences with the gadgets. The string might become wrapped around the bowsight, for instance, ruining a shot. I've had similar experiences while using bowfishing gear. Unless you've seen an arrow stopped in midflight

Marking yardage sightings on your bowsight can help your shooting accuracy.

Replace Allen bolts on your bowsight with slot-head bolts. The change facilitates any field repairs or adjustments.

Inset photo, top: Attaching Molefoam to the riser reduces noise if the arrow falls off the rest. Note Molefoam is also placed on cushion plunger. Inset above left: A Berger button or cushion plunger makes it easier to tune your bow and reduces chance of arrow fishtailing. Inset above right: Some bowhunters use a rubber string silencer, designed to reduce bowstring twang and ensure quiet.

by heavy bowfishing line and shoot back at your head, you don't know what quick reactions are!

The factory finish on many bows is glossy and could alert wary game. I've seen hunters more than a mile away when their uncamouflaged bows flashed in the sun. Some archers are reluctant to ruin the beauty of their bows, so they camouflage them with tape or cloth limb covers. Both add weight to the limbs and slow arrow speed.

My choice of camouflage is dull-finish spray paint. By using stencils or masks made of leaves or twigs, you can make a camouflage paint job very attractive.

To put the final touches on your bow before the hunting season, get a tiny squirt bottle of Triflon lubricant and a package of Molefoam, made by Dr. Scholl's. Triflon leaves particles of lubricating Teflon, which work well even at below-zero temperatures, so it is marvelous for silencing your eccentric wheels and their axles.

Molefoam can work wonders to quiet-proof your bow, too. Most cushion plungers, for example, have hard plastic tips that screech when aluminum arrows are drawn against them. To cure the problem, cut a narrow strip of the self-adhesive Molefoam and apply it across the button. Be sure to sight in your bow after the Molefoam is attached.

Wrap the bottom part of your pin guard with Molefoam, too, and cover the shelf of the sight window as well as the bare metal above and below your arrow rest. This alone has helped me to take my game several times. Once, when I was pivoting to shoot at a deer, my arrow fell off its rest and silently struck the shelf. Because the shelf was padded, there was no metallic ring to spook the animal. When nocking an arrow, I'm sometimes clumsy and tap the arrow against my bowsight or pin guard. When those metal parts are protected, there is little or no game-alerting noise. If your cables make a noise as they rub each other or the cable guard, wrap portions of the cables with Molefoam.

Having the right archery gear won't guarantee that you'll become a big-name bowhunter, any more than buying a top-quality camera will make you an award-winning photographer. But it certainly can't hurt. After all, Ansel Adams didn't get famous by shooting an Instamatic.

Background photo by Leonard Lee Rue III

Bowhunting The Early Season Slump

By Dan Brockman

Where did the deer go?

Five weeks ago, when I was scouting this farm, twenty or more deer fed in the alfalfa field each evening, with half of them young bucks. Even two weeks ago, when the archery season opened, there was plenty of deer activity, though the deer spent more time in the oaks along the edge of the field than out in the field. Now, during an unusually warm last week of September, the deer have seemingly disappeared. I know they're still in the area; I'm just having a difficult time finding them.

With the low average success rates of bowhunters, most states provide the archer with long seasons. These long seasons often begin in late August or September and continue through December or January. The season starts in late summer, runs through autumn, and ends in winter. Through the change of seasons, deer change their habits which affect how and where we hunt them.

The change of seasons means a change in average temperatures, length of daylight (which triggers the rut), a change in food and cover available to deer, and an increase in human activity in the woods when hunting seasons begin.

These seasonal changes affect where deer feed, travel, and bed, the time of day they carry out these activities, how active and cautious they are, and which other members of the herd they travel with. These changes in daily habits can greatly influence the success of the hunter pursuing them.

Even though we may scout throughout the year, we may still be thrown off track during these seasonal changes by not heeding what our scouting reveals. We humans love to get into a pattern of doing something and it's difficult for us to change. Because we saw deer from a certain stand last week, we believe it to be the best location this week as well. If one stand turns cold, it's time to move and find a hot one.

My experience has shown that here in central Wisconsin there is a period from about September 25 through October 25 when the deer activity slumps. This time period coincides with the seasonal change from summer to autumn, during which time leaf drop occurs, average temperatures drop and frosts become more common, some farm crops ripen and are harvested, and acorns and other mast crops begin to fall. This slump period ends when rutting activity suddenly increases near the end of October. Another activity which affects the deer at this time is the increase in human activity in the woods as small game, upland game, and waterfowl seasons begin.

Last fall I spent some time hunting the farm referred to at the beginning of this chapter. I had scouted it in spring and summer. The summer scouting showed the deer feeding primarily in the alfalfa field and bedding within 200 yards of the field in some hazelnut brush in the woods. A small creek runs along one side of the alfalfa field so the deer had plenty of food, water, and cover within a few hundred square yards.

I found a few promising stand sites about 50 to

Reprinted courtesy of DEER & DEER HUNTING magazine.

A good, sturdy portable stand will help make your early season bowhunt a sucessful one. The trick is not getting too comfortable with a particular location; if it turns cold, it's time to move on to hot one.

100 yards from the field, along trails leading from the bedding areas to the field. I sat in some of these stands in late August and early September, prior to the opening of the bow season, and observed plenty of deer within easy bow range. Even during the first few days of the archery season, these stands produced sightings and I passed up does and small bucks which passed by my stand.

About one week into the season, I noticed the activity around the stands was beginning to taper off. Thinking I somehow spooked the deer in the area of the stands, I tried hunting other locations along the trails leading to the alfalfa field. Still no luck. It

was time to find where the deer had gone.

A short scouting trip revealed some interesting facts. The trails I had been hunting that led from bedding areas to the alfalfa field were now getting little use. Instead, the deer were now using trails that came from bedding areas deeper in the woods, led through oak stands, then on to the alfalfa field. Also, I found a few rubs along these trails and noticed that the acorns were beginning to drop and that there was a lot of deer sign in the oak stands. The deer were apparently feeding first in the oaks, then heading to the fields after dark if they were still hungry. The old bedding areas were beginning to open up as the hazel brush lost its leaves and the deer found new bedding areas deeper in the woods.

I also noticed at this time that the bucks weren't traveling in the large bachelor groups as in summer. The hierarchy had been established, the velvet shed, and the first urges of the rut were being felt.

I moved my stands to cover the trails leading from the new bedding areas to the oaks and I immediately began seeing more deer, but not as many as I thought I should have considering all the signs present. Scratching out the deer tracks on the trails in the evening and checking them again before daylight showed that many of the deer moved during the night. The night movements may have been caused by the warm weather. The deer now wore their new winter coats and may have been waiting to travel until it cooled off at night. Also, the increased human activity in the woods as the archery, squirrel, grouse, and woodcock seasons opened may have caused the deer to become more nocturnal.

Hot, dry weather seems to adversely affect deer movements, with cool or cold, damp weather maintaining good activity. Of course, a heavy rain will usually dampen the deer activity in more ways than one, but a light drizzle often seems to cause an increase in deer activity.

The early part of the season will often be warm, with the woods the thick, lush green of summer. This thick growth makes it easy for the hunter to hide, but also easy for the deer to hide. The warm weather also works against the hunter by causing him to perspire with the slightest activity, which leads to body odor. Warm weather also means mosquitos and other insects which can make hunting uncomfortable. A good insect repellent will help keep the bugs at bay, but the odor may also spook the deer. One thing in the hunter's favor during the first week or two of the season is that the deer haven't been hunted for several months and may be less cautious than later in the season.

After shedding their velvet in early September, the deer begin to feel the first urges of the upcoming rut, with the urges getting stronger as autumn progresses. You will notice an increase in rubbing activity and may begin to find a few scrapes in early October. It may be possible to hunt these early scrapes with some success, though I've never observed much action around them. Most of them seem to be once-made, soon-forgotten scrapes.

Throughout October here in Wisconsin the leaves drop, resulting in a great change in the forest and in the deer's daily habits. As the leaves drop, feeding and bedding areas open and the deer often move to thicker, more secure cover. They may continue to feed in open areas but seem to prefer doing it under cover of darkness.

This is also the time of year when corn begins to harden and become more attractive to deer, and they seek the cornfields for both food and cover. If many of the local deer move to the cornfields, you will often notice activity in other areas drop to almost nothing. A few years ago, a couple of deer man-

agement units here in Wisconsin had unusually low kills during the gun deer season. Department of Natural Resources game managers attributed this to an unusual amount of standing corn in the area due to a wet autumn. About the only way to hunt deer living in cornfields is to try still hunting them on dry, windy days when the noise of the wind-rustled leaves covers the noise of your approach.

As the cornfields are harvested, deer are forced back into the woods and you may witness a couple days of very good hunting as the deer try to settle into their new environment.

Often, just before the first good rutting activity starts (about October 25 where I hunt), deer activity plummets. One old-timer told me that this is caused by the does hiding from the bucks. He said the bucks are chasing the does and trying to breed but the does aren't ready for the aggressive bucks. His theory does make some sense, but I can't prove it one way or the other.

The early part of the archery season, during the transition from summer to fall, can be one of the toughest times for the bow hunter. With plenty of food and cover available, the deer don't have to travel far to find either. The rut hasn't started, there may be an influx of other hunters in the woods as small game seasons open, the weather may be warm, and insects may be thick; everything seems to be against the bow hunter.

While there may be three or four weeks of tough hunting, there are ways to be successful.

It's important to maintain an active scouting program to learn when and where the deer change their habits. Remember where you found them at this time other years and check those areas. If there are farm crops in your area, watch how they progress and if the deer are utilizing them. When the acorns and apples start dropping, watch for deer feeding on them. In hot weather the deer usually move very early and very late in the day, so set up as close to bedding areas as possible to catch the deer moving during daylight hours. One area where I've had consistently good early-season luck is in river bottoms where there are stinging nettles and oak trees. The deer feed heavily on the nettle flowers and acorns and the thick canopy of large trees keeps it a few degrees cooler in the lowlands. The only problem with hunting the river bottoms in the early season is the mosquitos are often bothersome.

Wherever you hunt during the early season—oak ridges, river bottoms, old orchards, or farm crops— a quality portable stand will be a great aid in your hunting success. A portable stand allows you to change locations as the deer move, which is an important factor if you're going to keep track of the early season deer.

Careful attention to details and a willingness to change hunting locations to follow the deer can produce good results for the bowhunter hunting the early season slump. You may not find the almost frenzied activity that you'll find during the rut, but the deer are still there and you can find them.

PART 6

SAFETY AND SURVIVAL

Staying Warm In A Tree Stand

By Jeff Murray

It was quite a jolt when I first stepped outside of the deer shack that morning; my comfortable Minnesota Indian summer had turned into a squaw winter almost overnight. Just two days ago, the old outdoor thermometer, bearing a faded Marilyn Monroe figure with her classic ruby lipstick smile, had reached a balmy 64 degrees. This morning, she read only 10 degrees.

Undaunted, I forged on. Had to get to that deer stand . . . running late . . . overslept.

Although my mind was still groggy from a lousy night's sleep, my step was light and lively. Adrenaline surged through my veins while I recalled all the bucks taken off that tree stand over the years. The only trick was to stay on it all day without coming down for even a moment, for its location was strategically chosen: Hunter pressure from the east, north, and south could virtually be counted on to push deer along the brushy creek bed that it overlooked. Sooner or later, a buck with my number on it would try to sneak by, and experience had taught me that it could be any time of day.

But this day would not go as planned. Instead of being the victor, I would become a victim, of sorts. Oh, a buck came sneaking by all right, and I even got off a decent shot. At least that's what I thought I did. I can't remember the details, although I've tried a million times. To this day, it still plagues me. Only recently, breakthroughs in medical research have

A winning combination of proper dress and diet can turn a vigil in a tree stand from ordeal to fun.

148

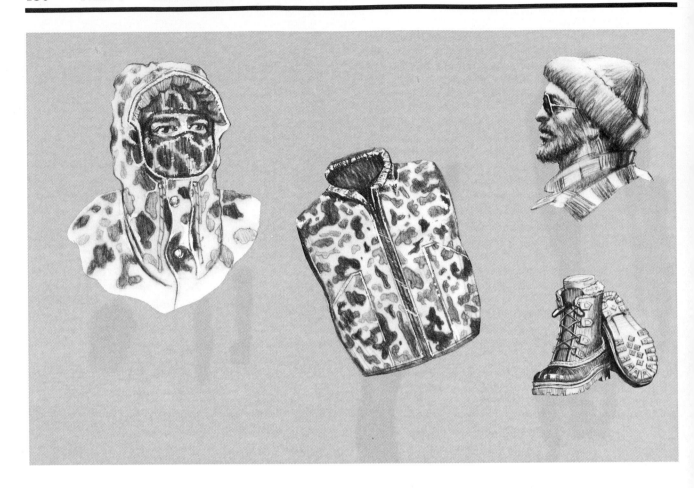

helped to unravel the mystery, so there shouldn't be a repeat performance.

What does medicine have to do with deer hunting? A lot. And if you do much hunting from a stand during cool weather, chances are mighty good that you have been or could be victimized as I was.

Dr. Robert Pozos, a nationally known researcher on hypothermia from the University of Minnesota, has studied the human body's defense system with respect to how it copes with extreme cold. From my conversations with him, I think I learned why I missed that buck.

He started by asking a series of probing questions, to which many a hunter would probably have had to answer yes: Were you in a hurry that morning? Did you work up a sweat? Was there a wind? Did you hunt from an elevated stand? Did the weather suddenly turn cold? Did you drink coffee that morning? Did you find yourself experiencing moderate or severe shivering?

"It's really no mystery," Dr. Pozos concluded. "You were obviously suffering from the initial stages of hypothermia."

"Hypothermia?!" I said in disbelief. "I thought only lost arctic travelers or drowning victims suffered from that."

"Well, those are the classic cases most often cited," he said. "But you deer hunters are especially vulnerable because you hunt during marginal weather in the fall. Of course, most guys come down from their stands well before succumbing to hypothermia, but it still affects performance and makes life miserable. Hypothermia is a threat when the weather is less severe and you can be caught off guard."

According to Dr. Pozos, temperatures below 40 degrees, coupled with a little wind and a wet body, are all it takes. That potentially includes an awful lot of hunters across the nation at one time or another, and not just North Woods hackers like me. Fortunately, Dr. Pozos had some practical advice that could help us to stay warm and, it is hoped, keep us on our deer stands until that buck drops by.

First we need to know a few things about heat loss and heat generation. Body heat loss is accomplished primarily through five processes: radiation, conduction, convection, evaporation, and respiration. Body heat, on the other hand, is generated by only two means: radiant heat and metabolic rate. Obviously, the two aren't in perfect balance. The whole key is to evaluate each component in an effort to minimize heat loss while maximizing the opportunities for heat generation. By doing this, we can come up with a systematic approach that really works for us.

Radiant heat loss is influenced mostly by shape. Heat always flows from warm objects to colder ones, and uniform, spherical objects lose their heat proportionately faster than those that are irregularly shaped. Tests have shown that billiard balls cool off four times faster than other objects of a similar size and weight. That's why a bareheaded hunter—especially a bald one—who is in the woods without a warm hat or cap is going to get chilled no matter what he's got on his back, hands, or feet. Even if you have a head of hair like a Greek god, you won't be much better off; the brain requires 25 percent of the body's hot blood. So, perhaps more serious consideration ought to go into what goes on your head. Stocking caps are popular but, if there is a strong wind, a ski mask under an insulated hat might be a wiser choice.

The neck is often overlooked but, due to the closeness of large arteries there to exposed air, it is just as important as the head. Parkas are best for extreme conditions and, at the very least, a heavy turtleneck dickey (which can be added or removed easily) should be standard gear.

Heat loss by conduction occurs when something cold touches something warm. It is the least concern for most cold-weather activities, but not for the deer hunter on a stand. You simply can't avoid sitting or standing on something that's colder than you are. The best way to handle conduction is by blocking the heat flow from your fanny and your feet with a good insulator. The most effective material I've found to date is Styrofoam. I carry a two-inch-thick chunk into the woods to sit on and it really helps. Once broken in, it will conform to my body shape and be quite comfortable. On occasion, it may be necessary to wrap a wool blanket around the Styrofoam to keep noise at a minimum.

Cold feet have caused the not-so-grand exit of many a dedicated stand hunter, and I think that the problem will always be with us to kick around. Although much of the problem is physiological, much is psychological. As Dr. Pozos said, "Some guys can live with pain and some just can't stand it." I'm one who can't, so you can imagine how many different styles of footwear—from Moon Boots to Army-surplus models—I've tried over the years. I know I don't stand alone in this department, yet I see many hunters who will spend $150 on a nice jacket or parka and walk around in a pair of $19.95 specials. Boots are no place to scrimp. Felt-lined packs have provided yeoman service for years, and they should be satisfactory for short walks over dry ground. But for longer treks into the back country, where swamps and creeks might be encountered, I prefer the new Thinsulate-insulated Guide Boot, which is available from mail-order houses. The boots are lightweight, warm, and almost waterproof with their rubber lug soles. When sizing these boots, though, be sure to go two full sizes larger than your street shoes so two pairs of wool socks can be worn when necessary; too many hunters make the mistake of pinching their toes and reducing vital circulation. You can go a step further and cut Styrofoam to the contour of your foot and wedge it in the bottom of the boot. Or you can add a Thinsulate/Gore-Tex sock to further increase warmth and dryness. If you stick with regular wool

socks, however, be sure to buy them in two sizes, with the smaller one going on first. And by all means carry extras—your feet have more than 250,000 sweat glands capable of excreting a half pint of liquid in one day.

Heat loss by convection, or circulation, became well known in the outdoor community when weather forecasters first started indexing the so-called windchill factor. That was a darn good idea; it's a factor to reckon with. Who cares if the temperature is going to be 20 degrees tomorrow when the dang wind is going to make it feel like 15 degrees below zero? (That's precisely what a 25-mph wind will do.) Smart deer hunters don't hunt with their backs to the wind, but they still can do two things to thwart the chill of the wind. First, they can dress in layers instead of wearing one or two thick garments. That will not only trap more air—nature's best insulator—but will also provide you with the flexibility to put on and take off clothing as conditions dictate.

Secondly, by slipping a raincoat under your overcoat, you can cut wind penetration and stay dry, even if it rains. Rainwear made from breathable materials, such as Gore-Tex, would certainly make sense. This intermediate layer should also include those insulating materials that trap the most air with the least amount of loft, thus increasing maneuverability. Bowhunters especially appreciate this. Traditionally, down has been the top insulator, but there's a little jingle that backpackers like to sing: "Up with down till it gets wet, for then you can bet you've got a threat . . . yet when it's dry, you'll have few regrets." If getting wet can be a problem where you hunt, consider Thinsulate, pile, Insulite, Bunting, or Polar Fleece. These materials retain thermal-resistance properties even when wet.

When the body does get wet, it falls prey to the worst heat-loss mechanism of all—evaporation. A wet body will lose heat 200 times faster than a dry one and, when you combine that with the windchill factor, you've got double trouble. Sweating, a primary cause of evaporation, is the biggest no-no for the deer hunter, according to Dr. Pozos.

"If hunters knew how vicious the sweat cycle was," he told me, "they wouldn't take it so lightly."

What's so vicious about a litte moisture buildup? According to Dr. Pozos, the process starts out as simple water vapor excreted through the skin but, when it reaches the layer of clothing that's below the dew point, it condenses and wets that layer. Latent heat is liberated and released into the air—unfortunately, well away from the skin. Eventually, your clothing wicks the moisture back to your skin, where latent heat is again drawn from your body in order to evaporate the moisture. This goes on until your clothing dries out, even though the body is trying to conserve heat, not give it away as it did when it decided to sweat.

This cycle commands respect, not just mere understanding. Interestingly, the key to its defeat is the underwear that you put next to your skin, which experts now believe to be the most important component of the anticold system. If moisture can be kept away from the skin, most heat loss initiated by evaporation can be eliminated. For many years, a good wool union suit, for those who could handle the itching, used to be the only undergarment found in deer camps. And wool still makes some sense—its wicking properties are well documented. But some of the new synthetics do a better job of transmitting moisture—both vapor and liquid—and feel soft to the skin. Polypropylene is one. Du Pont's Thermax, the latest entry on the market, is reported to be one-sixth the diameter of human hair with hollow center. Indeed, these new miracle fabrics do a marvelous job of keeping the skin dry, but the best thing about them, I think, is their ability to combine with other insulating materials. Last winter, I tried Kenyon's Strata, a line of polypropylene that adds an additional layer of Insulite which is a Meraklon synthetic. Sure I stayed dry, but I was just as impressed with its thermal properties. I may never go back to the woolies again.

Finally, respiration, or ordinary breathing, can be an important heat-loss factor in cold weather. When you inhale cold air, it is warmed by thousands of tiny blood vessels and brought to 100 percent humidity before it is exhaled. Even here, Dr. Pozos had a few practical recommendations for conserving heat. Because the lungs have the surface area of a tennis court, they can deliver the moisture needed to condition intake air. But to do that, they need lots of water. Pozos suggested drinking large quantities of water to assist the lungs in that function. Covering your mouth with a scarf or face mask can also cut down on respiratory heat loss.

On the plus side of the heat loss/heat gain equation, we have only radiant heat and metabolic heat to play with. Radiant heat can only be garnered by placing your stand in a sunny area, when possible. Body metabolism, however, is a much more controllable factor, with diet and exercise as its vehicles.

Most kinds of exercise are obviously out of the question. Every buck in the country is going to avoid a red-jacketed figure doing calisthenics in a tree. But you can do isometric contractions of different muscle groups without raising a flag. Just be sure to keep it up for 20-minute intervals or you won't notice any lasting benefits—wiggling toes included. Another good idea is to hunt out of two stands in fairly close proximity to one another. That way, you can sneak-hunt from one location to the other, warming yourself up in the process, and keep your scent out of the area that you intend to hunt. You should also be able to stay on top of the deer without letting them weasel by you when other hunters are likely to be moving them your way.

Diet selection isn't as cut-and-dried as I once thought it was. Standard advice for combating the cold has been to load up on "high energy" foods—whatever that means. Carbohydrates, such as candy bars, and beverages such as coffee and cocoa are often mentioned. Again, Dr. Pozos had an interesting perspective to offer.

"I have found no scientific basis for recommending sugars as a cold-weater dietary aid," he said. "There may be some empirical, or practical, evidence that suggests such a course for some individuals, but I'd be tempted to go with more fats than carbohydrates. And I would strongly discourage both coffee and chocolate."

Fats are also a good bet, according to commercial fisherman Stanley Sivertson, who has worked the frigid waters of Lake Superior for more than 50 years. He eats plenty of oil-rich herring when he is going to be on the water for long periods of time. Further evidence from research involving Eskimos, who generally eat a lot of high-fat foods, might give credence to Sivertson's theory. In one study, Caucasians and Alaskan Indians were tested to see how long they could keep their hands in 50-degree water. Some Eskimos fell asleep, while the longest a non-Indian could take it was about one minute!

Liquids should be carefully chosen, too. Recently, the Mayo Clinic confirmed the findings of Mount Sinai Medical Center's research on chicken soup: It's not only good, but *good for you* because it is clinically effective in clearing stuffy nasal passages.

Coffee and chocolate are bad for one simple reason: They have significant amounts of caffeine, which blocks a hormone that enables the body to restrain urination. And the less you get caught with your pants down, the less bare surface area you'll be exposing to the elements. The same obviously goes for bowel movements. You have some control here, too, believe it or not. The solution involves acclimation. When the deer season rolls around, most hunters are not accustomed to the early hours required for reaching their stands by sunrise. Consequently, their digestive systems are out of whack. But by keeping earlier hours *before* the season, bodily functions can be put into line so that elimination can be accomplished before climbing that stand.

Dr. Pozos added that the body's defensive strategy against the cold can be acclimated, too. By purposely underdressing before the season and spending time in the woods, you can prepare other bodily functions—including metabolism and the repiratory system. This way, when the first wintery cold front hits, it won't seem like a January storm. In fact, a recent poll somewhat confirmed this. Respondents were asked which was the mildest month, November or March. Nearly 80 percent of the participants said that March was milder. In most of the states where the interviews were conducted, however, November had a higher mean temperature. What's going on here is acclimation: By the time March arrives, the body has long since become conditioned by previous winter months.

There's a lot more to the hunt than picking a good spot for your deer stand. After strategies have been drawn, go ahead and climb that stand, keeping these ideas in mind. And stick to it. You *can* stand it.

Hypothermia!

By Kent Horner

Hypothermia refers to the lowering of one's body temperature below the normal setting of 98.6 degrees Fahrenheit. This physiological condition can strike the deer hunter while he sits on stand in cold weather.

Should your body temperature fall to 85 degrees F, you'll pass out and remain in suspended animation until you warm. At a body temperature of 75 degrees F, the heart and body functions stop and death occurs.

While on stand, of course, the deer hunter must remain motionless, else the wary whitetail may detect the hunter's movements. The technique of stand-hunting is based on surprising one's prey through nondetection. The two coinciding factors of the deer hunter's immobility and cold temperature can cause both discomfort and danger during his wintertime hunting.

THE WHITETAIL'S SECRET

The whitetail deer evolved ways and means to protect himself during winter. The hunter, however, has lost some of his more primitive means of escaping the cold and must now use his reasoning ability more in staving off the severity of the elements.

The whitetail, for instance, after eating nutritious fall foods, enters winter with a few pounds of fat packed along his backbone. This calorie supply, coupled with very little wintertime movement and his wintertime browse—even if sparse—usually enables the deer to survive. A cold-weather calorie supply, from either internal fat or from their diet, is important to whitetails in winter.

A deer also has the ability to erect the hair on his body. This physiological process is called piloerection, which means that the deer's hairs stand on end. This traps a layer of warm air around the deer's body, forming an insulating coat that protects the deer from the cold surroundings. Also, deer sweat very little, which helps them maintain their body heat in winter.

Here, then, we see that the production and maintenance of body heat are critical factors for any warmblooded animal during cold weather. That goes for both the whitetail and the hunter.

We know that not all animals are warm-blooded; therefore, some creatures must hibernate during periods of cold weather. Snakes, for example, are cold-blooded. The deer hunter can rest a little easier when he knows that no poisonous snakes are around. In my case, living in Alabama, I don't have to worry about the rattlesnakes after cold weather begins.

WHAT REGULATES BODY TEMPERATURE

The ability for warm-bloodedness is regulated by the hypothalamus region in the lower, more primitive part of an animal's brain. Cold-blooded animals, through the course of evolution, did not evolve this ability. For those animals that did evolve warm-bloodedness, however, a great breakthrough was reached, for it enabled their wintertime mobility.

The nerve tissue in the hypothalamus that regu-

Reprinted courtesy of DEER & DEER HUNTING *magazine.*

WIND CHILL CALCULATION CHART

Equivalent Temperature (°F)

Windspeed (Miles per hour)	Calm	35	30	25	20	15	10	5	0	−5	−10	−15	−20	−25	−30	−35	−40	−45
5		33	27	21	16	12	7	1	−6	−11	−15	−20	−26	−31	−35	−41	−47	−54
10		21	16	9	2	−2	−9	−15	−22	−27	−31	−38	−45	−52	−58	−64	−70	−77
15		16	11	1	−6	−11	−18	−25	−33	−40	−45	−51	−60	−65	−70	−78	−85	−90
20		12	3	−4	−9	−17	−24	−32	−40	−46	−52	−60	−68	−76	−81	−88	−96	−103
25		7	0	−7	−15	−22	−29	−37	−45	−52	−58	−67	−75	−83	−89	−96	−104	−112
30		5	−2	−11	−18	−26	−33	−41	−49	−56	−63	−70	−78	−87	−94	−101	−109	−117
35		3	−4	−13	−20	−27	−35	−43	−52	−60	−67	−72	−83	−90	−98	−105	−113	−123
40		1	−4	−15	−22	−29	−36	−45	−54	−62	−69	−76	−87	−94	−101	−107	−116	−128
45		0	−6	−17	−24	−31	−38	−46	−54	−63	−70	−78	−87	−94	−101	−108	−118	−128
50		0	−7	−17	−24	−31	−38	−47	−56	−63	−70	−79	−88	−96	−103	−110	−120	−128

lates body temperature in warm-blooded animals differs from that of cold-blooded animals. In the warm-blooded animals, the hypothalamus region that rests just below the brain at the top of the spinal cord acts as a heat thermostat. In short, this neural thermostat controls body hormones that regulate the amount of heat generated in the body cells and carried by the blood.

That thermostat is tuned to the seasons, too. When seasonally cool weather arrives, it causes the hypothalamus to stimulate the thyroid gland and its hormone production. Within a few weeks, the hunter's rate of heat production increases about 30 percent as winter begins. Thus, we say that we are conditioned to the cold weather.

Heat loss is regulated by controlling the rate of blood flow in the skin. This, in turn, regulates the rate at which heat transfers from the body core to the body surface.

COLD-WEATHER FOODS

Body cells can produce more heat if an increased amount of dissolved foods are carried to them. Thus prior food intake *does* help keep the hunter warm while he's sitting on stand.

Skipping breakfast before going to your stand is not a good idea during cold-weather deer hunting. Also, a high protein diet of bacon, sausage, or some other protein food for breakfast increases the hunter's metabolic rate about 30 percent. In contrast, a meal of carbohydrates (pancakes and syrup) only increases the hunter's metabolic rate by about five percent. Carbohydrates such as a chocolate bar, however, provide a quick burst of energy when you're tired. This effect is referred to by the medical profession as the specific dynamic action of foods.

After a protein meal, the hunter's metabolic rate remains elevated for up to ten hours. That sure helps while you sit several feet up in the air in a cool breeze waiting for a buck. For a carbohydrate meal, the metabolic rate is elevated for only about two hours.

WARM-UP EXERCISES

The best stimulus for increasing the hunter's heat production is exercise. This, though, can create a Catch 22 dilemma unless the hunter works it right. Under intense exercise lasting a few moments, the hunter's metabolic rate may increase to forty times its normal, basal rate. Further, under less intense but still very rigorous exercise, the hunter's metabolic rate may be maintained at 20 times its normal, basal rate. That's when you really sweat because the basal metabolic rate for most humans is about 60 to 70 calories per hour under resting conditions.

The hunter, however, should sweat as little as possible before reaching his stand. But that often is quite impractical. When we do sweat profusely, there's a price to pay. The cost? About 540 calories of heat loss for every quart that you sweat. When under intense physical activity, the hunter may sweat 1.5 quarts per hour. That's about three pounds of liquid.

The maintenance of muscle tone can raise your metabolic rate by 400 percent. You can increase this even further by doing isometric exercises while sitting in freezing weather and waiting for a deer to come by. While doing isometrics, you don't noticeably move—or at least not much. Thus, you can do this if you're careful and still scan the woodland for deer. One good way to do isometrics while sitting 15 or 20 feet up in your tree stand is to push and pull with your hands and arms on the side bars of your stand. Too, I push on the bottom of the stand with my feet and legs. This arm and leg action uses energy from the larger muscles.

As always, when up in a tree stand you should be careful. Never exert any force that might cause you to take a tumble. Should that happen when you are cold, it makes matters worse because your reflexes are slowed. Another isometric exercise is to simply clasp your hands together and push and pull. This contracts the arm and back muscles. The idea is to contract your larger muscle groups so they will

Photo by Leonard Lee Rue III

The whitetail, after eating nutritious fall foods, enters winter with a few pounds of fat packed along his backbone.

burn more calories within them. The heat will then be carried by the blood to your other body parts.

Isometrics do work. And naturally your increased heat production depends upon how hard you work at it. After ten or fifteen minutes, you do feel yourself warming up.

FIRST SYMPTOMS

Some of the first symptoms of hypothermia include slurred speech and uncontrolled shivering. Uncontrolled shivering is the body's attempt to maintain normal body temperatures. These shivering movements increase the rate of heat production by about 300 percent or more.

Perspiring is a problem for the deer hunter any way you look at it. When we sweat, diluted nitrogenous body wastes are given off through the skin.

Sweat, in a sense, is similar to a dilute solution of urine. Both carry waste products from our body. Bacteria soon invade these waste products and give us our peculiar human odors. Further, a white-tailed buck can match a bloodhound in sniffing out these human odors. The hunter adage, "a deer lives or dies by his nose" is, for the most part, true. Sweating, then, not only helps cause hypothermia later when the liquid evaporates and cools your body, it can also cost you a buck through odor detection.

LAYERED CLOTHING

Most deer hunters soon learn that layered clothing is effective in combating the cold. Goose down and wool are good natural insulators for the deer hunter, showing once again that Mother Nature knows how to take care of her creatures. Some synthetic fibers are also quite effective for warding off the cold. The important point is not so much the composition but whether or not the material remains dry.

The layers form an envelope of warm air around the hunter as he maintains his own body heat. This works as long as the layers of clothing remain dry. Earlier, I mentioned that the whitetail can perform piloerection of his body hairs and make them stand on end. This insulation of warm air protects him from the cold. The hunter cannot effectively do this because, in contrast to a deer, he has relatively little body hair. What hair you have, though, does help in insulating you from the cold.

Your boss may not socially or philosophically agree with your wearing a beard during deer hunting season, but that tonsorial item does come in handy in forming some insulation over your face and head when you're sitting on stand. You might consider taking your boss deer hunting in cold weather. Chances are he'll better appreciate the reason for your beard.

Sufficient layers of dry clothing, however, provide the best answer to your comfort when you're out in the cold. During freezing weather, should your clothing become waterlogged with sweat, you could have a real problem with hypothermia. The envelopes of air between the clothing layers then fail to act as an insulator. Surprisingly, should your clothing become totally soaked, the heat loss from your body is nearly the same as if you were nude in cold weather. In that case, the hunter should waste no time in either changing clothes or drying out immediately in a warm place.

In researching the hunter physiology aspects of this chapter, I interviewed Dr. Carlos Zeller, a medical doctor who lived in Kotzebue, Alaska, and worked with the Eskimos. His statements on the hunter combating hypothermia follow.

STEPS TO FOLLOW

"In extremely cold weather the hunter should reduce his body surface exposure to the cold as much as possible. Some tips for the hunter in the extreme cold: protect your head; keep your ears flattened against your head (a skull cap and face mask work fine); make your hand into a fist instead of spreading your fingers; wear mittens instead of gloves (manufacturers now make modified shooting mittens for both bowhunters and gun hunters); keep the body as free of sweat as possible (if possible, buckle your tree stand up the night before you climb, or wear lightweight clothing while hiking to your stand, then put on your heavyweight coveralls immediately before climbing or sitting on stand; if it's a long way to your stand, stop a few times and rest to keep from sweating much); while sitting on stand, drink warm liquids (a thermos of coffee or hot chocolate helps; if your body can tolerate it, some caffeine does alleviate fatigue); drink no alcohol—you may feel warmer but you're losing in the long term. Alcohol dilates the blood vessels in the skin and exposes

more blood to the cold. Keep your body core warm—the chest, heart, lung, kidney, and liver regions; your own body fat helps to keep you warm too. If you're going to gain weight, gain it during cold weather. Some medical doctors contend that humans become hungrier for meaty foods during winter. Give in and eat more meat during cold weather."

I've incorporated Dr. Zeller's medical advice with some of my own field and hunting experience. As a hunter, however, I know that there are many times in the excitement of the moment when it isn't practical to stop and either add or subtract layers of clothing. Sometimes the hunter just has to "gut it out," and suffer a certain amount of sweat and cold.

Example: You've just shot a buck from your stand after six hours of sitting and waiting, and you decide to check for a blood trail. You feel half-frozen already so, naturally, you don't care to make matters worse by stripping off a lot of clothes. Besides, you may not have to walk very far, you think. So you start tracking. After 200 yards, you jump the buck; this time he runs toward your hunting buddy's stand.

What follows then is a dramatic mountainside scenario of running, hollering, falling over a rock, rolling down a cliff, and getting slapped in the face six times as you run through "sapling city." Then, a mile down the mountainside, you finally come upon "your" buck after another hunter has already dispatched him.

By now you're drowning in your own lather and upset that an unknown hunter shot your deer. Further, your hunting buddy looks back up the terrain whence you came and secretly hopes that in the ensuing negotiations you lose. For him to help you tote the deer back up the mile-long mountainside strewn with rocks and cliffs is going to take hours.

But you believe that the hunter who drew first blood should be the owner of the deer. Finally, after the unknown hunter looks back over the rough terrain where his vehicle is parked, he too becomes a believer in first blood. He then declares you owner of the deer.

So, four hours later—carrying your outer, heavy camo overalls, three wool sweatshirts, two pairs of pants, four long-john tops—but minus your canteen (you left it at your tree stand), you arrive at your vehicle with your deer and dying of thirst.

The questioning words of your beloved spouse ring in your head. "Honey, why do you want to leave a warm bed at 3:30 A.M. and go sit in the top of a tree and freeze?"

But you know the answer. It's lying there on the tailgate of your truck. Five very long tines adorn each side of its head. Too, you know that those tines will grow even longer when you retell your heroics among other bearded brethren on other hunts.

Furthermore, memories of the morning's freezing cold and the four-hour uphill tote are fading fast as you borrow your hunting buddy's canteen, replenish your body fluids, and promise him and the rest of the hunting party a dinner later if they'll just give you one sandwich now.

How To Prevent Hunting Accidents

By Kirk H. Beattie

Sam and George began hunting for the elusive buck just as the sun came over the ridge. They walked abreast, Sam taking one side of the small valley and George taking the other. The buck arose from its bed in front of them and began to run back between them. Sam quickly raised his scoped .30/06, found the buck in the sights, and fired. The 180-grain bullet missed the buck and smashed into George's chest, killing him instantly.

Joe thought it would be quicker and easier to drive around the back roads looking for deer. After driving for a half-hour, he saw a nice six-pointer cross the road in front of him. He raced up to where the buck crossed. Joe grabbed the barrel of the uncased, loaded 12 gauge semiautomatic lying on the passenger-side floorboard. The slug entered right above the bridge of the nose and took off the back of his head.

John was a veteran deer hunter, in this case meaning he had hunted many years but had yet to kill a buck. It was only the third day of the firearms season and his four buddies back at camp already each had a deer. They always pestered him about coming back to camp with little more than the makings for "pellet soup."

A motion to John's left startled him. He quickly raised his open-sighted .30/30 and fired in the brush at what he thought was a buck digging in the snow for acorns. The buck turned out to be another hunter looking for his fallen glasses. Blood from the fatal wound quickly colored the snow.

Eight of the 12-member hunting party lined up 75 yards apart to begin the drive through Harbor Swamp. Frank and three other standers lined up about 100 yards apart at the end of the swamp where the drivers would come out. Not more than two minutes after the drivers started hooting and hollering, Frank saw a high-racked ten-pointer moving quickly in front of the drivers toward him. His semi-automatic .308 barked five times and the big buck went down. At the same time, one of the drivers screamed. Frank's eleven-year-old son died soon after the bullet passed through his belly.

These four accounts of Wisconsin deer hunting accidents are true, with the exception of fictitious names, and are representative of accidents that occur in Wisconsin and other states. Recently, I analyzed accidents like the above, which happened over a 31-year period from 1951 through 1981. Unless deer hunting accidents are specifically mentioned, the following results refer to accidents for all game species combined.

AGE AND HUNTING ACCIDENTS

Young deer hunters are more likely to be involved in hunting accidents than the veteran deer hunter. Like the old buck who has seen six winters pass, the veteran hunter has learned safety in the woods. For example, hunters 20 years old or younger make up 23 percent of all Wisconsin deer hunters but are involved in 53 percent of the self-inflicted accidents. Hunters ranging in age from 12 to 16 are not more likely than older hunters to become involved in two-

Reprinted courtesy of DEER & DEER HUNTING magazine.

Table 1. Age distribution of Wisconsin firearm deer hunters and those involved in accidents

Age	Hunters	Self-Inflicted Shooters	2-Person Judgment Shooters	2-Person Victims
12–13	3%	10%	3%	4%
14–15	6%	16%	4%	8%
16–20	14%	27%	23%	21%
21+	77%	47%	70%	67%

Table 2. Wisconsin hunting accidents prior to, during, and following the start of hunter education programs

Year(s)	Average Number of Accidents	Average Annual Number of Accidents per 100,000 Hunters
1951–1966	161	27.2
1967[a]	197	30.4
1968–1981	143	19.1

[a]Start of Wisconsin Hunter Education Program

person accidents. But 16- to 20-year-olds are more likely than either younger or older hunters to be involved in a two-person accident as either shooters or victims. The fact is that the younger hunter (less than 21 years old) is more likely to be part of a hunting accident. This is a good reason for youngsters, and even older first-time hunters, to complete a hunter education course.

HUNTING EXPERIENCE

At least 50 percent of all deer hunting accidents involve hunters with five years or less hunting experience. Deer hunters involved in accidents tended to not only have less hunting experience but also started hunting later in life. The old adage is true: There is no substitute for experience.

HUNTING FATALITIES

Don't be misled into thinking that hunting is more dangerous than other recreational activities. Some Michigan researchers found that deer hunting was 2.5 times safer, in terms of fatalities, than driving an automobile. Hunting ranks low among sports activities and ties with college football, both have 0.3 fatalities per 100,000 participants. About one of every ten Wisconsin hunting accidents produces a fatality. More than one-half of the fatalities occur during the nine-day deer gun season, possibly because of high-powered rifles, high-velocity ammunition, concentrations of hunters, and high excitement levels.

One factor common to virtually all deer hunting accidents is that those involved are males. It doesn't take a Ph.D. to figure this out. Most hunters are males and men hunt more frequently than women.

One important factor stands out when analyzing deer hunting accidents: Three out of every four accidents involve members of the same hunting party. This is a good reason for knowing the location of your hunting partners at all times.

HUNTING ACCIDENT NUMBERS

The number of hunting accidents occurring annually in Wisconsin changed greatly between 1951 and 1981. In 1967, the Wisconsin Department of Natural Resources began a voluntary hunter education program and has educated over 200,000 hunters, primarily youngsters, since then. The number of annual hunting accidents declined from a high of 265 in 1966 to 111 in 1981, in spite of an increase in licensed hunters from 600,000 to 800,000+. The annual number of accidents declined 60 percent while hunter numbers increased 33 percent. A similar situation exists for deer hunting accidents. Although Wisconsin averaged 44 deer hunting accidents per year from 1951 through 1966 and 48 accidents per year from 1968 through 1981, deer hunter numbers have increased considerably. Thus, the accident rate (number of accidents per 100,000 hunters) has declined significantly.

I personally feel the major factor has been the hunter education program, but I can't prove it. Statistics show that graduates of Wisconsin hunter education programs are more likely to have a hunting accident than a person who hasn't completed the course. This does not mean that taking the course causes somebody to have a hunting accident. Graduates are much younger, on the average, than non-graduate hunters and younger hunters have more accidents. Graduates may also hunt more frequently than nongraduates and, thus, be at risk for a longer period of time. Therefore, because graduates are younger and may hunt more often, they have more accidents. One major advantage of the program is that trained hunters can then teach safety-related ideas and behavior to other members of their hunting party.

CAUSES OF ACCIDENTS

What causes hunting accidents? A hunting accident report form is completed for each deer hunting accident in Wisconsin. An investigator determines what caused the accident. More than 50 percent of deer hunting accidents involved a judgment error by the shooter. In 16 percent of the accidents, the shooter swung on a deer and hit another person who was in the line of fire. In another 20 percent of the accidents, the victim was out of sight of the shooter. This is called a judgment error because a hunter is supposed to know what is behind the deer he shoots

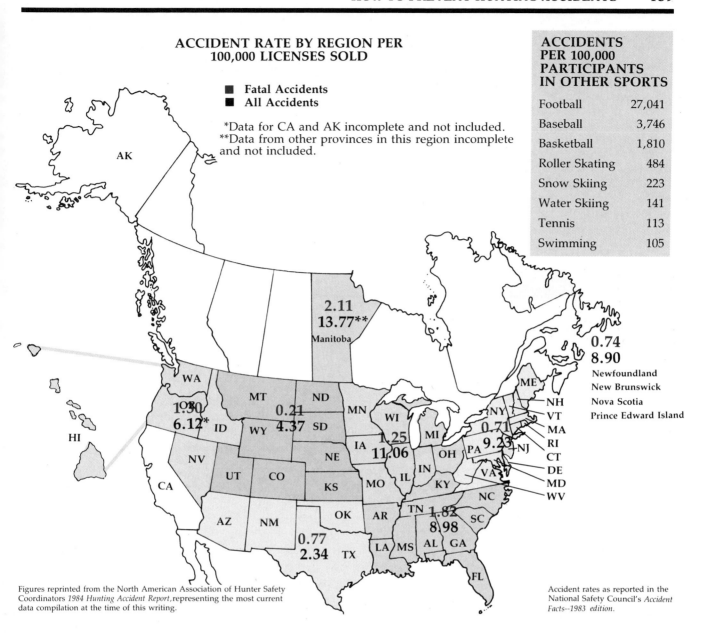

ACCIDENT RATE BY REGION PER 100,000 LICENSES SOLD

■ Fatal Accidents
■ All Accidents

*Data for CA and AK incomplete and not included.
**Data from other provinces in this region incomplete and not included.

ACCIDENTS PER 100,000 PARTICIPANTS IN OTHER SPORTS	
Football	27,041
Baseball	3,746
Basketball	1,810
Roller Skating	484
Snow Skiing	223
Water Skiing	141
Tennis	113
Swimming	105

2.11
13.77**
Manitoba

0.74
8.90
Newfoundland
New Brunswick
Nova Scotia
Prince Edward Island

1.30
6.12*

0.21
4.37

1.25
11.06

0.71
9.23

1.82
8.98

0.77
2.34

Figures reprinted from the North American Association of Hunter Safety Coordinators *1984 Hunting Accident Report*, representing the most current data compilation at the time of this writing.

Accident rates as reported in the National Safety Council's *Accident Facts--1983 edition.*

at. In six percent of the accidents a victim was mistaken for a deer. Many accidents are self-inflicted—the hunter shoots himself. Three out of every ten accidents happen this way. A hunter wounds himself when he stumbles and falls, when he doesn't unload the gun before crossing a fence, and when he unloads the gun improperly or drags it by the barrel. These *should* be the most preventable types of accidents.

FLUORESCENT ORANGE

Beginning July 1, 1980, all firearm deer hunters in Wisconsin were required to wear fluorescent orange. Many hunters wore it even before the law was passed. For all Wisconsin deer season accidents studied, nine of every ten victims in judgment accidents wore some prominent color of clothing. Many victims were mistaken for deer even though they wore red, orange, or yellow clothing. However, it is obvious to any deer hunter that you can pick

out blaze orange in the woods much quicker and easier than camouflage clothing.

EQUIPMENT USED

Rifles were involved in 61 percent and shotguns in 32 percent of all deer hunting accidents since 1968. This does not necessarily mean that rifles are more dangerous than shotguns, because the number of deer hunters that use each is not known. For deer hunting there may be no difference since large projectiles are used in both. Because of this, the National Safety Council advises that a shotgun loaded with a slug should be treated as a rifle.

TIME FACTORS

A large proportion of hunting accidents occurred during the opening day (25 percent) or the second day of a hunting season (15 percent). This is probably the time during which the largest number of hunters are afield and, as a result, more accidents occur then. Also, hunters may be less safety conscious than at other times because of heightened interest to be the first in entering new hunting territory and in bagging a deer, or because familiarity with their firearms or safety precautions decreased during the time between seasons. Furthermore, most hunting seasons open on weekends. Throughout seasons for all game, the majority of accidents occurred on Saturday (36 percent) or Sunday (31 percent). Accidents occurred at nearly every hour of the day. At least 75 percent happened between 9:00 A.M. and 5:00 P.M., though no single hour was predominant.

ACCIDENT SCENE CHARACTERISTICS

Analysis of accident scene characteristics is limited by the quantity of data available for the entire hunter population. It is not known how hunters distribute themselves in relation to topography and vegetation and what amount and type is accessible by hunters.

In Wisconsin, some hunters suggest that public hunting areas are too crowded and may promote unsafe hunting conditions. Our analysis does not indicate these public hunting areas are less safe than private areas. About one-quarter of Wisconsin's hunters spend most of their time hunting on public lands and 22 percent of all accidents occurred on public lands.

Weather and light conditions at the accident scene suggest that accidents occur when hunters are likely to be active. The sky was clear in more than 50 percent of hunting accidents. Most accidents (88 percent) occured during daylight hours and nine percent occured at dawn or dusk. Less than six percent of the accidents since 1973 occurred when rain or snow was falling or when it was foggy. The ground was snow-covered in one-quarter of these accidents. Thus, hunters are probably more active during days with good weather than with poor weather if conditions at the time of accidents are indicative of hunter-effort.

Most accidents occurred where the topography was level or rolling. Swamps and steep hills accounted for 18 percent of the acccident sites. Hunters may avoid harsh landscapes while hunting and access, such roads and trails, may also tend to be located in places with gentle topography.

A NATIONWIDE DECLINE

The number of hunting accidents in North America averaged 9.35 for every 100,000 licenses sold from 1981–83. By 1984, that number had dropped to 5.86. Leutentant James Dabb, Michigan Hunter Education Program Administrator and President of the North American Association of Hunter Safety Coordinators, credits the sharp drop in accidents to ongoing hunter education programs and increased use of hunter orange clothing. "Hunting has never been safer than it is today," he asserts.

So why the continued emphasis on safety training and research? "Because hunting patterns and activities change. You're looking at more hunter days and new seasons for blackpowder and turkey hunting. You have to adjust for these increasing activities and meet the needs of society today. And besides," adds Dabb, "even one hunting accident is one too many."

PREVENTING HUNTING ACCIDENTS

What can you do to prevent hunting accidents? First, take a hunter safety course if you haven't done so already. Enroll your young son or daughter in one if he or she plans to hunt. After the course, continue to teach your kids and friends how to hunt safely. I believe a hunter safety course once saved me from killing my father accidently.

My dad and I were hunting blue grouse in western Colorado and he was walking in front of me. I was walking with my gun pointed toward the ground and decided to pull the trigger to see if the safety was on. The 12 gauge went off but no damage was done, other than my father walked *behind* me for several years after that. I did a foolish thing that could have caused me lifetime grief; apparently I learned the lesson well in the hunter education course about keeping the muzzle pointed away from others but had to relearn the lesson about how to make sure the safety is on.

Finally, use common sense and think safety. Deer drives are common in many states. Drivers go through a patch of woods and standers wait at the other end. Common sense dictates that you don't shoot toward the drivers, that you know where other drivers and standers are, and that deer will always be available, but an exceptionally good hunting partner and friend is one in a million.

THINK SAFETY

If more deer hunters thought about the safety considerations of their actions, they would have fewer accidents. I'm as guilty as the next guy. While deer hunting in Colorado as a teenager, I came upon the hide and entrails of a mule deer. Wanting to get the hide tanned, I wrapped it around the upper part of my body and began walking down the mountain with the deer's tail bouncing against the back of my knees. After several hundred yards, I suddenly realized, *I look like a deer!* I quickly discarded the hide and never mentioned the incident to anyone. I acted without thinking about the safety of what I was doing.

The head of our deer hunting camp, who happens to be a conservation warden, constantly tells us to think safety, practice safety, think before acting, and to remember that a deer is not worth an accident. I don't think a day goes by when this isn't drilled into our heads. We pass up many deer because the situation isn't completely safe, but we have a clean slate as far as accidents.

I'm reminded of the now-deceased shift commander on the television show, "Hill Street Blues," who ended every morning session with, "And remember, let's be careful out there."

Have a good deer hunt this fall. And be safe.

Game Robbers: What If It's Your Buck They're After?

By Douglas Zimmer

I was sitting in my kitchen drinking coffee and the man on the other end of the telephone was someone I knew and hunted with for nearly 15 years. He was telling me about his latest hunting trip into the mountains of northern Idaho. Mostly he was telling me about the three "sportsmen" who stole his cow elk at gunpoint.

As I listened in mounting frustration, he related how he and his hunting partner hiked to their favorite spot each morning for three days. On the third morning they spotted several elk crossing a clearing about 250 yards away. Both men fired and two elk went down. Seconds later, one struggled to its feet and disappeared in a stand of jack pines.

Reprinted courtesy of DEER & DEER HUNTING *magazine.*

Each year stories continue to circulate around campfires, shooting benches, and gun-store counters involving incidents of game theft. A few simple marking tricks like the one this hunter is using could help ensure that you keep your buck this season.

Photo by Dan Brockman

Leaving his partner at the firing point to act as a reference, my friend set out to follow the wounded animal. His own cow dropped at his shot and hadn't so much as kicked since, but my friend knew he was a better tracker than his novice partner and he wanted to catch up to the wounded animal as quickly as possible. In the interest of speed, he passed his own cow without tagging her, continuing instead to follow the blood spoor of the wounded elk.

The amount and color of the blood on the snow indicated that the cow wasn't going far and within 15 minutes he found her lying where her heart finally ran out of blood. After marking the kill and signaling his partner, he set off back down the hill toward his own kill, intending to tag it.

But when he got there, three other hunters, men he never saw before, stood over his kill. One slipped a tag on the animal's ear.

"I walked up and asked them what they thought they were doing," he said. "The one leaning against a tree with his rifle in his hands asked me what the hell it looked like they were doing; they were tagging their elk. I told them I thought they were mistaken, that they had the wrong elk. By this time they were all standing up with their guns in their hands, and they told me they weren't mistaken about anything; this was their elk and they were going to take it.

"Suddenly I realized that these men were out-and-out game thieves. I knew my partner and I had fired the only two shots we heard all morning, and I realized these men weren't even going to make a pretense of having shot that elk. They were three against one and they were simply going to take it.

"I worked plenty hard for that elk and when I realized I was being robbed, my blood started to boil. Then I thought about it for a moment. I thought about my family and decided it wasn't worth it. So I just walked off."

He paused for a moment, and when he spoke again the frustration and disbelief in his voice were nearly tangible.

"I've heard stories about this kind of thing, but I never thought it could happen to me! I mean this is Idaho for cryin' out loud! I never thought this kind of thing could happen here," he lamented. "What is it coming to when hunters are robbing each other out in the woods?"

I didn't have the heart to tell my friend that, while such a confrontation may have been new to him, reports of similar incidents have been filtering back from the field for years. But because of their rarity, they receive little attention from anyone but the outraged victims. In fact, for years game department officials considered reports of such incidents so rare that few, if any, records of such complaints were kept. Most states followed a policy of benign neglect concerning any reported incidents and blandly assured anyone trying to investigate that such things just never happen.

Yet, each year stories continue to circulate around campfires, shooting benches, and gun-store counters about just this kind of incident. For years they were relatively rare, but with ever-greater numbers of people hunting in ever-smaller areas, in the last few decades such stories have become almost commonplace. But despite what appears to be a significant increase in the number of such reports, game-department officials continue to turn a blind eye. At the same time that officials in five western states denied that such things happen in their states, conversations with hunters in the same five states produced an entirely different point of view. Nearly every gun club seems to have at least one victim of such an incident, while some claim as many as seven or eight.

Part of the reason for this disparity may be that many game stealing incidents are never reported to game authorities, partially because many victims don't know where or to whom to report the crime and partially because they don't think anything will be done about it. One angry Washington state hunter wrote down the license number of two men who took his deer and reported it to the first game-checking station he found. The ranger in charge calmly told him the two men checked the buck through 20 minutes earlier and suggested that he contact the local sheriff's department with his complaint. When he did, the deputy who took his complaint told him such incidents were under the jurisdiction of the game department.

While some of this confusion on the part of law enforcement and game officials may be understandable (Wyoming, for instance, does not cover such incidents by statute, but suggests that a victim might have recourse to a civil court), part of it may be due to buck-passing of another kind. The top wildlife enforcement official of one West Coast state called reports of such robberies a myth created by two people shooting at the same animal at the same time. His counterpart in a neighboring state called it a matter of hunter ethics and suggested sportsmen get closer to their game before shooting to minimize confusion. Neither would admit to any significant number of incidents in his state.

But while game officials deny that the problem exists and talk of hunter ethics, elsewhere tempers are rising. Typical of this new attitude is the following story, which was overheard recently at a blackpowder shooting competition.

The shooter told how he dropped a nice two-point buck on the edge of a clear-cut with his .58 caliber half-stock Hawken, a nice shot of nearly a hundred yards. As he recharged his rifle, preparatory to walking up on his kill, he was astounded to see a four-wheel-drive truck with a camper on the back come roaring out of the trees and slide to a stop beside his deer. Too startled to move, he watched two men jump out of the truck and run over to his animal. One slipped a tag onto the antlers and the two men started dragging the carcass toward the truck.

"When I realized what they were doing, I just saw red," he said. "I decided I was damned if they were going to get my buck and without thinking any further I fired the charge I had loaded into the bank behind them and started yelling, running, and reloading all at the same time. They just threw the buck into the back of the camper and took off down the skid trail. I was so damned mad I fired the second charge at the back of their camper, but I was puffing pretty good and I doubt if I hit anything.''

While he may have left justified in shooting at the thieves, the frustrated hunter can be glad he didn't hit either of them. Thieves they may be, but if the law seems murky concerning game theft, it is quite clear about what would lie in store for the hunter if his bullet had connected, or if one of those game robbers had decided to file a complaint about being fired upon.

Laws vary from state to state, but the general rule is that a citizen can use deadly force against another person only when his life, or that of another, is threatened. Shooting at a man stealing a deer hardly qualifies as self-defense and, however righteous he may have felt at the time, the shooter could easily have wound up facing a murder or manslaughter charge.

On the other hand, if the two game robbers had stopped long enough to return his fire, he might not have lived long enough to tell his story.

It is exactly this kind of escalation that worries game officials most when game-stealing incidents are mentioned and, although they prefer to say such things don't happen, they all counsel extreme caution if such a situation should arise. To a man, they recommend reporting the pertinent information to local law-enforcement and game officials, although admitting that unless the number or reports increases significantly, little will probably be done about them.

Game and law-enforcement resources are already stretched too thin in most areas to allow much follow-up on the complaints that do come in, especially since the evidence in many cases is too insubstantial to stand up in court.

"It gets to be a matter of one man's word against another's," admitted one law-enforcement officer. "How do you build a case that will stand up in court on something like that?"

So what should a hunter do, faced with such a situation? To begin with, stealing a deer is *theft*; if it is done while armed, it is *armed robbery*. The proper authorities to deal with this are the police, not the game wardens. But the wardens can be summoned to testify in preliminary hearings and at the trial, if any. In only a very few states, game wardens have the status of full-fledged peace officers in addition to their conservation duties. In any case, if you can present evidence that you did indeed shoot the buck and had possession of it, you have the basis for a criminal charge.

In some areas where game theft is common, hunters put their tags on the animal the first chance they get—which is also required by the game laws. They also mark the buck in some way not readily apparent to a game robber. Some ways are: put your business card under its tongue or write out your name and address on a small piece of paper with ink and do the same. Always put your hunting license number on whatever you use. But knowing thieves often look in the mouth for such things, so other methods have been developed. For instance, you can roll up a piece of paper with your name, address, and hunting license number and insert it in a goose quill, then slide the quill into an ear or nostril. You can also make a small slit in the hide and tuck the quill under the skin. Seal the cut end of the quill with wax to prevent damage to the paper. There are hundreds of variations on this method, and if you can think of a new one, you're better off.

If your buck is stolen, follow the thieves if you can. Sometimes you can track them down to camp or to their vehicle. Write down hunting license numbers from back tags as well as the vehicle license, if possible. Then make for a phone and call checking stations and wardens in the area. Describe the thieves, give the numbers, and tell them exactly how you can identify the buck as your own. If you do follow game thieves, try to stay back and remain unseen. The idea is to confront them with a warden (who can later testify) in their camp or other home base. At the confrontation, disclose your hidden card or note and immediately ask the warden or wardens to testify. Get their numbers and names so you can identify them to the police. When you do this, the more witnesses you have the better, so take along a few friends if possible. Then make a formal complaint to the police about theft or armed robbery. The hidden-card trick doesn't always work, but it has worked so often that game thieves in some areas are wary of taking a buck that has actually been handled by the man who shot it.

Quite often, it is possible to locate the thieves by driving around and simply looking for their vehicle or the men themselves at the end of the hunting day.

Take time to think carefully about what you might do if faced with such a situation. Consider your proposed plan of action from a legal standpoint. While you might feel you have a moral right to certain actions, if you end up in court, the decisions will be made on a legal basis. If you aren't sure about your legal position, consider discussing the matter with your attorney. At the very least, familiarize yourself with game and state laws covering areas where you hunt and find out which governmental agencies have jurisdiction where. Make a list of details you feel would be helpful to remember if you ever had to file a legal complaint, and make a habit of noting those details about hunters you meet in the field—a handy practice that can also pay off if you are ever involved in a search for a missing hunter.

But above all, remember to remain calm. It won't console your family that the big buck you died trying to defend really was yours, nor is a judge or jury likely to accept such a claim as a viable defense in a murder trial.

Besides, there's always next year.

PART 7

THE VENISON

How To Tame A Gamey Buck

By Valerius Geist

Three fine pronghorn bucks lay outside the tent. We had been successful as well as lucky. In Alberta, antelope licenses are distributed by drawing, and you have to be lucky to be chosen. My friend Ron, my two boys, and I had drawn permits; we had planned the hunt well and, on the morning of the first day, Ron and the boys had each shot a fine buck. I took a large buck on the second morning of our hunt.

We were in camp at dusk of the first evening. We were tired, happy, and very hungry. As always, after killing any big-game animal, I had kept the livers, hearts, and kidneys. I sliced one liver and dusted the slices with flour, pepper, and salt. The heavy skillet was hot, and a generous lump of fresh butter was melting in it. Soon the slices were sizzling in the bubbling butter. Quckly, I got out the sourdough bread and cut it up. This would not be a fancy meal—just sound fare for hungry mouths. The liver was quickly fried and I distributed the slices. Then I turned to fry a second batch.

An odd sound made me turn around. A less-than-happy expression distorted the faces of the crew.

"Anything wrong?" I asked.

"It's a bit strong," Ron said with a gulp.

"Yeech," was the comment from Karl.

"Dad, you better try some yourself." said Harold, my youngest.

Abandoning the frying pan, I reached for my plate and bit into the first piece of buck antelope liver that I had ever tasted. Phew! Awful! Filthy!

Had I ever bitten into anything as ghastly before? Nothing had ever equaled this liver taste. It was as if I had sunk my teeth into the hairy, oily rutting gland that each antelope buck carries below his ears. (This is the black spot just behind the hinge of the jaw, the secretions of which an antelope buck rubs on twigs and grass stems to mark his territory.) This was no sage taste in my mouth. The sage taste is bearable; the rutting taste of antelope liver and meat is not.

I grabbed the frying pan and flung the liver slices into the ravine. "May the coyote make a feast of it, or the badger, or the bobcat, or whoever," I thought.

As I looked over those sleek, beautiful antelope bucks, my mind was filled wih foreboding. It did turn out that the meat of all three bucks had a penetrating, horrible rutting taste. Harold's buck, a fine 14-incher, was almost edible. Karl's buck, an old, regressed fighter with 11-inch horns and a broken fork, was the worst. The buck had a gaunt body that was covered with bruises from a fight. To make matters worse, Karl's first shot had drifted off target because of the strong prairie wind and had hit the gut. After Karl killed the buck, he had discovered that he had lost his knife and had to run some miles to camp to get another one. Meanwhile, the contents of the gut soaked the meat. My own buck, a large-bodied, fat fellow with heavy 14½-inch horns, had been hit lengthwise and low. I cleaned the carcass at once, and yet the meat was almost as foul-tasting

as that of Karl's buck. This was all the more pity because the meat was tender, had a beautiful texture, and contained relatively little fat. Chemical analysis has shown that antelope meat is higher than beef in protein content, vitamins, and minerals.

Mountain goat billies killed in the rut—not outside of it—have meat that, when cooked, exudes a filthy odor and tastes horrible. I had experienced that, but the antelope meat from our Alberta hunt, on the other hand, surpassed even the bad goat meat. What was I to do? In our family, the rule is: If you kill it, you clean it and you eat it. If you do not want to eat it, you simply do not kill it.

After butchering the three bucks, I hauled 30 pounds of meat to a local Austrian butcher. He added beef shank and pork to the antelope meat and made classical German bratwurst or frying sausage. To my surprise, it turned out excellent. In fact, that was the best batch of frying sausage he made for us that year. I would have gladly brought all the antelope meat to him but, by then, it was in the deep freeze. To make frying sausage, fresh meat is required. Anyway, we had more than enough elk and moose sausage already.

When in doubt, call friends. Only then did I dis-

cover that foul-tasting antelope is not uncommon. Some of my acquaintances had quit hunting antelope on that account. Others continued hunting, celebrated every edible antelope shot, and spiced and stewed every other one—and suffered through it. Nobody in my immediate circle of acquaintances knew how to deal with foul-tasting antelope meat. I had a problem.

The first roast I cooked like hasenpfeffer (hare stewed in a vinegar marinade). That is, I marinated the meat in a mixture of dark stout and wine vinegar, with plenty of fresh onions and black pepper as well. It didn't work.

Next, I tried a soy-sauce marinade on lean slices of antelope meat, and I stir-fried them in a wok. It didn't work.

I boiled the hearts in a rich mixture of garden herbs and vegetables. It was awful!

Next I cooked the tongues in sour cream. Horrible!

A Swiss colleague, hearing of my plight, recommended buttermilk as a marinade. He had used it on antelope meat with good results, he told me. Off I rushed and bought two liters of buttermilk. For seven long days, I marinated antelope steaks in buttermilk. It didn't work.

I made a *terrine de pâté.* (That's French for meat loaf.) Half of the meat I used was ground pork. I doubled the amount of brandy that the French would normally use and went a bit heavy on the spices. The *terrine* was rather snappy. It was served at a party, and the adult guests liked it. The taste of the rut was gone, but the children detested my *terrine.* They said that the taste of the brandy was overpowering. Scratch that one! The meat loaf was not family fare.

Next, I took some thin steaklets, rubbed mustard all over them, rolled them in fine bread crumbs, black pepper, and salt, and fried them crisp. With the meat, I served a spicy white sauce—just in case. My wife liked this dish. I did not. I could still taste buck.

At a downtown dinner talk I gave, I met a lady in the audience who had a long acquaintance with the ways of Indians. Antelope? Why yes, some can be quite gamey, but a couple of days marinating in tomato juice will cure that, she told me. That's how her Indian friends treated antelope. Tomato juice? People use that to deodorize clothes and dogs that have been sprayed by skunks. Maybe it would work. Eagerly, I headed home and marinated a roast for three days in tomato juice. It didn't work.

Why didn't I think of it earlier? I'd have to consult game cookbooks. Off I went in search of antelope recipes, but pronghorns are conspicuously absent from cookbooks. I finally found one recipe, but it had obviously been concocted for nongamey antelope meat because it treated the meat as if it were bland veal.

At that point, I remembered Schroeder. I had seen my friend Schroeder in Italy the summer before. We were both at a conference on mountain ungulates—that is hoofed mammals such as wild sheep, mountain goats, chamois, gorals, serow, and the like. Dr.

Wolfgang Schroeder is head of the Wildlife Institute at the University of Munich in Germany and, like me, is an avid hunter and cook. Dr. Schroeder had mentioned a marinade used by the backwoods residents of the Alps in order to make rutting chamois bucks edible. Schroeder had used it on ibex, which can be exceptionally filthy. A rutting ibex buck is reputed to smell and taste like an uncastrated domestic billy goat, only worse. Since I have shot a good many feral goats, some big billies included, I had an inkling of what rutting ibex would taste like.

A friend in need is a friend indeed! Schroeder wasted no time. Within a few days—bless the postal service—I had his letter in my hand. Not only had he written down the recipe for the marinade, but he also included several ways to prepare rutting ibex or chamois meat. Would this time-tasted marinade work on rutting pronghorns, too? It did, but only when the meat was braised (browned in fat and then simmered in a covered pan with liquid). The results were so good that even my finicky kids ate it. They were actually grieved when the last of the meat was eaten and they were eager to apply for another hunt! If this recipe will work on rutting antelope, it will work on any strong-tasting game you might shoot.

MARINADE SCHROEDER

You need one quart of red wine. I prefer a heavy, full-bodied dry wine. Add one quart of fresh orange juice. (Schroeder used apple cider or apple juice. Both work fine, but I prefer good orange juice.) Add one six-ounce cup of good wine vinegar. No ordinary cider vinegar, please! Add one handful of juniper berries (about 25). I collect mine from the prostrate juniper in the foothills, but the common juniper will do. Add one handful of whole cloves (about 25), two bay leaves, and four medium carrots that have been scraped and shredded. Do *not* add salt!

Bring the ingredients to a boil, reduce heat, and let the mixture simmer for 15 minutes. I use an enameled steel pot—no aluminum, please. Let the marinade cool, and add the antelope meat. Store in a cool place for at least two days, but there's no harm in keeping the meat in the marinade for up to seven days. If you use apple cider or apple juice instead of orange juice, the marinade will turn cloudy by the second day. That's a good sign—it means that the marinade is working. This marinade draws the albumen out of the meat. The albumen appears as scum that comes to the surface when you boil meat or bones for stock. This scum must be skimmed off and discarded.

The marinade can be used for a second batch but not for a third. To use it a second time, bring the marinade to a boil again and remove the thick albumen scum that rises to the top. Taste the marinade. You may have to adjust the taste with a shot of port wine or brandy. After the second use, I have found that the marinade is no longer usable because it tastes like antelope buck, even after the albumen scum is removed.

Marinating the meat, however, is only half the battle. With thick chunks of meat, even seven days of marinating will not remove the deep-seated buck taste. To do this, you must also braise the meat. That is, you cook the meat in such a fashion that the fibers rupture and allow the deep juices to seep out, and the braising liquid to seep in. You exchange the tissue juice for the braising liquid of your choice. Properly braised meat is very tender. The following two recipes are both braises.

ANTELOPE ALBERTA

Drain the marinated three- to four-pound roast thoroughly and remove as much surface moisture as possible. If need be, use a towel. Set the meat aside. Use a ceramic pot that will just barely accept the roast as well as the vegetables that will be used. There must be no space between the meat and the sides of the pot.

To prepare the vegetable bed, clean and cut into chunks six medium carrots, one large parsnip, and one large onion.

In a pan, melt some fresh butter and add a little olive oil. Add some salt and sugar (I use about one-half teaspoon of each, but a little extra sugar doesn't hurt). Heat the vegetables gently in the hot butter; they must be carefully watched so that they will be browned but not burned. Remove the browned vegetables and place them in the bottom of the ceramic pot. I use a crock pot for this because it is handy.

Now sear and brown the meat thoroughly. Yes, you must have a brown, hard crust all over it. Do not stop until you get it. Marinated meat often sizzles on and on without browning. Persevere! When the roast is finally browned all over, put it on top of the vegetables in the ceramic pot.

Thin a four-ounce can of tomato paste with a splash of port wine or sherry. Brandy works fine, too, if you only have adults to feed! Add two heaping teaspoons of brown sugar to the diluted paste, stir, and pour over the roast. Add one uncrushed, large clove of garlic. Cover the pot and put it into the oven at 325 degrees. When using a crock pot, turn it on high and leave covered.

About one hour after the meat has been put in the oven or crock pot, check to see if the meat has given off juice and has sunk down into the pot. If not, continue until it does. Then pour some of the liquid in the pot over the meat and let it simmer.

About two hours into the process, I make my final arrangements by tasting the braising liquid in the pot and adjusting its taste with lemon juice, salt, and brown sugar. If the braising liquid is too thin, I let the meat bubble away without a lid until the juice has thickened; then I adjust the taste. Thereafter, I let the braise simmer on—the longer, the better. Five hours is good.

With antelope Alberta, I recommend rice—wild rice mixed with brown rice, if it is to be a festive dish—a crisp, light salad, and an aromatic, dry red wine.

The taste? It tastes something like very good barbecued beef.

ANTELOPE FOR HUNTERS

Take three pounds of cubed antelope meat and marinate it *à la Schroeder*. Dice one-half pound of good-quality bacon. Fry the bacon until it is crisp and put it into the pot. In the bacon fat that remains in the frying pan, brown three large diced onions and two diced stalks of celery, and put them into the pot. Brown the antelope meat in small batches in the remaining bacon fat, to which I add a lump of butter. Put the meat in the pot and add one large, crushed garlic clove. I also like to add a generous handful of dried mushrooms. If you have no dried mushrooms, fry a half pound of meadow mushrooms in butter until they are brown. Next, brown three large tablespoons of flour in the remaining fat in the pan. You may have to add some butter to get a good brown roux. With a cup or two of lukewarm beef stock, make a sauce base with the browned flour and strain through a sieve to get rid of the lumps. Season the sauce with black pepper and salt, and pour over the meat and vegetables in the pot. Close the pot and turn on the heat. One hour later, adjust taste with salt and add two tablespoons of brandy—a little more does not hurt. Let the pot simmer slowly. You can stir the ingredients around a little. A beautiful, brown sauce should form.

This dish can be served with fresh potatoes boiled in salt water, broccoli, and fresh crusty bread. Depending on the occasion, serve a dry red wine or some hearty ale or beer.

ANTELOPE WESTPHALIA

There is at least one more way to obtain a superb product from the gamiest antelope that there is. The albumen in the meat gives it the bad taste, and albumen can also be extracted by salting. Coarse, noniodized salt is rubbed into the meat and extracts a lot of fluid in only 24 hours. The meat is then washed thoroughly to remove the salt, and it is used with an equal amount of ground pork in hamburger dishes. However, if you have a smoker, you can do as I did.

After salting the antelope meat for 24 hours, drain and briefly rinse the meat with water. With one-half pound of brown sugar, one ounce of baking soda, and one ounce of liquid vitamin C, make a paste and pour it over the meat. Let stand in an earthenware pot in a cool place for four days. Turn the meat daily.

Drain meat and let its surface dry. Place it in a preheated smoker for 24 hours, keeping the heat *low*.

The result is a very dark, shriveled chunk of meat, greatly reduced in size. On the inside, however, it is deep red and flavored just like an old-time ham.

To our sorrow, the antelope meat vanished all too rapidly. Be it gamey or not, I am now looking forward to my next antelope.

11 Marinades For All Seasons

By Roxanne Anton

Many factors must be considered when choosing the proper method to prepare and cook game. Tenderness, taste, and quality all vary with the species, its food supply, and its age. The hunter who truly enjoys dining on wild game soon learns to evaluate the quality of his bag.

Grandpa knew many methods of determining the palatability of his harvest. He checked feathers, skin, legs, and feet of birds for signs of age. He evaluated the color of the fat, the size of the bird, and the overall appearance. If the area under the wing was tender, he knew that he had a young bird. When the breast bone was soft and pliable, a tender dinner was in store. Yellow legs and dark bills were yet another indication of young birds.

When he bagged the special Thanksgiving turkey, with light skin and smooth black legs, he was properly thankful. Soft, loose spurs on a male meant that the bird was prime eating. Even if his turkey was a tough old tom with a purplish cast to the flesh and long hairs, Grandma would rise to the occasion and transform it into a succulent meal. She had her secrets, too!

Grandpa was an early naturalist. As he walked his woods and fields, whether hunting or farming, he observed the animals. He came to recognize that young squirrels had very light bellies, while those of older ones were shaded from creamy to dark. Less than three hairs above the dewclaws of squirrels indicated a young animal.

When bird season closed and Grandpa went deer hunting to provide the main meat supply of the winter, he considered the size of the animal and the condition of the coat and hoofs in determining age. He counted the prongs of the rack, believing that each prong represented one year of life. When the deer was young, according to Grandpa, the fat would be thick, clear, and close, while the meat would be fine textured.

Just as any hunter, though, Grandpa hoped to bring home the biggest, grandest, and oldest buck. Grandma would have preferred a younger, more tender doe, as she judged that the sweetest and most tender of meats.

Experienced hunters can easily identify a game animal as young or old. An older creature will certainly have tougher meat, more muscular tissue, and generally be stronger flavored, so you'll need to take steps in your preparation and cooling to tenderize and improve the flavor.

The most tender cuts will be found in the areas of the body that have been the least exercised. Meat from these areas will have less muscle and connective tissue and will be the choice cuts. These cuts may often be broiled, roasted, or fried with good results.

More muscular cuts may be tenderized by cooking with moist heat. They lend themselves well to recipes that call for stewing, braising, sautéing, or moist roasting. These cuts are also tenderized and flavored when cut into small portions and cooked in casserole dishes or in game pies complete with gravy. They may also be ground and used in sausage or made into burger.

A vinegar marinade helps break down tissue, be-

Photo by Rodale Press

Whether you choose a cooked or uncooked marinade depends on how much tenderizing your game needs and how much time you're willing to put into it.

sides adding flavor to the meat. I use a marinade for all game animals and for older, tougher fowl. Parboiling is another means to tenderize meat prior to cooking, as is soaking meat in salt water with a small amount of baking soda.

A strong, unpleasant flavor is found in the fat of most wild game. Remove as much fat as possible before cooking. As you cook, you may replace this animal fat with butter, oil, or bacon grease, basting by rubbing it into the meat. Game may also be larded by covering the meat with bacon strips or by inserting small pieces of salt pork into the tissue.

Even tender cuts, such as steaks or chops from young deer, should be cooked with low heat when they are cut thin. A high, fast heat will cause these sections to become leathery and dry. They should

be braised, sautéed, or pan-fried at low heat for best results. Use high temperatures only for quick browning or for quick cooking of very tender cuts.

Hibernating animals such as bears have extremely fatty meat. Waterfowl may also contain some fat under the skin. This can be removed by skinning or by piercing the skin of the fowl as it cooks. Excessive fat should be discarded from drippings before you make gravy. Excessively fatty meat from larger animals should be parboiled before cooking to allow the fat to be rendered. A rack in a roaster will allow fat to cook away and drop to the bottom of the pan for easy disposal.

Some hunters let game hang to enhance the flavor. When the meat was high enough to suit their palates, it was dressed for cooking. Modern knowledge of food quality and preservation indicate that game should be cleaned as soon as possible after the kill and stored at cool temperatures. Game that has been hung will have a more defined and usually wilder flavor, however.

Before you cook any game, be sure that it is free of all traces of blood, entrails, shot, feathers, fur, and hair. The finest dish can be ruined, otherwise.

When you dress your game, the carcass should be washed under running water until the water runs clear. You will find some cooks who disagree, but the average contemporary appetite demands this attention to cleanliness and custom. Cut away all damaged areas of meat, and any area that seems excessively bloody. Take a sharp, pointed knife and dig down into areas where shot was lodged to remove blood, fur, or feathers—and the shot itself. If an off smell is present in any portion of the meat, cut away that section.

Game should be marinated or cooked only when the meat appears as clean and appetizing as cuts from a store. Naturally, game that will be stored for very long should be frozen.

Modify cooking time for the size and quality of your game, and for your personal preference. Your oven is another factor to consider because temperatures tend to vary with different stoves. The fork test is a time-honored method that will serve you well: When the meat is tender, it's done.

SELECTING THE MARINADE RECIPE

There are two types of marinades; cooked and uncooked. Cooked marinades are often the best choice for game that will need a lot ot tenderizing or seasoning. Select a recipe from this category for best results when you prepare old critters. Use a cooked marinade also for species with strong or unpleasant flavor, tough cuts from large game, or for flesh that has yellowed or off-color fat or appears excessively lean, stringy, or muscular. An uncooked marinade mixture may also be used in these instances, but the cooked marinades will do a better job.

Uncooked marinades are quick to fix, store well in your refrigerator, and are a good choice for young and middle-aged game. These are also good for choice cuts from large game, game that has been pretenderized by parboiling, and game that will be cooked by a long, slow moist-heat method (such as stewing, braising, covered moist roasting, or casseroles, for example).

Select your marinade and cooking recipes before

MARINADE NO. 1

½ cup chopped celery	1 tsp. thyme
1 medium chopped onion	1 tsp. basil
¼ cup olive oil	1 tsp. ground cloves
4 cups white vinegar	1 tbsp. garlic powder
4 cups water	6 whole peppercorns

For this cooked marinade, chop onion and celery, combine with olive oil, vinegar, and water. Blend in remaining ingredients. Bring mixture to boil. Reduce heat; simmer for 30 minutes. Place mixture in refrigerator until well cooled. Place game in bowl or pan, cover with marinade mixture, refrigerate. When marinade time is completed, remove game from marinade, rinse, and proceed with the cooking recipe you have selected.

MARINADE NO. 2

1 chopped onion	2 tbsp. brown sugar
1 cup catsup	1 tbsp. dry mustard
2 tbsp. Worcestershire sauce	1 tbsp. basil
½ cup white vinegar	1 tsp. garlic powder
½ cup water	1 tsp. allspice
½ cup oil	1 medium chopped onion

Combine catsup, Worcestershire sauce, vinegar, water, and oil. Blend in basil, garlic powder, allspice, and onion. Mix well. Bring mixture to a boil; reduce heat and simmer for thirty minutes. Cool well in refrigerator. Place game in bowl or pan, cover with marinade mixture, and refrigerate. Turn game fre-

quently during the marinade period. Remove game from marinade mixture, drain, and follow cooking recipe selected.

MARINADE NO. 3

1 medium sliced onion	1 cup oil
1 sliced lemon	2 tbsp. lemon juice
4 tbsp. red wine	2 tbsp. sugar

Pierce lemon with fork and squeeze out juice. Slice lemon. Mix wine, oil, lemon juice, and sugar. Blend well. Pour marinade over meat, then lay lemon slices and onion on top. Place in refrigerator. Turn the game as it marinates to expose all areas. Replace lemon and onion on top of meat after turning. Remove game from marinade, drain, and follow the cooking instructions of your recipe.

MARINADE NO. 4

1 chopped onion	3 bay leaves
1 tbsp. dry mustard	2 tbsp. Worcestershire sauce
1 tbsp. brown sugar	1 cup water
1 tbsp. oregano	2 cups vinegar
3 whole cloves	½ cup salad oil
3 peppercorns	

Slice onion and combine with all remaining ingredients except oil. Mix well. Place in large bowl and add meat. Pour salad oil over top of marinade. Put marinating meat in refrigerator and allow to stand from 12 hours to four days. Turn meat daily.

you start. This ensures that the seasonings used in the marinade mixture compliment those to be used in cooking.

PREPARING AND USING THE MARINADE

Use a porcelain or glass container to prepare and use the marinade recipes. Stir and blend with a wooden spoon; the acid base of the marinade mixture can corrode untreated metal.

Select a container that is large enough to hold the game without overcrowding. I like a flat glass container at least one inch deep for marinating steaks, roasts, and chops, and a large wide bottom bowl for small whole birds or cut-up birds and game.

Pour the marinade mixture generously over the top of the game, then turn the meat over and saturate the other side. Add enough marinade mixture to cover the bottom of the container. Game that will be marinated over one hour should be stored in the refrigerator. Although room temperatures will hasten the action of the marinade, they increase the risk of bacterial activity and *should be avoided.*

For thick roasts or tough cuts, pierce the flesh with a fork before marinating. This allows the mixture to penetrate deep into the flesh. Turn the game over frequently during the marinating period to allow all areas equal exposure. When marinating is completed remove game from the mixture, drain, and follow instructions in your cooking recipe.

Use left-over marinade to baste game as it cooks. It also makes an excellent base for a delicious sauce or gravy to serve at your game meal.

STORING MARINADES

Uncooked marinade mixtures made with wine or vinegar base can be prepared in advance and stored in the refrigerator. I usually make a double batch to have on hand for the next game meal.

Cooked marinade mixtures, marinades made with dairy products or other perishable ingredients, and any marinade mixture that has been in contact with game *should be discarded and not stored.* This is a safety factor as these marinades have an increased risk of contamination.

One final thought before we proceed to the marinade recipes. If hunting is poor, game is scarce, and your bag is empty, you can still enjoy some good eating by using the marinade recipes to add a special touch to conventional meats or poultry.

MARINADE NO. 5

4 cups white vinegar	1 tsp. pepper
4 cups water	1 large onion
2 tsp. salt	1 sliced lemon
1 tsp. sugar	2 tbsp. cooking oil

Mix all ingredients. Add meat and place in large bowl in refrigerator. Marinate meat from 12 hours to four days, turning occasionally.

MARINADE NO. 6

1 cup tarragon wine vinegar	2 tsp. salt
1 cup water	3 bay leaves
1 sliced lemon	½ tsp. basil
2 sliced onions	½ tsp. caraway seed
1 minced garlic clove	4 peppercorns

Proceed as in Marinade No. 5.

MARINADE NO. 7

1 bottle dry white wine	1 tbsp. celery seed
1 cup vinegar	3 sprigs chopped parsley
1 large onion, sliced	4 peppercorns
1 tsp. rosemary	1 tsp. salt

Proceed as in Marinade No. 5.

MARINADE NO. 8

1 tsp. allspice	½ tsp. basil
1 tsp. caraway seed	1 cup vinegar
1 tsp. salt	¼ cup cooking oil
½ tsp. pepper	2 tbsp. brown sugar
¼ tsp. paprika	1 minced onion

Proceed as in Marinade No. 5.

MARINADE NO. 9

½ cup salad oil	¼ cup lime juice
1 tbsp. dry mustard	½ tsp. Tabasco
½ cup red wine	½ tsp. salt
½ tsp. marjoram	4 peppercorns
¼ tsp. thyme	

Proceed as in Marinade No. 5.

MARINADE NO. 10

½ cup soy sauce	½ cup pineapple juice
½ cup brown sugar	1 tsp. salt
½ cup vinegar	1 tbsp. garlic powder

Mix all ingredients. Simmer for one hour. Cool and add meat.

MARINADE NO. 11

2 cups tomato juice	½ tsp. pepper
1 tsp. dry mustard	2 tbsp. Worcestershire sauce
4 tbsp. vinegar	1 tbsp. garlic powder
2 tbsp. grated onion	2 tbsp. oil
1 tsp. salt	½ cup dry white wine
½ tsp. paprika	dash Tabasco sauce

Mix and simmer for 30 minutes. Cool and add meat.

20 Quick 'N Easy Venison Delights

By John Weiss

EASY ROAST VENISON

1 3-pound rump roast
8 strips bacon

Use one of the tenderest rump roasts you have. Drape the top of the roast with the bacon strips, held in place with toothpicks. Or, in preparing a rolled rump roast, drape the meat with the bacon before you make your string ties. Insert a meat thermometer in the thickest part of the meat, set it on a roasting pan, then place in an oven preheated to 350 degrees. The roast is finished when its internal temperature reaches 145 degrees. Transfer roast to a hot serving platter and remove bacon. Slice roast very thin. Then slice bacon into squares and sprinkle over the top of the meat slices. Finally, take any remaining pan juices and pour over the meat. Serves 4 (with enough leftovers for sandwiches the next day).

4-STEP POT ROAST

1 2-pound shoulder or neck roast
1 envelope dry onion soup mix
1 cup water

This is the fastest, easiest pot roast I know how to make and, happily, one of the most delicious. Place your roast in the center of a square sheet of heavy-duty aluminum foil and bring the edges up around the sides to form a pouch. Pour one cup of water over the top of the roast, then sprinkle on the dry soup mix. Now pinch together the edges of the foil to form a tight seal to trap steam, and place the pouch in a shallow roasting pan. Place in a 325 degree oven for 1½ hours. When you open the pouch to slice the meat, you'll find it tender beyond belief, and as a special surprise you'll have a good quantity of perfect gravy you can ladle over noodles or potatoes. As with all venison, remember to serve on a hot platter. Serves 4.

EASY VENISON RIBS

2 rib plates
1 bottle Open Pit Barbecue Sauce

Place the ribs in a roasting pan, cover with the barbecue sauce, and bake at 325 degrees for 1½ hours. Serves 4.

VENISON SHISH KABOB

3 pounds tenderloin or sirloin tip steak
4 large onions, quartered
4 large tomatoes, quartered
4 green peppers, quartered
4 apples, quartered
Italian salad dressing
white wine
garlic powder

This is a fantastic, all-in-one meal that's perfectly suited to backyard or camp use, and if you've got kids they'll have great fun doing most of the work.

4-STEP POT ROAST

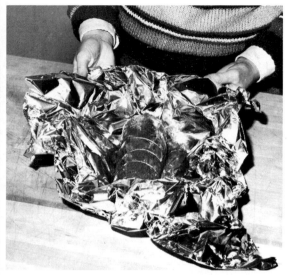
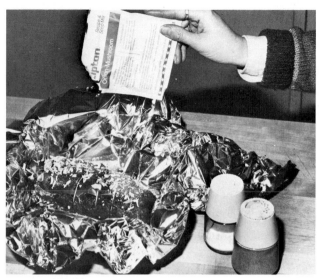

1. *Place the roast in the middle of a sheet of foil and bring up the edges to form a pouch.* **2.** *Pour in one cup of water and sprinkle the roast with a package of dry soup mix. Add salt and pepper if you wish.*

3. *Pinch the foil edges together to form an airtight seal and carefully set the package in a shallow roasting pan.* **4.** *Not only is the roast incredibly tender, but you also get a good quantity of perfect gravy.*

In a deep pan, blend a bottle of white wine and a bottle of Italian salad dressing, then stir in just a little garlic powder. Meanwhile, on shish kabob skewers (or peeled, green willow branches) begin impaling chunks of venison, alternating the meat with the vegetables and fruit. As each skewer is finished, lay it in the pan to slowly marinate in the wine mixture, turning them frequently. The marinating time should be at least 45 minutes. Then carefully lay the kabobs on a grill over a bed of glowing coals. Every ten minutes, rotate the skewers one-fourth turn, and use a brush to frequently baste the kabobs with more marinade from the pan. Total cooking time should be 45 minutes to 1 hour. Serves 4–6 very generously.

MEL MARSHALL'S VENISON ROLL-UPS

2 pounds round steak
2 cups breadcrumbs
1 stick margarine
3 cups mushrooms
1 onion, chopped
1 tsp. garlic powder

½ tsp. parsley flakes
1 tsp. salt
½ black pepper
meat tenderizer
cooking oil

The round steak should be sliced thin. Then sprinkle the pieces with meat tenderizer and pierce deeply with a fork. Now use a meat hammer (in camp, a pop bottle works fine) to pound the meat out flat. Remove the stems from the mushrooms and chop them along with the onion. Make a stuffing by kneading with your hands the breadcrumbs, margarine, mushroom stems, onion, seasonings, and as much water to make the stuffing moist. Lay a glob of stuffing in the center of each piece of round steak and roll up, securing each with toothpicks to hold everything together. In a large skillet or oval pan, sear the venison roll-ups in hot cooking oil until they are browned on all sides. Now reduce the heat by turning down the campstove burner or raking away some of the coals and continue to cook very slowly until the venison is tender. Meanwhile, in a separate pan, gently sauté the mushroom caps. Transfer the meat rolls to a hot plate, and surround them with the mushrooms. Serves 4.

MEL MARSHALL'S VENISON ROLL-UPS

1. *Sprinkle tenderizer on the meat and pierce it deeply into the steaks. Then pound the steaks thin with a meat mallet.* **2.** *Remove the caps from the mushrooms and dice the stems, then chop the onions.*

3. *Prepare the stuffing mix, place several spoonfuls onto steaks, roll them up, and secure with toothpicks.* **4.** *Sear the roll-ups in a large skillet, rake some of the coals away, and continue cooking on low heat until the meat is tender. In a separate pan, saute mushroom caps and serve as a side dish.*

VENISON ITALIANO

2 pounds tenderloin or sirloin tip steaks
½ cup olive oil
½ tsp. garlic powder
½ tsp. Worcestershire sauce

Thoroughly blend the olive oil, garlic powder, and Worcestershire sauce in a bowl. Then use the mixture to baste your steaks as you broil them in the usual manner. Serves 4.

LIVER PARMESAN

1½ pounds liver
1 cup white wine
¼ cup seasoned breadcrumbs
¼ cup grated Parmesan cheese

Place liver slices in a bowl, cover with the wine, and let sit for 1 hour. Remove the slices and shake off excess liquid, then dredge in a mixture of the Parmesan cheese and breadcrumbs. Next, fry in the usual way in cooking oil or butter. Serves 4.

VENISON CANTONESE

2 pounds sirloin tip steak, sliced in thin strips
2 tsp. meat tenderizer
4 tbsp. cornstarch
¼ cup sherry
6 large onions, sliced
¼ cup cooking oil

Mix together the tenderizer and cornstarch and thoroughly dredge the steaks, then gently pound them with your meat hammer. Place in a deep dish and pour the sherry over the top and let stand for 15 minutes. Meanwhile, separate the onion slices into rings and fry in the cooking oil until they are clear in the middle and crisp around the edges, then transfer them to a plate in your oven where they will stay warm. In the same skillet, now fry the thin strips of steak for 5 or 6 minutes, stirring continually. Place the onion rings on top of the meat strips, toss gently, and serve. Serves 4.

AUTHENTIC MEXICAN-AMERICAN CHILI

2 pounds venison   *½ tsp. oregano*
2 tbsp. chili molida powder   *½ tsp. cumin*
1 garlic clove, chopped   *1 tsp. salt*
1 large onion, chopped

(Note: If instead of molida you use regular chili powder, omit the cumin, garlic, oregano, and salt, and add 1 teaspoon red cayenne pepper)

Cut venison into inch-square cubes, then brown them in a Dutch oven or pot containing just a little lard or fat. When the meat chunks are browned on all sides, spoon off as much of the fat as possible. Sprinkle the chili molida powder on top of the meat, stir thoroughly, then reduce the heat to very low, cover the pot, and allow the seasoning to cook into the meat for 20 minutes. Now add to the pot just enough water to cover the meat, and then add the remaining ingredients. Cover the pot again and continue simmering for an absolute minimum of one hour. Authentic chili is one dish that improves after being allowed to cool overnight before being reheated the following day. Serves 4.

RIO GRANDE VENISON WITH NOODLES

1 pound deerburger   *1 4-ounce can mushrooms*
cooking oil   *½ tsp. chili molida*
1 green pepper, chopped   *1 tsp. salt*
1 onion, chopped   *½ tsp. black pepper*
2 stalks celery, chopped   *1 8-ounce package noodles*
1 small can red kidney beans
1 16-ounce can tomatoes, with juice

In a deep skillet, brown the deerburger in a bit of cooking oil. Stir in the pepper, onion, and celery, then reduce the heat, and simmer until they are tender. Add the remaining ingredients (except the noodles), stir thoroughly, cover the pan, and slowly simmer for 30 minutes. Meanwhile, prepare the noodles according to the package instructions, then drain. Place the nooodles on a hot platter and ladle the meat and vegetable sauce over the top. This recipe serves 4.

TEXAS RED WHISKEY DEER STEAKS

4 large sirloin tip steaks   *½ tsp. Worcestershire sauce*
1 onion, finely chopped   *2 tsp. chili sauce*
tarragon vinegar   *1 tsp. wet mustard*
½ tsp. Tabasco sauce   *½ cup bourbon*

Place the steaks and onion in a skillet and pour in tarragon vinegar until the steaks are barely covered. Simmer over low heat for 20 minutes. Add all the remaining ingredients, except for the bourbon, and continue to cook until the sauce becomes thick. Now spoon half of the sauce into a shallow pan, arrange the steaks on top, then spread the remaining sauce on top of the steaks. Pour the bourbon over the steaks and cook, uncovered, in a 350 degree oven for 1 hour. Serves 4.

TENDERLOIN CHEESE-STEAKS

2 pounds tenderloin or sirloin tip steaks
2 eggs, beaten
½ tsp. salt
¼ tsp. black pepper
1 cup seasoned breadcrumbs
¼ cup Romano-Parmesan cheese

Thoroughly mix the salt and pepper with the beaten eggs. In a separate bowl, thoroughly blend the breadcrumbs with the grated cheese. Dip the steaks individually in the egg batter, then roll in the bread crumb and cheese mixture. Fry in just a bit of cooking oil over medium-high heat until the exterior breading is golden brown, turning frequently. Be careful not to allow the breading to burn. Serves 4.

CRACKER-FRIED STEAKS

4 large chops or sirloin tip steaks
2 eggs, well beaten
1 cup saltine crackers, finely crushed
cooking oil

Dip each steak into the beaten egg, roll in the cracker crumbs, then pound very gently with a meat hammer. Dip the steaks a second time in the egg, then roll again in the cracker crumbs. Fry in a skillet until the cracker coating has a roast-like appearance, no longer! Serves 4.

SAVORY STEAK SANDWICHES

Venison tenderloin, particularly the mini-tenderloins from that part of the backbone inside the chest cavity, make superb steak sandwiches. I like to take these mini-tenderloins and pound them flat with a meat mallet so they are uniformly about ½ inch thick. Then either broil them, pan-broil them, or panfry them, for the most delicious sandwiches your crew ever enjoyed.

Any tenderloin steak, sirloin tip steak, or rump roast left over from a meal can also be served as sandwiches the following day. It's fine cold, after sitting overnight in your refrigerator. But you may prefer to slice the steak or roast into very thin strips, then place the meat in a skillet with just a bit of cooking oil over medium-high heat. Cover the pan and let the meat become very hot as you occasionally stir and toss it.

We like to serve our steak sandwiches on fancy steak rolls with just a light touch of horseradish or other conventional sandwich fixin's, but they are equally delicious when served between slices of buttered rye toast.

EASY MEAT PIE CRUST

1⅓ cups flour
½ tsp. salt
½ cup shortening
3–4 tbsp. cold water

Blend the flour and salt in a bowl, then cut in the shortening thoroughly with a fork. Sprinkle in the water, one tablespoon at a time, until the dough is moistened and there is no flour clinging to the inside of the bowl. Gather the dough into a ball and then shape into a flattened round on a floured work surface. Dust a rolling pin with flour and begin rolling the dough until it is as round as possible and just slightly larger in diameter than your pie plate. Now gently fold the dough into quarters.

Lightly butter the inside of your pie plate, then spoon in the venison stew and spread it around so it is equally distributed. Lay the pie crust on top of the stew and gently unfold it so the four quarters now form a round that entirely covers the pie plate. Pinch the edges of the crust around the diameter of the plate. With a knife, make numerous slits in the top of the crust. Bake in a 425 degree oven for 15 minutes or until the crust just begins to brown. Now turn the oven temperature down to 350 degrees and bake 15 minutes longer. Serves 4.

Occasionally you may like to make a meat pie with a double crust—that is, one on the bottom and one on top as with a conventional berry or fruit pie. In this case, simply make a double quantity of Easy Meat Pie Crust, divide it in half and after rolling it out lay the first half in the bottom of your pie plate. Sprinkle on top of this ¼ cup of dry breadcrumbs, which will prevent the stew or other meat pie ingredients from making the bottom crust soggy. Then proceed as usual in laying the second pie crust dough on top and pinching together around the edges.

QUICK MEAT PIE

3 cups venison stew
pastry crust

See facing page for step-by-step sequence.

QUICKIE VENISON STEW

2 pounds venison, cubed
4 potatoes, cut into chunks
1 large can cut green beans
2 carrots, cut into chunks
1 onion, chopped
1 envelope dry onion soup mix

Brown the venison in a skillet containing a bit of cooking oil. Transfer the meat to your stew pot along with the other ingredients, cover with water, and simmer over low heat 1 hour. Let each guest add salt and pepper to his own taste. Serves 4.

EASY VENISON CASSEROLE

1½ pounds deerburger
1 onion, chopped
1 stalk celery, chopped
2 8-ounce cans tomato sauce
2 tsp. flour
1 4-ounce can mushrooms
1 tsp. salt
½ tsp. black pepper
¼ tsp. oregano
1 package frozen tiny, tender peas
1 package "tube" biscuits
1 cup shredded mild cheddar cheese

Brown the deerburger in a skillet, then stir in the onion and celery and cook over low heat until the onions are clear. Drain off any grease, then stir in the flour, tomato sauce, seasonings, mushrooms, and peas. Pour this into a deep casserole dish. Arrange the biscuits on top, then sprinkle on the cheese. Bake at 350 degrees for about 20 minutes (be careful that the biscuits and cheese topping do not burn). Serves 4.

QUICK MEAT PIE

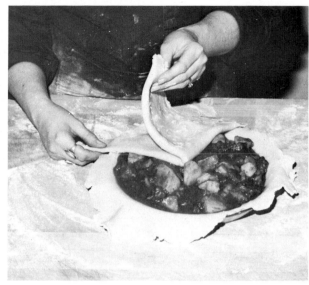

1. *After mixing and rolling out the pie crust, lay it in a pie plate and sprinkle it with breadcrumbs. Then ladle your stew into the pie plate.* **2.** *Drape pie crust over top of stew. Note how the crust, after being rolled out flat, is folded into quarters, then laid on top of the pie filling and unfolded. This evenly distributes the crust and prevents it from tearing.*

3. *With the top pie crust in place, make flutes around the edge of the pie plate by using the fingers to pinch together the edges of the top and bottom crusts.* **4.** *A perfect meat pie, ready for the table.*

4-STEP COUNTRY CASSEROLE

1 pound deerburger or bulk sausage	*½ cup tomato juice*
1 onion, chopped	*½ tsp. salt*
1 green pepper, chopped	*½ cup grated mild*
1 16-ounce can baked beans	*cheddar cheese*
1 8-ounce package elbow macaroni	

In a skillet, brown the deerburger in a bit of cooking oil, then stir in the onion and green pepper and continue to cook on low heat until they are tender. Stir in the beans, tomato juice, macaroni, and salt and mix thoroughly. Pour into a casserole dish and bake in a 400 degrees oven for 20 minutes or until the casserole begins to bubble. Then sprinkle the cheddar cheese on top and bake five minutes longer. Serves 4. (For an entirely different taste treat, use the same recipe but substitute some of your own venison sausage for the deerburger.)

COUNTRY CASSEROLE

1. *In a skillet, brown the burger or sausage, then stir in onion or green pepper. When the vegetables are cooked, stir in beans, tomato juice, and seasonings.* **2.** *Blend in the cooked macaroni.*

3. *Transfer to an oven-proof pot and begin baking. When casserole begins to bubble, sprinkle cheese on top and bake until cheese melts.* **4.** *Country Casserole is a hearty meal for winter nights that is fun to make.*

4-STEP PEPPER STEAK SUPREME

4 large tenderloin or	2 tbsp. butter
sirloin tip steaks	2 tbsp. olive oil
black pepper	1½ ounces brandy

Sprinkle just a bit of black pepper on both sides of the steaks and then gently pound it into the meat with your hammer. Add the butter and olive oil to a heavy skillet and sear the steaks on both sides over medium-high heat. Turn the heat down to low and continue cooking the steaks until they are medium-rare inside. Meanwhile, warm the brandy in a small saucepan. When the steaks are ready, transfer them to a preheated platter and pour the juices from the pan equally over the tops of them. Bring the platter to the table and, before your guests, pour the brandy over the top of the steaks and ignite it; be careful, and use a long stick-match because the brandy may flare up slightly. Allow the brandy to completely burn itself out, then serve. Serves 4.

PEPPER STEAK SUPREME

1. *Begin by pounding black pepper into sirloin tip steaks.* **2.** *In a skillet, sear the steaks in butter and olive oil, then turn the heat down and continue cooking.*

3. *Meanwhile, warm a bit of brandy.* **4.** *Transfer the steaks to a platter, pour warmed brandy over them, and ignite. Allow flames to die out before serving.*

Index